Instructional Computing for Today's Teachers

Instructional Computing for Today's Teachers

EDWARD L. VOCKELL, Ph.D.
ROBERT H. RIVERS, Ph.D.

PURDUE UNIVERSITY CALUMET

MACMILLAN PUBLISHING COMPANY
New York

COLLIER MACMILLAN PUBLISHERS
London

Copyright © 1984, Macmillan Publishing Company, a division of Macmillan, Inc.
Printed in the United States of America

Macmillan Publishing Company
866 Third Avenue, New York, New York 10022

Collier Macmillan Canada, Inc.

Library of Congress Cataloging in Publication Data

Vockell, Edward L.
    Instructional computing for today's teachers.

    Bibliography: p.
    Includes indexes.
    1. Computer-assisted instruction. I. Rivers, Robert H.
II. Title.
LB1028.5.V57   1984   371.3'9445   83-17532
ISBN 0-02-423090-1

Printing   2 3 4 5 6 7 8   Year: 4 5 6 7 8 9 0 1 2

ISBN   0-02-423090-1

To Alice and Majel.

PREFACE

The computer can be a valuable tool in instruction. Teachers carry out instruction in classrooms; but numerous other persons (including parents, counselors, and various training specialists) also engage in instruction. This book is written for anyone who needs help in the instructional endeavor. The purpose of this book is to enable such people to use the computer as an effective tool to enhance learning.

Computers are complex tools, and this book assumes that readers are relatively unfamiliar with those complexities. In addition, it assumes that readers do not imagine that they will become computer technologists simply by reading this single volume. Rather, this book introduces readers to the basic instructional applications of the computer and to the basic programming principles needed to write common instructional programs.

Instructional Computing for Today's Teachers differs from computer manuals and other introductory programming books in two important respects. First, it begins at an extremely nontechnical level. Some moderately complex ideas are discussed, but the text provides ample information for readers with no background whatsoever in computing to understand these concepts. Second, this book uses examples that focus on instructional activities. There are numerous excellent introductions to computer applications; but they all seem to focus on examples dealing with checkbooks, airline schedules, and mailing lists. This book uses educational drills and simulations as examples. This will enable readers to apply the information more directly to their own instructional activities.

Acknowledgments

We wrote this book because we felt that educators need a nontechnical introduction to computers focusing on instructional activities. For six years, we have taught a course to provide such an introduction to inservice teachers, and we have been unable to find a suitable textbook. This book arose out of our attempt to meet the needs of our students. The acceptance and encouragement from those students has led us to pursue the line of presentation which provided the basis for this book.

During the writing of this book several people were extremely helpful. Bob Bechtel, Sam Paravonian, and Eileen Schwartz read each chapter and made helpful suggestions. In addition, Steve Nowacki and Dan Luncsford made helpful comments on specific chapters. Mildred Blosky patiently and accurately typed most of the original text from dictation; and Sandy Hooper and Paula Wells typed preliminary versions of several chapters.

We would especially like to thank our families for their patience and support as we tried to transfer field-tested ideas into a written format. Finally, we would like to thank the students in our Computer-Assisted Instruction course. They have reacted to trial versions of this book, and their constructive criticism has eliminated ambiguities and helped us make the book as practical as possible for instructors who want to use the computer to enhance learning.

Edward L. Vockell, Ph.D.
Robert H. Rivers, Ph.D.
Purdue University Calumet

CONTENTS

Instructional Computing for Today's Teachers

Chapter 1
Computers for Teachers and Educators

The rapidly expanding availability of computers in schools makes it increasingly important for teachers and educators to learn to use them effectively. In future years, some teachers will use computers only to run programs purchased from commercial sources. Others will find it necessary to modify existing programs, and still others will write programs entirely on their own. Finally, some teachers will actually teach learners to use the computer in various ways as part of the learning process. Regardless of their level of involvement in using computers, it is obvious that teachers and educators who know how to use computers will be able to help learners more than will those who do not possess such knowledge.

Of course, teachers can be considered good teachers if they have never written a textbook or developed an educational television program. Likewise, teachers can be considered master teachers without ever writing a computer program. To use microcomputers well, teachers must be able (1) to recognize a good program when they see one, (2) to supplement the weaknesses of an otherwise good program, and (3) to take advantage of a program's strengths by using it creatively and appropriately in achieving educational objectives.

To develop such skills, teachers and prospective teachers should spend time examining computer applications in education and in developing criteria for selecting hardware and software. In addition, it has been our experience (Vockell and Rivers, 1980; Vockell, Rivers, and Kozubal, 1981; Vockell, Rivers, and Kozubal, 1982) that one of the best ways to teach educators how to use computers for instruction is to teach them how to write actual programs. This appears to be true even if the teachers themselves may never have the need or opportunity to program a computer without commercially available materials or professional help. Our research also indicates that such teachers are able to think more critically and creatively after learning to program computers. We are not arguing that it is of paramount importance that teachers become skilled programmers. Rather, we are suggesting that by understanding how computers work, teachers can often teach more effectively.

One of the major advantages of the approach used in this book is that it encourages *active* interaction with the computer. We have found that teachers often display very negative self-concepts with regard to computer technology. They assume that computers are mysterious machines that only geniuses can master. They often view computers as threatening enemies. However, once these same teachers understand how computers work and once they develop some basic programming skills, their attitudes change. They not only feel equal to computers, they feel that they are the master. These teachers become eager to use computers as tools to solve their instructional problems (Vockell, Rivers, and Kozubal, 1981).

Most readers of this book will be users rather than writers of instructional computer programs. (We emphatically do not advocate requiring all teachers to write most of their own programs.) This means that learning to write actual programs is irrelevant, right? Wrong. The need for users to have programming skills can be understood by examining analogies with other fields of learning.

Reading teachers provide a good comparison. Those who know how to write good instructional exercises can make more intelligent decisions about textbook selection and can use their textbooks more effectively than can other teachers who are incapable of developing their own materials. This is why teachers spend time learning to design reading materials, even though their school systems will supply them with most of the materials they will actually need. Likewise, automobile owners who know how to pinpoint and remedy automotive difficulties usually have cars that run better, even if they hire someone else to do the actual repair and maintenance work. In addition, more sophisticated car buyers are more easily able to spot gimmicks—items which boost the cost of the car without any real advantage and at little cost to the dealer.

A similar phenomenon occurs in the field of instructional computing: teachers who know something about what goes on inside a computer program are more likely to be intelligent users of the computer, even if they have access to commercially available materials and extensive professional help. Teachers who possess the skills taught in this book are able to recognize that the computer can assist the instructional process in a variety of ways. They raise questions. They recognize gimmicks. They aggressively employ computers as a means for solving their problems. These skills are not difficult to acquire, and it is worth the effort to develop them. Therefore, even educators who have no intention of writing a program of their own should master many of the programming skills presented in this book.

This book is designed to help educators (1) become familiar with what is possible in instructional computing, (2) recognize and apply good instructional computing in their classrooms, and (3) develop initial skills in computer programming. This text offers numerous examples of good instructional programs and describes their structure. In addition, readers will examine the criteria used to evaluate, select, and implement good courseware. Readers will also learn to write educational programs of moderate complexity and will be prepared for advanced books or courses which would develop much more complex and comprehensive skills in selecting good courseware and integrating it into their instructional programs.

Finally, this book will prepare readers to develop more comprehensive skills in computer programming if the need should arise. The reference manuals that seem too difficult for inexperienced programmers will become intelligible to those who have mastered the contents of this text.

What Educators Can Do with the Computer

Taylor (1980) has outlined three roles that the computer can play in education: those of the tutor, the tool, and the tutee. The computer acts as a tutor when it provides educational information for learners, as a tool when learners use the computer to solve problems that arise during their educational endeavors, and as a tutee when learners organize information in such a way as to "teach" the computer to model or react appropriately to some aspect of experience or knowledge. In actual practice, these roles overlap and merge. Sometimes, for example, the computer may serve as both a tool and a tutor. Another way to describe the role of the computer is with regard to the person who controls the learning situation. In some applications, the computer (or programmer) exercises a great deal of control over the learner who uses the program, but in others, the learner has a great deal of freedom and can actually be regarded as controlling the computer.

Tutorials

Tutorials and drills are examples of situations in which the computer controls or structures student learning and achievement. In tutorials, the learner who wishes to master a subject or acquire certain skills interacts with the computer in much the same manner as he or she would interact with a teacher or tutor. Just as it is theoretically possible for a learner to acquire information or skills by merely reading a good book on the subject, without ever consulting a teacher, it is also theoretically possible to acquire information from a properly programmed computer without ever consulting a teacher. However, students learn best when they interact with teachers at critical times during the learning process instead of only reading textbooks. In the same way, a computer will become an effective means of instruction only if a competent teacher can employ it as a useful supplement to the overall curriculum. Likewise, counselors or librarians can tell students to "go read a book" in order to acquire some information or some form of self-help, but they are more likely to use books to supplement their own services and expertise. The same thing is true of the computer: it is best viewed as a valuable supplement to rather than as a replacement for teachers, counselors, and other educational personnel.

Most readers will be familiar with the concept of branching programmed instruction, which presents small segments ("frames") of instruction to which a student is asked to respond. The learner is directed to the next relevant frame or branch of the instructional sequence based on each response. Tutorials and drills based on branching programmed instruction have been developed to teach concepts and processes in such areas as science, mathematics, social studies, and language arts. Despite the obvious benefits of such a strategy, researchers have been hard pressed to demonstrate its effectiveness. One deficiency in many such programs is that most written materials do not branch very effectively, and this is when the computer can implement and improve such programmed tutorials. The computer is able to evaluate a learner's performance very quickly and then offer the next piece of information that will be most helpful. Although it is possible to incorporate entire courses of instruction into such computerized programs, the most practical approach seems to be to program only those instructional units that will benefit from the interaction and branching that the computer can provide.

A similar application appears in counseling and various educational support services. Computers can be used to give to a learner or client information based on the response to a previous question. For example, the computer can help students make career choices or select colleges by systematically offering pertinent information. (SIGI is a professionally developed program that does just this.) Likewise, librarians can use computer programs to help library patrons select appropriate reference books. Another library application is to provide a tutorial program that can teach a patron how to use a reference book once it has been selected.

Drills

In recent years drills have become unpopular among both students and teachers. This is partly because they often focus on factual information that can be boring to students, especially those who have already mastered it. In addition, devising a large number of drills (especially individualized drills) presents a formidable task for the teacher. But despite such unpopularity, repeated practice in understanding and applying concepts and principles is often an important teaching method, and therefore drills can often have a useful purpose. A properly programmed computer can offer drills that are varied and are interesting and that can easily be tailored to the needs of the students who will use them. These drills can be used as remedial work for students who have trouble understanding a concept, as individualized practice for a wide range of students, and for makeup work missed during a class session. This book will discuss creative strategies for developing such drills.

Simulations and Tool Applications

In addition to drills and tutorials, the computer can often simulate a real-life situation or event. There are numerous settings in education in which it would be desirable for a student to engage in some sort of problem-solving activity but in which practical considerations such as time, money, or danger prohibit it. For example, students could learn a great deal about various scientific and mathematical concepts if they could land a vehicle on the moon, and it is possible for a computer to simulate such a landing and for students to apply their knowledge and skills. Likewise, studying the comparative numbers of predators and prey in forests, fields, and open woodlands is important to understanding population biology. Students could learn about predator-prey interactions, ethics, and economics if they could manipulate such variables as the density of forest vegetation, initial numbers of predators and prey, and human interference. This scientific manipulation would permit them to examine the impact of these variables on the balance of organisms in a natural environment. With the assistance of the computer, a learner can easily perform such experiments and can replicate them as often as necessary and with variations in order to understand the concepts, principles, and scientific processes under investigation.

The computer also can be used to search data bases to find bibliographic citations or find and evaluate information that enables learners to make various decisions. The computer can also be used as a sophisticated calculator for complex mathematical computations. The computer has the advantage over the simple calculator that once a student enters a formula into a program, the amount of work needed to repeat similar computations is greatly reduced. Likewise, the computer can be used as a word processor. Students can enter essays or term papers into the computer, store their work, make revisions, and generate a final copy without a lot of unnecessary drudgery. By introducing the computer as a tool in such situations, students can spend their time thinking about and solving problems rather than having to focus on the details that such activities often entail.

Computer as Tutee

Finally, it is possible to use the computer as what Taylor has called a *tutee*. Nearly all teachers can cite examples of concepts or principles that they never really understood until they were required to teach them to someone else. But a computer can do only what it is taught to do. Therefore, the person who does the programming has to understand the principle well enough to be able to teach it to the computer. During this teaching (programming) process, programmers often learn the concept or principle more thoroughly than ever before and even explore ideas that had not previously occurred to them.

As you read this book and try to write programs of your own, you will probably find yourself benefiting from teaching the computer to teach someone else. For example, to write a good drill or tutorial, you must consider each of the following questions:

1. What kinds of questions should you ask, and how can you formulate these questions clearly enough that the learner's focus will be exactly where you want it to be?
2. What is the correct answer, and how can you recognize its many variations?
3. What are the incorrect answers that could be given?
4. What feedback will you provide for both correct and incorrect answers?
5. What will you do after the learner gives the correct answer?
6. What sort of remediation will you provide if the answer is incorrect?
7. What can you do to enable the learner to have all the necessary information to make a response?
8. How long should the learner be allowed to continue, and who should terminate the learning session?
9. How should information regarding the learner's performance be stored (if at all), and to whom should this information be given?

These are questions that must be answered by both teachers who program the computer and those who work without computers. We have found that when teachers program a computer to teach something, they learn how to teach more effectively.

A similar phenomenon occurs when learners at any level teach the computer to do something. Rather than learning about teaching, learners come to understand the process that the computer must "learn." Students who can program a computer to draw a circle must understand the mathematics behind the circle. Students who can program a computer to simulate a horse race or baseball game will better understand the dynamics of those activities—as well as the theory of probability required to make the simulations resemble the actual activities. Likewise, students who can program a computer to simulate the balance between predator and prey in nature will be able to understand the principles involved in this balance better than will students who just read a textbook or watch a film.

By teaching the computer to do something, the learner acquires not only specific information about the subject itself but also (and perhaps more importantly) generalized thinking skills. Because computers are always logical, learners who program computers learn to diagnose problems and synthesize knowledge to solve problems.

LOGO is a commercially available programming language that can help young children develop generalized thinking skills. Not only can LOGO be used to teach programming skills it can also serve as a modeling tool that young children can use to simulate real-world activities and processes. In one of LOGO's applications, the child directs a "turtle" to move around the screen according to his or her instructions. While the turtle moves, it makes geometric patterns on the screen. As young children become more proficient at LOGO, they can create more and more intricate geometric patterns. Children painlessly and almost automatically learn increasingly complex rules of logic, art, geometry, computer programming, and the like.

This book will offer numerous examples of these structured and unstructured applications of the computer to education.

Computer Literacy

Most educators have grown up in a world without computers. We are aware that the IRS uses computers to calculate and correct our taxes more quickly than ever before; that the phone company and most large universities use computers to keep our records; and that if we commit a crime, the FBI will probably catch us by tracing our fingerprints through its computer system. However, we have not grown up in a world in which we can access the computer in our living room or bedroom to find about business projections, current news items, or personal tax and medical records or to store a manuscript that we may want to reissue in a different format at a future time. The children we teach, on the other hand, are growing up in a world of computers, and thus it is important to us as educators to understand this world and to help children make more appropriate and effective use of computers.

As we examine the many advantages of computers, we shall also look at its disadvantages. The most obvious is that if the computer is programmed incorrectly, it can make more errors more rapidly than can other modes of teaching. And when a computer makes errors, it may make them internally, and they may go unnoticed and therefore uncorrected. Of course, careful quality control can eliminate such errors. In addition, the computer may reduce spontaneity and creativity. For example, if children are required to make only one-word (or single-letter) responses to the computer's prompts, this could reduce their capacity to express themselves in complete, well-thought-out sentences. However, the solution is not to avoid computers but, rather to use programs that require various modes of thinking and responding. The actual response at the terminal is not as important as the type of mental activity that precedes the response. In addition, the computer should not be used alone, but with other ways of thinking and responding.

Finally, if students interact with computers in one-to-one situations, will they stop interacting with teachers and classmates? The answer is maybe, but not if computers are used as creative supplements to other effective kinds of instruction. For example, a teacher could use computerized simulations that require students to interact with one another as they prepare the simulations, collect data at the terminals, and analyze the process after the data session.

Ironically, the criticism that computers are a threat to the educational process was also made in regard to books when they were introduced into our culture and schools. If students learned to read and to rely on books, they might forget how to hold a lively discussion or how to listen. Students might not bother to remember facts if they could easily look them up in books. Students might not listen to lecturers or talk with other students if they could curl up in the corner with a good book. Yet few people now argue for the elimination of books from our schools. Computers will have a similar impact. Used unwisely, they will result in shortcomings and poor education. But used wisely, they will lead to more effective learning than has ever before been possible.

The Structure of This Book

Advocates of computer literacy among teachers have two goals:

1. Teachers should know what applications are possible in their field of instruction and should learn how to integrate these applications into the flow of classroom instruction.
2. Teachers should be able to program computers at a moderate level of expertise, to modify programs to suit their needs, or to write simple programs.

Many educators agree with the first goal. A smaller number agrees with the second. The premise of this book is that the two goals interact and overlap. By learning to program, you can profit more from exposure to examples of instructional computer applications; and by being exposed to instructional computer applications, you will acquire the motivation to develop programming skills.

This book offers examples of programs in specific categories and then demonstrates the underlying structure of these programs. The reader should learn how to write or modify programs similar to those discussed in the text. The programming sections of the book are obvious, and the reader could skip them. However, our experience has been that educators who merely read about computers do not understand instructional computing as well as do those who try writing or modifying such programs. We therefore urge you to study the programming chapters and to carry out the proposed activities.

There are many books on how to program computers, and many persons have acquired programming skills without reading any book cover to cover. Rather, they learned by interacting directly with the computer. They sat down at the computer terminal with a goal in mind, wrote programs containing mistakes, and learned by debugging them. The computer itself and its accompanying manual are the best textbook for such learners, and the computer's logic is the ideal teacher for prospective programmers.

So why write this book? Why not let educators learn from currently available books or by "hacking away" at the terminal with the manual close at hand? The answer is that teachers and other educators learn to program most easily when they focus their attention on educational problems. Other books employ examples that use the computer to schedule airline flights, balance checkbooks, compute population projections, and generate lists of prime numbers. This book, on the other hand, uses educational examples: drills, tutorials, and simulations that have direct educational applications.

Most readers will find it best to read the book from beginning to end while practicing the principles at a computer terminal. The best idea is to enter the sample programs into the computer, run them, and make appropriate modifications to produce different outcomes. The book emphasizes actively interacting with the sample programs by running them and modifying them according to prescribed guidelines. By modifying a program, you can demonstrate your understanding of the underlying principles without writing the entire program. With a minimum amount of physical effort and in very little time, you can actually make a computer do something you want it to do. After a few modifications, you can try your hand at some programs of your own. In addition, skill at modifying programs will help you adapt existing programs to your own educational goals.

If necessary, the reader can enter each sample program into the computer. Whenever possible, however, we recommend omitting this step. For example, when this book is used as a course textbook, the instructor should simply provide copies of the sample programs in a format (such as a cassette tape or floppy disk) ready to run on the computers available for the course. In addition, on request, we will supply (at low cost) the sample programs in an appropriate format (whenever this is possible for a specific computer), with permission to reproduce additional copies of the programs. Further information can be obtained from the Instructor's Manual or by contacting Edward L. Vockell (see the Vockell entry in Appendix F for the address).

The next four chapters introduce general programming strategies: Chapter 2 focuses on tutorials, Chapter 3 on drills, Chapter 4 on simulations, and Chapter 5 on strategies for letting students take greater control of the computer. These four chapters cover these topics without explaining the programming strategies necessary to write such programs. Chapters 6 through 9 discuss BASIC programming. The overall goal is to help readers understand the logic of the programs in the previous chapters and to write or modify moderately complex programs. No previous knowledge of programming is assumed. "Graduates" of these chapters will be able to use their manuals to program in BASIC on the computers to which they have access. Chapters 10 and 11 apply the nonprogramming chapters (2 through 5) to the programming chapters (6 through 9). Chapter 10 contains a case study of how one program evolved to serve the needs of a specific learner, and Chapter 11 shows how a single format can be easily modified for many diverse needs. Chapter 12 answers questions that arise in selecting hardware and software for instructional computing and offers guidelines for purchasing hardware and evaluating software.

The appendices are isolated at the end of the book, not because they are unimportant, but rather because readers will wish to refer to them in conjunction with different chapters. Appendix A is a glossary of terms likely to be encountered by educators as they begin to use computers for instruction. Appendix B describes the most important BASIC commands. Appendix C contains several modules that can be "plugged into" the programs you write or wish to modify. Appendices D and E discuss technical information for computer programmers and users. Finally, Appendix F lists the sources from which educators can obtain useful materials related to instructional computing.

Most readers will want to read the first twelve chapters in the order in which they are presented. The appendices, on the other hand, should be used as resources as the need arises. Throughout the entire book, we have tried to present the information in such a way as to be comprehensible to the complete novice. No prior programming knowledge or experience is assumed. In writing this book, it was necessary to use concrete examples. In the programming chapters (6 through 9), our examples required us to select a specific computer, and so we chose the TRS-80 as our main source of examples. We made this choice for several reasons: (1) the TRS-80 is widely available in homes and in schools; (2) the disk-operating system accompanying the TRS-80 gives the novice programmer effective error messages and editing strategies; and (3) it is easy to transfer knowledge from the TRS-80 to other computers.

Because many readers will use systems other than the TRS-80, we have taken pains to avoid unique features or commands that will not be available on other systems. Everything written in this book can easily be transferred to any computing system that supports BASIC on a cathode ray screen. To help readers make such transfers, we included cross-references to the Apple and other popular computers. By using their manuals, readers can easily apply this information to their systems.

References

Taylor, R. P. *The Computer in the School: Tutor, Tool, Tutee.* New York: Teachers College Press, 1980.

Vockell, E. L., and R. Rivers. "A Computer Simulations Course for Inservice Teachers." *The Computing Teacher* 7 (1979): 53–55.

Vockell, E. L., R. Rivers, and D. Kozubal. "A CAI Course for Teachers: Stimulus to Creative and Critical Thinking." *The Computing Teacher* 9 (1981): 35–39.

Vockell, E. L., R. Rivers, and D. Kozubal. "Computer Literacy for Teachers: An Intensive Program." *Proceedings of NECC '82.* Kansas City, MO, June 1982, pp. 326–330.

Chapter 2
Tutorial Programs

One common usage of the computer in education is for educational tutorials. From the perspective of programming logic, tutorials are among the easiest of all educational programs to write. However, this does not mean that "any fool can easily write one." Quite the contrary, writing a good tutorial is actually very difficult. This difficulty, however, arises not from the complexity of logic involved in writing the program, but from the need for adequate tutorial content.

Simply stated, the computerized tutorial puts programmed instruction on the computer. In a few cases, this will be linear programmed instruction, although there is little real gain in using the computer instead of written materials for such linear instruction. Therefore, most computerized tutorials are examples of *branching* programmed instruction. The computer offers a question or stimulus, and the learner responds. Then, depending on the learner's response, the computer decides what information to give next. This interaction continues until the tutorial has achieved its goal.

In this book, the term *tutorial* will apply to (1) programs designed to tutor students by helping them learn new subject matter or conceptual material and (2) programs that tutor students by guiding them through a decision-making process that gradually narrows their range of choices and helps them make a wise selection. Strictly speaking, only the former are true examples of tutorials; the latter are often actually guided searches of databases. However, since both represent attempts to lead students or clients through a set of information and since both branch on the basis of previous responses, we have decided to treat them together in this chapter. Examples of the first type of tutorial include programs written

- To help young children learn basic geometric shapes.
- To help students learn the grammar of a foreign language.

- To help students understand the measurement theory behind correlation coefficients.
- To help students understand important scientific principles.
- To help students learn to program a computer in BASIC.

Examples of the second type of tutorial include programs

- To help students select a course in their educational program or even to select a college or other career training.
- To help persons who must use educational statistics to select the best statistic for a given problem.
- To help persons decide whether a given tax deduction applies to them.
- To help students find a specific reference source in a library.
- To help teachers select a good educational strategy for a certain learning situation.

In any of these cases, of course, it is possible to combine tutorial strategies with other strategies (such as drills or simulations), discussed elsewhere in this book.

Tutorials vary in length and complexity. For example, it is possible to write a tutorial to cover only one point of Spanish grammar, which would be a very short computer program. On the other hand, it is possible to put portions of an entire Spanish course on a computer, which would be a very long program. Likewise, tutorials designed for counseling can differ in their complexity. At one extreme, a counselor may write a short program to help students determine which of several elective courses they should take. At the other extreme, SIGI is a long, professionally developed computer program that helps the student or client at the terminal make intelligent decisions about career plans.

Examples of Tutorial Programs

SIGI (System of Interactive Guidance and Information) is a comprehensive guidance and counseling program that incorporates many of the features of a good tutorial. Its purpose is to help adolescents and adults clarify their thinking and make intelligent and self-fulfilling career plans. Although SIGI has many components, we shall discuss only a few of them here.

Counselors of those making career plans often find that an important early step in career preparation is "value clarification." This means that the clients should ponder their values and determine how they will fit into various career fields. SIGI incorporates this value clarification into one of the program's first steps. The computer displays a series of characteristics one at a time and asks the clients to indicate how important each is to their choice of career. After the clients have gone through the set of ten characteristics, the computer returns with the display shown in Figure 2.1. This enables the clients to obtain an overall view of their values as related to their career selection.

In addition to providing this overview, the computer can compare the clients' values with those of persons successful in many career fields and to generate a list of careers that are closely suited to these values.

At important points in the counseling process, SIGI gives a summary to the

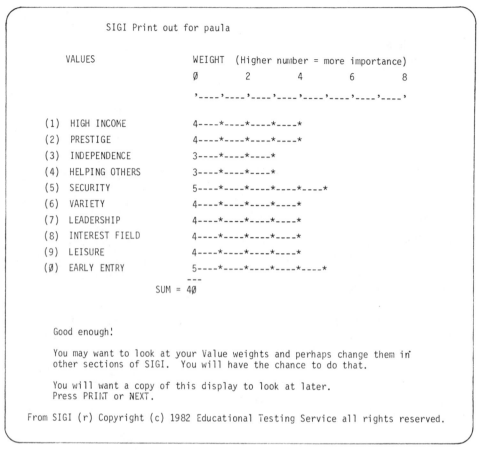

```
                SIGI Print out for paula


        VALUES                      WEIGHT  (Higher number = more importance)
                                    Ø         2        4        6        8

                                    '----'----'----'----'----'----'----'----'

    (1)  HIGH INCOME                4----*----*----*----*
    (2)  PRESTIGE                   4----*----*----*----*
    (3)  INDEPENDENCE               3----*----*----*
    (4)  HELPING OTHERS             3----*----*----*
    (5)  SECURITY                   5----*----*----*----*----*
    (6)  VARIETY                    4----*----*----*----*
    (7)  LEADERSHIP                 4----*----*----*----*
    (8)  INTEREST FIELD             4----*----*----*----*
    (9)  LEISURE                    4----*----*----*----*
    (Ø)  EARLY ENTRY                5----*----*----*----*----*
                                    ---
                        SUM = 4Ø


    Good enough!

    You may want to look at your Value weights and perhaps change them in
    other sections of SIGI.  You will have the chance to do that.

    You will want a copy of this display to look at later.
    Press PRINT or NEXT.

  From SIGI (r) Copyright (c) 1982 Educational Testing Service all rights reserved.
```

Figure 2.1. SIGI's summary of values regarding career.

client (Figure 2.2). These summaries enable the learner to change answers, and they increase self-awareness, which is considered to be an important part of the career selection process.

Because SIGI is a time-consuming program (often requiring an hour and a half to three hours of interacting with the computer), the computer provides a "place-holder" (Figure 2.3) for clients who do not want to go through the entire guidance process in a single session.

Eventually, SIGI zeros in on specific career fields, providing information regarding such factors as salaries, level of training needed to enter a field, and geographical distribution of possible job openings within that field. Figures 2.4 to 2.6 show examples of this information. Note that in every case the clients are permitted to make a printed copy of the screen display.

Another good example of tutorial programming is COMPUTER LITERACY. This is one of the PLATO programs that have recently become available for microcomputers. This program helps learners develop literacy in the areas designated by the menu in Figure 2.7.

A person who chooses "Computer Uses" (number 2 in the menu) soon sees the

```
                SIGI PRINT out for nancy b

   To summarize what you've said about yourself:

        Value:          "I have thought about my Values, and I know what
                        I want from an occupation."

        Information:    "I know one or two occupations that might fit my
                        Values, and I know quite a lot about them."

        Prediction:     "I think I could predict my grades accurately in
                        any program of study I might take."

        Planning:       "I know which program to enroll in, which courses
                        to take, and most of the other steps necessary
                        to reach my occupational goal."


   You will be able to get copies of certain displays as you go through SIGI:
   This is the first.

   If you want a copy of what you see now, press PRINT.

   If you do not want a copy, press NEXT.

   From SIGI (r) Copyright (c) 1982 Educational Tesing Service all rights reserved.
```

Figure 2.2. Summary of what the client has said about himself or herself after about fifteen minutes or a half hour of interacting with SIGI.

```
              SIGI Placeholder Number: 8675 5564 4655



       Two copies of your Placeholder Number are being printed for you.
   This number tells SIGI which sections you had completed so you can pick up
   where you left off.

   Please bring this number when you come to use SIGI again.  If you would
   like you may leave one copy here, in case you forget.



                When the printer stops, Press NEXT.



   Date:                             SIGI Session Number:



   From SIGI (r) Copyright (c) 1982 Educational Testing Service all rights reserved.
```

Figure 2.3. A "placeholder" to make it easier for a client who leaves the terminal to resume at the same point in SIGI.

```
                    SIGI Print out for Sandra Denise Hooper


                        Definition of occupation?
        181 Nurse, Licensed Practical
   A licensed practical nurse (LPN) provides direct patient care to the sick or
   infirm in simple nursing situations under the direction of a physician and/or
   registered nurse (RN).  Assists RN with acute cases.  LPN may direct nursing
   assistants, aides & orderlies.  In California & Texas called licensed voca-
   tional nurse (LVN).


        193 Nurse, Registered
   A professional nurse (RN) administers nursing care to patients following a
   doctor's instructions.  May supervise licensed practical nurses, aides and
   orderlies.  May work in a hospital or nursing home, on private duty, or as a
   public health, school, or industrial nurse.


        243 Physician's Assistant
   Working under the supervision of a licensed physician, assumes many tasks
   once performed only by physicians.  Specialties include primary care, surgery,
   pediatrics, orthopedics, internal medicine.



   For a copy of this information, press PRINT; otherwise press NEXT.

   From SIGI (r) Copyright (c) 1982 Educational Testing Service all rights reserved.
```

Figure 2.4. A SIGI summary description of three career fields likely to be of interest to a client.

```
                    SIGI Print out for Sandra Denise Hooper

                        Personal qualifications?
        181 Nurse, Licensed Practical
   Dependability, maturity, common sense, and self-control.  Strong desire to help
   people, and ability to follow orders to the letter.  Must be calm during emer-
   gencies; show warmth, patience and tolerance.  Good health and stamina
   essential.



        193 Nurse, Registered
   Must be alert, self-controlled, and responsible, with a great desire to help
   the sick and injured.  Good health, both physical and mental, is essential.
   Must be able to handle emergencies calmly and work well with the medical team.



        243 Physician's Assistant
   Good judgment, maturity, ability to act calmly in emergencies, solve clinical
   problems.  Concern for sick people and ability to relate to them.  Skill in
   listening and counseling.  Good health.



   For a copy of this information, press PRINT; otherwise press NEXT.

   From SIGI (r) Copyright (c) 1982 Educational Testing Service all rights reserved.
```

Figure 2.5. Summary of personal qualifications of the three career fields shown in Figure 2.4.

```
            SIGI Print out for Sandra Denise Hooper

                    Level of work with data, people, things?
        181 Nurse, Licensed Practical
Data:  Medium--keep medical charts.
People:  Medium--give personal nursing care.
Things:  Medium--sterilize, assemble, use simple equipment.



        193 Nurse, Registered
Data:  Medium--record observations, carry out instructions.
People:  Medium--inform, confer with doctors and patients; give nursing care.
Things:  Medium--prepare equipment and instruments for doctor.



        243 Physician's Assistant
Data:  High--collect, record, discuss, assist in diagnosing.
People:  High--examine, counsel.
Things:  Medium--use of equipment varies.  High for surgical assistant.




For a copy of this information, press PRINT; otherwise press NEXT.

From SIGI (r) Copyright (c) 1982 Educational Testing Service all rights reserved.
```

Figure 2.6. Summary of several characteristics related to the career fields shown in Figure 2.4.

screens shown in Figures 2.8 and 2.9. The sequence shown in Figure 2.8 comes with animation: as the little person at the right of the screen enters data at the terminal, the learner watches the data make their way to the storage area. The learner has the option of reviewing previous information, by pressing control R (which restarts the "Computer Uses" sequence), or returning to the main menu, by pressing control B.

```
            Lesson Instructions 1 of 6

        This lesson has five sections
        following this short introduction.

        * Examples of computer uses
        * Limitations of computers
        * The nature of computers
        * Where computers come from
        * How computers affect us

        Each section can be selected
        from the index by typing its
        number then pressing the RETURN
        key.

        Press the RETURN to continue
```

Figure 2.7. The introductory menu from COMPUTER LITERACY.

```
              Examples of Computer Uses 4 of 10

The Lone Pine Lumber Yard sells
building supplies to its regular
customers on a charge basis.  Each
time a customer comes in, a list
of the supplies being purchased
is entered into a terminal by a
clerk.


Storage                    CPU
 9/2/82 Smith              whirr        9/13/82 Jones
Saw and nails


9/2/82 Doaks              The CPU uses a


pipe stretcher           program (written by a
                         person) to record the
                         information about each
                         purchase in storage.




CTRL   R       to review
CTRL   B       to return to the index
```

Figure 2.8. Sample of output that a learner receives by requesting "Examples" in Figure 2.7. This is the fourth of ten examples.

```
            Examples of Computer Uses 3 of 10

The characteristics of these computer
parts help determine what the
computer can do.

To store a lot of information,
You need a big  MEMORY

Yes.  That's right.

To do a complicated task, you
need a fast  CPU

That's it.

RETURN      to continue
CTRL R      to review
CTRL B      to return to the index.
```

Figure 2.9. An example of the output that the learner receives by requesting "Examples" in Figure 2.7. This is the third of ten examples.

In general, COMPUTER LITERACY makes good use of the learner's time. It gives immediate responses to the learner's input and helpful feedback for errors. The learner receives several opportunities to give correct answers, but repeated failure brings the right answer before frustration sets in. In certain cases, the program actually recognizes "probable errors" and uses these to direct the learner toward the correct understanding of concepts and principles. Finally, the program is accompanied by sound effects, such as the click of the keyboard and the whirring of the disk drive (Figure 2.8), although the sound can be turned off.

Guidelines for Writing and Selecting Tutorials

An educational tutorial should (1) clearly state each question (or other "prompt"), (2) permit the learner to make the desired response, (3) evaluate the learner's input, (4) provide feedback to the learner, and (5) decide its next step based on the evaluation of this input. The programs displayed in Figures 2.1 to 2.9 appear to do an exemplary job of meeting these requirements. It is only fair to point out, however, that not all tutorials possess these qualities.

In evaluating tutorial programs, therefore, some guidelines may be helpful. Although this chapter does not examine specific programming techniques, because many readers will wish to write or modify tutorial programs, we shall occasionally refer to future chapters that will show them how to write programs that follow these guidelines. The following are designed to help you write or purchase educational tutorials:

1. The computer should be programmed to respond to all of the possible responses the learner can make. Failure to cover all possible responses will cause the program either to go to a wrong step or to come to an abrupt stop. For example, in the program HELLO (Chapter 6), the computer will accept absolutely any answer. If the response is one that the computer will accept, it will act upon this answer; otherwise it will recycle the learner to force him or her to provide the input desired by the computer.

2. The program should be as "user friendly" as possible. This means that the learner should be able to decide easily what kind of input to give to the computer; and when errors occur, the learner should be able to decide easily how to correct them. One example of a violation of this guideline occurs when the computer simply stops running or "breaks" when the learner provides faulty input. Another example occurs when the computer recycles the learner by continuously showing "?" in response to faulty input. In both cases, before recycling the learner, it would be much better to explain what the error was or what kind of input should have been provided. In general, learners should be protected from technical messages that they will probably not understand (such as "Syntax error in line 3030"). Rather, they should be given simply stated, grammatically coherent sentences that tell them what to do next. User friendliness requires that the programmer spend more time writing the program in order to reduce the learner's effort in running the program.

3. The program should be written as efficiently as possible. For example, whenever possible or appropriate, the program should use subroutines to accomplish the tutorial's goals. (Subroutines are discussed in Chapter 7.) In addition to the

other advantages of subroutines, if the program is efficiently written, it will usually be much easier to change the tutorial content when revisions are necessary.

4. When using a cathode ray (television) screen, the tutorial should use the screen so as to focus attention where it should be focused. Sometimes the limited space of the screen can impede instruction. But on the other hand, the limited space of the screen also enables us to eliminate distractions by placing on the screen only what the learner should be focusing on at a given time. The best procedure, therefore, is to put the relevant information on the screen and permit the learner to call for additional information as it is needed to pursue a particular task.

5. To avoid cluttering the screen with too much information, the program should provide a means for controlling the rate of delivery and for erasing information that is no longer necessary. For example, the program could use a "Press Enter to Continue" option to provide two or more screenfuls of information.

6. The steps in the program and the points to which the learner will be branched must be logically and pedagogically correct. Following this guideline requires more skill in the content or subject matter area than in computer programming. Nevertheless, this is probably the most important step in developing a good tutorial program. A program that runs successfully but is pedagogically unsound is of little educational value to anyone. When learners actually learn effectively from a program, then that program can be considered finished (at least until someone notices an exception).

7. The program should allow learners to review important parts of the tutorial whenever it is necessary to do so. If the learner asks to review some information, then it should be displayed on the screen before he or she is required to continue to the next step. If the learner makes no such request, the program should proceed immediately to the next step. Such assistance is usually offered through subroutines (see Chapter 7).

For example, many programs include a "help" routine. The learner is told during the instructions near the beginning of the program (or in written instructions) to input the word *help* at any point at which he or she needs assistance. The

```
WHAT KIND OF HELP DO YOU WANT?

        1.   REVIEW OF A PREVIOUS UNIT.
        2.   DEFINITION OF A TERM.
        3.   INSTRUCTIONS TO USE TERMINAL.
        4.   CHANGE ANSWER TO PREVIOUS QUESTION.
        5.   TERMINATE SESSION.
        6.   RETURN TO PROGRAM.

ENTER A NUMBER AND PRESS THE ENTER KEY.
```

Figure 2.10. An example of a HELP menu. In response to the HELP request, the computer presents this menu. The action the computer will take depends on what the learner chooses from the menu. For example, if the learner selects "1," then the computer will offer further prompts to identify the unit to be reviewed and eventually will review that unit before returning to the original point at which help was requested.

computer examines each response to determine whether or not the word help was entered. If the response is anything other than the word help, the computer will simply continue with the program. But if the word help occurs, the computer will then present a "menu" listing the possible types of help available. The learner selects the appropriate type of help from this menu, and the computer provides the information. This process continues until the learner indicates a willingness to go back to the regular program, and then the computer returns the learner to the original program. The successful implementation of useful help routines makes a program very user friendly. An example of a help menu can be found in Figure 2.10.

Closing Comment

This chapter indicated settings in which educational tutorials can be helpful, showed examples of some good tutorials, and provided guidelines for writing or purchasing tutorials. At the present time, however, there are not many good tutorials on the market, though there are several excellent drills and simulations that use tutorial techniques for small units of instruction or remediation. Perhaps this is where tutorials should be used in instruction: as suppliers of short units of supplementary tutoring at exactly the time when such tutoring is required. Therefore, as you read the next chapters, keep in mind that whenever a part of a program is designed to tutor a learner, the principles discussed in this chapter should be applied.

Chapter 3
Educational Drills

In this book, the term *drill* refers to any exercise in which learners repeatedly attempt to solve problems according to a prescribed pattern and receive feedback after giving their answers. Such educational endeavors as vocabulary and spelling drills fall into this category. In addition, many games really are disguised drills that require students to give answers to related problems.

The term drill has negative connotations for many who associate it with rote learning and who wish that education would focus on more worthwhile activities. On the other hand, the same term has positive connotations for those who advocate getting back to the basics. In fact, the value of a drill depends on its contents and how it is designed and presented. Although many useful drills focus on the simple retention of factual information, others concentrate on higher levels of learning by requiring the application of important principles.

The computer has the capacity to provide extremely effective educational drills. Once properly programmed, the computer can supply a degree of accuracy, variety, feedback, record keeping, and even patience that is often difficult for a human teacher to maintain. By allowing students to use computers for drills, teachers can free themselves to work toward educational objectives that are not easily attained through drills.

Random Selection of Questions

The simplest computerized educational drill merely inserts into the linear tutorial format a series of questions to which the learner responds. The computer then evaluates each response and proceeds to the next question, finally determining the learner's overall performance on the series of questions. However, just as computerized versions of linear tutorial programs are not necessarily superior to the written format of the same programs, these linear drills usually do not take advantage of the unique features that a computer offers.

A good educational drill will offer a different set of problems related to the same skill or set of objectives each time the drill is run. This variation discourages the rote memorization of trivial information. For example, a drill on state capitals could start each run of the program by asking for the capital of Alabama, then the capital of Alaska, and progressing through the alphabet until it reached Wyoming. But, it is obvious that the constant repetition of the drill in the same order will give clues that can interfere with actually learning the information. It is also possible that interruptions may prevent the learner from reaching the end of the drill, and therefore information regarding the last three states would be less likely to be covered by the drill than would information about the first three states. Extraneous clues become an even more serious problem when the drill requires the application of principles to solve problems. In such cases, an invariant order of presentation may enable the learner to give the answers without even working out the problems. From this brief discussion, it should be clear that a drill should usually present the questions in a different order each time it is run. In addition, it is really not very difficult to arrange for the random presentation of questions. It is surprising, therefore, to find how many commercially available programs use an invariant sequence of presentation in their drills. We therefore urge you to be aware of the value of altering the order in which questions are presented and to incorporate such variation into the programs you acquire or develop.

Games Versus Drills

Some drills have academic orientations, and many of these have useful purposes. For example, computer programs can easily offer addition or subtraction problems for the student to solve, require a learner to indicate a synonym or antonym for a word the computer places on the screen, or ask a child to name the capital of a given state. In addition, effective drills can be put into a game format which enhances student interest and motivation.

For example, TRAP (which is discussed in greater detail in Chapter 7) presents a number-guessing game in which the learner is asked to "trap" a number by entering a pair of numbers. The computer then indicates whether the number it is thinking of is above, below, or within the range of the trap numbers (see Figure 3.1). Learners may start by guessing wildly, but they soon discover that they can improve their chances of winning by using a strategy combining addition, subtraction, and division. By playing TRAP, therefore, learners are able to practice these mathematical skills while playing a fun game.

The use of games to promote learning is not new to teachers. Mathematics games, logic games, word games, board games, and (more recently) electronic games often enable learners to practice important skills. The computer merely makes these games accessible in a convenient format. It is worth noting that many of the games that you may consider to be educationally useful (such as word games, logic games, and mathematics games) can be programmed into the computer and that in many cases, these programs are already available.

```
I AM THINKING OF A NUMBER BETWEEN 1 AND 100.

TRY TO GUESS MY NUMBER.

ON EACH GUESS, ENTER 2 NUMBERS,
TRYING TO TRAP MY NUMBER BETWEEN THE TWO NUMBERS.

I WILL TELL YOU IF YOU HAVE TRAPPED MY NUMBER,
OR IF MY NUMBER IS LARGER THAN YOUR TWO NUMBERS,
OR IF MY NUMBER IS SMALLER THAN YOUR TWO NUMBERS.


ARE YOU READY TO CONTINUE (PRESS ENTER)?
```

Figure 3.1. A sample screen from TRAP. This is one of the sample programs described in Chapter 7.

Another gamelike drill is PIZZA, which is described in greater detail in Chapter 7. In this game, the player is presented with a map (Figure 3.2) and receives an "order" for a pizza from one of the "customers." The player has to deliver the pizza by entering the geometric coordinates of the customer's location. By playing games like this, young learners come to enjoy learning to read and interpret geometric coordinates. A slight modification in the program (described in Chapter 7)

```
MAP OF THE CITY

----1---2---3---4----

1   M   N   O   P   1

2   I   J   K   L   2

3   E   F   G   H   3

4   A   B   C   D   4

----1---2---3---4----

THE ABOVE IS A MAP OF A CITY.

A CUSTOMER WILL ORDER A PIZZA.
YOUR JOB IS TO TELL THE DRIVER WHERE TO DELIVER IT.

ARE YOU READY TO CONTINUE (PRESS ENTER)?
```

Figure 3.2. A sample screen from PIZZA. A "customer" on the map—such as H—orders a pizza. The learner has to give the correct address (geometric coordinates) to which the pizza is to be delivered. This program is described in Chapter 7.

enables the computer to present the names of students in a given class, rather than the letters of the alphabet, as the potential "customers" on the map.

Although computerized drills may sometimes be useful for memorizing information, they can often teach students how to apply concepts, principles, and other information. A learner working at such drills is given a series of problems and is required to understand and apply important principles in order to solve them. The learning that results from a drill does not have to be trivial, even if it is purely factual.

For example, history courses that require nothing beyond the rote memorization of dates are of little use, because the reasons for studying history go far beyond memorization. At the same time, however, it is important for learners to be able to put events in a chronological perspective. The history teacher, therefore, is often faced with the dilemma of wanting to avoid undue emphasis on dates, yet realizing that the students must know some dates in order to discuss history intelligently.

One way to resolve this dilemma is to use a program like HISTORY (see Figure 3.3) as an adjunct to a history course. If you try to put the events in Figure 3.3 in their proper order, you can do this by merely memorizing the dates. On the other hand, most persons who try this game start making intelligent guesses. For example, a player may reason: "I know that the firing on Fort Sumter occurred at the beginning of the Civil War, which means that it must have come before the Emancipation Proclamation, as Lincoln issued that as a military measure when things were going badly during the war. Therefore D comes before B. The Kansas-Nebraska Act was concerned with a compromise over slavery. A compromise would not have been needed if the war had already begun, and so the act must have come before the other two—probably by about ten years. Now, the Lincoln–Douglas debates. . . ."

Far from requiring mere memorization, therefore, this program can teach students how to put events in the proper historical perspective. The players do re-

```
LISTED BELOW ARE FIVE EVENTS FROM AMERICAN HISTORY

TRY TO PUT THEM IN THE CORRECT ORDER.

A. CONFEDERATES FIRE ON FORT SUMTER
B. LINCOLN DELIVERS GETTYSBURG ADDRESS
C. PASSAGE OF KANSAS-NEBRASKA ACT
D. LINCOLN-DOUGLAS DEBATES
E. COMPLETION OF TRANSCONTINENTAL RAILROAD

ENTER A,B,C,D, OR E FOR EACH CHOICE.

IF YOU WISH TO START OVER, ENTER X.

WHICH EVENT CAME FIRST?
```

Figure 3.3. A sample screen from HISTORY. In this example, the learner has already selected a level of difficulty. This example assumes that the learner has chosen a fairly difficult level, and therefore the events are tightly clustered. After the player has put the events in order, the computer will put them in the correct order and give the learner points based on the degree of accuracy.

member the dates, but they do not put a priority on memorizing them. This beneficial outcome is most likely to occur if the students perceive the program as a game that has the side effect of helping them learn history. If the teacher requires that in order to get an A in the course, students must score 90 or higher on HISTORY, then they will be more likely to resort to the rote memorization of dates. But a teacher who uses such a program effectively can focus class discussions on more complex issues and let the computer assist with some of the less difficult aspects.

Providing Clues and Help

Sometimes it is desirable to give learners information to help them solve a problem. On some occasions, you may wish to give such information automatically to all learners who will use a given program; but on other occasions you may find it desirable to give this information only to those who request it. This can be done by evaluating each of these learner's responses to determine whether the learner has requested assistance, before proceeding with the program. For example, in the CAPS program, a learner who enters the word *list* automatically receives the list shown in Figure 3.4. More detailed assistance may be a statement or description of the rules and information necessary to solve a problem. Even more thorough assistance may be a short tutorial that enables the learner to review the information necessary to solve the problem.

User Friendliness

Like tutorials, drills should be user friendly. One unfriendly feature of many drills is that a learner is considered to have made a wrong answer by merely misspelling a correct answer, as well as by actually giving an incorrect answer. For example, unless CAPS is programmed to contain some friendly features, a person

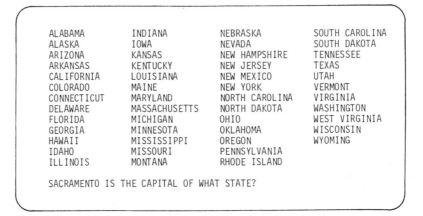

```
ALABAMA          INDIANA          NEBRASKA          SOUTH CAROLINA
ALASKA           IOWA             NEVADA            SOUTH DAKOTA
ARIZONA          KANSAS           NEW HAMPSHIRE     TENNESSEE
ARKANSAS         KENTUCKY         NEW JERSEY        TEXAS
CALIFORNIA       LOUISIANA        NEW MEXICO        UTAH
COLORADO         MAINE            NEW YORK          VERMONT
CONNECTICUT      MARYLAND         NORTH CAROLINA    VIRGINIA
DELAWARE         MASSACHUSETTS    NORTH DAKOTA      WASHINGTON
FLORIDA          MICHIGAN         OHIO              WEST VIRGINIA
GEORGIA          MINNESOTA        OKLAHOMA          WISCONSIN
HAWAII           MISSISSIPPI      OREGON            WYOMING
IDAHO            MISSOURI         PENNSYLVANIA
ILLINOIS         MONTANA          RHODE ISLAND

SACRAMENTO IS THE CAPITAL OF WHAT STATE?
```

Figure 3.4. An example of assistance provided by the computer.

who spells Massachusetts incorrectly will receive as little credit for his or her knowledge of state capitals as a person who thinks that Boston is the capital of Arizona. CAPS covers this possibility by checking to see if the student's response is a correct spelling of any state and displaying the message shown in Figure 3.5 if this is not the case. The person who spells the name of a state incorrectly is not considered to have given a wrong answer but is simply given an opportunity to supply a correctly spelled answer, either with or without first looking at a list of correctly spelled states. Notice that CAPS provides this friendly feature for the spelling of states but not for the spelling of capitals. In other words, a person who spells the capital of Kentucky as Frankfert is just as wrong as a person who spells it Louisville. The friendly feature was excluded from the spelling of the capitals because the programmer did not want to present learners with a list that would make their task unnecessarily easy by excluding Louisville as a possible answer. A different programmer might take a different approach to the same problem. One possibility would be to provide no spelling corrections and subsequent list for the first error on each state, but rather to supply these additional aids if the learner made an error a second time on the same state.

Another user friendly strategy is to permit the learner to terminate a drill session conveniently at any time and to obtain immediate feedback regarding his or her performance on that drill. It is also desirable to program the computer to accept alternative spellings of words. For example, CAPS accepts either the abbreviated or the unabbreviated version of the capital of Minnesota: St. Paul or Saint Paul.

It is often desirable to record the number of correct and incorrect responses made by the learner and to offer the students feedback on the correctness of their answers. In most cases this feedback should be given immediately after the learner's response. It can be the same for every correct response, can vary randomly, or can vary based on the number of correct responses (either overall or consecutively).

It is wise to avoid any feedback that reprimands the student for an incorrect answer. Although some teachers (and learners) may feel that it is "cute" to call a learner a "dummy" for making five wrong answers in a row or to say "I thought everybody knew that," such comments can have a harmful impact that the programmer will never see. For this reason, it is usually best simply to inform the

```
ALLASKA IS NOT THE CORRECT SPELLING
OF ANY STATE

ENTER A CORRECT SPELLING OR TYPE L
TO SEE THE LIST OF STATES.

?
```

Figure 3.5. The message that occurs as a result of the spelling feature in CAPS. A learner who enters L will receive the list shown in Figure 3.4.

```
 MAP OF THE CITY

 ----1---2---3---4----

 1   M   N   O   P   1

 2   I   J   K   L   2

 3   E   F   G   H   3

 4   A   B   C   D   4

 ----1---2---3---4----

 THIS IS N. I DID NOT ORDER A PIZZA.

 NOW TELL THE DRIVER WHERE H LIVES, ED.
```

Figure 3.6. Feedback for an incorrect response in PIZZA. The learner was asked to deliver a pizza to H, who "lives" at location 4,2. The learner has inaccurately entered 2,1 as the coordinates.

student that his or her answer is wrong or perhaps to state that "maybe you had better try that one again." Figure 3.6 is an example of realistic and informative feedback from PIZZA, and Figure 3.7 is a good example of very detailed feedback from the program BEHMOD (described in Chapter 11). The feedback shown in Figure 3.7 is vastly superior to the simple "Wrong. Do you want another question?" which is typical of many weaker programs. In a properly written program, such detailed feedback can often be supplied by adding only a few lines to the program.

As you read about these strategies that can be introduced into computerized drills, you will find that they all are strategies that good human teachers use when administering drills. You may therefore wonder why you should bother to use the computer to do what human beings can do perfectly well anyway. One answer is that the computer does all of these things automatically and is not influenced by

```
 WRONG.

 EXTINCTION IS DEFINED AS THE WITHHOLDING OF THE
 REINFORCERS WHICH MAINTAINED A BEHAVIOR

 SATIATION IS DEFINED AS ALLOWING A BEHAVIOR.
 TO OCCUR UNTIL IT LOSES ITS REINFORCING VALUE.

 SEE PAGE 45.

 DO YOU WANT ANOTHER QUESTION (Y/N)?
```

Figure 3.7. Feedback for an incorrect answer in BEHMOD. The learner was asked what technique is defined as "the withholding of reinforcers that previously maintained a behavior." The learner inaccurately entered "satiation," and the computer recognized the correct answer as a correct definition of another term. The computer was therefore able to give (1) feedback that the answer was incorrect, (2) the correct term that fits the definition, and (3) the definition of the term that the learner incorrectly answered. BEHMOD is described in Chapter 11.

momentary idiosyncrasies. The computer can be programmed to perform a variety of tasks such as (1) telling students how many questions they have attempted so far to answer, (2) notifying them how many they got right, (3) providing immediate feedback regarding the correctness of each response, (4) offering intermittent reinforcement based on varying numbers of correct responses, and (5) performing many other tasks that can be similarly systematized. Remember, however, that the computer cannot be programmed to do such things as stopping and encouraging the student who suddenly expresses extreme frustration over a series of incorrect responses.

A General Note on Drills and Tutorials

All of the sample programs (for which this textbook provides detailed listings in Chapters 6 through 12) should be regarded as drills or tutorials. They are clear examples of applications of fundamental BASIC programming strategies. These same strategies can be used in higher-level applications (such as simulations); but such applications are almost always more complex to program, since they often require complex mathematical formulas and assume a knowledge of the theoretical models underlying the programs. In addition, they often rely on graphic presentations, which are not discussed in this book. For these reasons, examples of higher-level applications have been omitted from the programming chapters, and the sample programs that are included have been drawn from areas with which almost all readers are likely to be familiar. By examining these programs and understanding their programming concepts, readers can learn the basic strategies of programming and the capabilities of the computer. An understanding of such concepts should help readers make informed decisions, not only about the drills used in the sample programs, but also about higher-level applications of similar strategies.

Chapter 4
Simulations

The preceding chapters demonstrated some creative ways in which the computer can present drills and tutorials, but the true potential of the computer in education will not become apparent until we examine computerized simulations.

When we use the computer to administer instructional drills, it is really serving as a "glorified flashcard"—a tremendously powerful flashcard, to be sure, but a flashcard nonetheless. Even the most creative drills merely enable learners to practice activities that normally occur in regular instructional settings. With simulations, on the other hand, the computer can allow learners to experience situations and solve problems that would otherwise be impossible because of considerations of time, danger, expense, or ethics.

Imagine the amount of learning possible if learners were able to perform the following activities:

1. Land a space module on the moon.
2. Give the earth a second moon, and examine what the impact would be on the earth's atmosphere, the tides, the other moon, and so forth.
3. Govern a nation, and manage its agricultural or industrial activities for a designated period of time.
4. Make the trip across the Oregon Trail under circumstances similar to those faced by the original settlers.
5. Pilot a jet airplane into a complex international airport.
6. Modify the density of vegetation in a forest, and examine its effect on the animals living in that forest.
7. Plan the strategy for a presidential election. Carry out this strategy in a historical context and compare the results with the actual ones.
8. Invent creatures with given genetic characteristics and examine the various mating patterns of subsequent generations.

28

9. Invest a million dollars in the stock market. Lose it all and learn from the experience.
10. Apply for a job, and on the basis of interview and communication skills, either be offered the job or be rejected.
11. Interpret advertisements in newspapers and receive quick feedback regarding what would have happened if you had acted on this interpretation.
12. Rewrite a passage in the style of a famous author.

Learners who could perform such activities would be able to see important principles in action. If they could perform the activities more than once, they could try different courses of action on each repetition and evaluate the underlying principles that led to the different outcomes. Undoubtably, persons who lose a fortune in the stock market and persons who mismanage a government or a presidential campaign have an opportunity to learn from their experience; and students can likewise benefit from such simulated experiences. Obviously, none of these experiences can easily be incorporated into the typical classroom; yet each of them can be simulated on the computer.

A computer simulation presents a set of information or series of events in a way that closely resembles real life. The learner is able to apply principles or suggest courses of action, and the computer almost immediately provides feedback indicating what would have happened if the learner had undertaken the same action within the context represented by the simulation.

Even without a computer, educators can help learners vicariously experience the situations described in the preceding paragraphs, through books, audiovisual sequences, games, live simulations, or lectures that describe such situations. Or they can encourage students in class discussions to suggest courses of action to solve a particular problem and explain what would happen if these were carried out. But a computer can enable learners (1) to manipulate important principles or variables, (2) to obtain immediate feedback regarding a particular course of action, and (3) to use this feedback as a basis for changing their strategy and repeating the experiment.

Simulating a Presidential Election

A social studies teacher can use a good book, film, or lecture to explain the principles that are thought to account for the outcome of the Kennedy/Nixon election in 1960. By using the computer, however, learners can actively manipulate various aspects of political strategy, lose the election, and then try a new course of action based on what they think they learned from their failure. These learners can see the political principles in action.

Figures 4.1 to 4.3 introduce ELECT3, a program that provides the simulation described in the preceding paragraph. Just as a book, lecture, or film probably uses a theoretical basis for such a discussion, this simulation also is based on specific assumptions. Indeed, the crucial element in this simulation is the theoretical model on which it is based. The person who wrote this program believed that there was an interaction among party affiliation, personal image, and political issues that could account for outcomes in the American electoral process. From this model

```
            Historical Elections—Twentieth Century

Do you want instructions (1 = yes, 2 = no)?  1

Your goal will be to choose the optimum strategy
for candidates in an historical election.

Each candidate's strategy consists of three numbers:
      The first represents the amount of emphasis to be
      placed on the candidate's image.
      The second represents the amount of emphasis to be
      placed on party affiliation.
      The third represents the amount of emphasis to be
      placed on the campaign issues.

                 Press Enter to Continue
```

Figure 4.1. The introductory screen from ELECT3. (Adapted from the Huntington Simulations.)

were derived mathematical formulas or other algorithms that led to precise predictions of outcomes. The programmer then incorporated these formulas and algorithms into a BASIC program. It is possible that the entire process, from the development of the model to the incorporation of the formulas into the program, was carried out by a single person, but it is more likely that the model and the program were developed by separate persons. The programmer simply incorporated an existing model into the format of a computer program.

When learners run this program, their first reaction is often that it is "marvel-

```
        Election of 1960

Candidate A                    Candidate B

Kennedy                        Nixon
Democrat                       Republican

Candidate A:
   Campaign strategy in all 3 areas (image, party, issues)
   should not exceed 100 total!

   Candidates Image (10-80)?  40
   Party Affiliation (10-80)?  40
   Campaign Issues (10-80)?  20
```

Figure 4.2. The main strategy in ELECT3.

```
The result of your strategy is:

Kennedy              Nixon
53 percent           47 percent


The vote for the two major candidates in the actual
election:

Kennedy              Nixon
50.1 percent         49.9 percent


Another Run (1 = yes, 0 = no)?  0
```

Figure 4.3. The feedback provided in ELECT3.

ous" that the computer can carry out such a simulation. But more experienced learners are usually quick to ask: How does the computer know? Someone had to program the computer, and that person had to decide who would win the election when I entered my numbers. How do I know that person didn't program the computer incorrectly?" This is the essential consideration in evaluating the usefulness of a computer simulation: to question the soundness of the model on which the simulation is based.

Some aspects of human and scientific experience present models of reality for which it is easy to develop the mathematical formulas needed for computer simulations. For example, the rules governing gravity, acceleration, and genetic reproduction are easily incorporated into mathematical formulas, and therefore it is relatively easy to develop good computerized simulations when well-known models are available. On the other hand, the principles underlying such topics as political theory, human psychology, and education do not lend themselves to simple mathematical formulation, because human behavior is determined by a very large number of variables, most of which are difficult to define and understand. In addition, when models are developed in these fields, they are often stated in terms of probability, and so random variables must be included in the mathematical formulation.

ELECT3 is a simulation based on an extremely simplified theory of the American political process, and it probably ignores some important factors. In general, ELECT3 is based on a model that states that the candidate representing the incumbent party should emphasize party affiliation, whereas the challenger should focus on the issues. Moreover, the model presumes that one candidate has a "positive image," whereas the other has a "negative image." Finally, the model presumes that there is an optimum strategy for each candidate, and that if both candidates followed their optimum strategy, the election would result in a tie. None of these assumptions is perfectly valid.

Do these considerations make ELECT3 useless? The answer is no. ELECT3 still seems to provide an accurate representation of a very limited model of presidential election strategies, and a person using the simulation would be able to achieve accurate insights regarding the principles underlying this model. As long as these limitations are understood and the limited model represents a valid step in the learning process, such a simulation can be useful.

Simulating Nature

Slightly over a hundred years ago, the full impact of the Industrial Revolution swept across England. Factories were built, and the smokestacks from these factories sprinkled generous portions of sooty contaminants over the countryside. Although this pollution merely annoyed the lords and commoners, it traumatized the pepper moths of the realm.

For centuries before the Industrial Revolution, the environment had favored white pepper moths, because they could easily blend in with the light-colored tree trunks, castle walls, public statues, and other features of the countryside. This ability to blend in made the light-colored moths nearly invisible to predators, thereby increasing their chances for survival. Thus they flourished.

But when the dark-colored pollutants descended, the tree trunks and building walls became blackened, and as a result, the white pepper moths became more visible; and their predators became fat. Within a few years, the countryside surrounding the factories was nearly free of the light-colored pepper moths; but numerous dark-colored pepper moths had appeared. Was this because the dirty pollutants had soiled the wings of the white pepper moths? Indeed not. A biological mechanism called *natural selection* had been hard at work. The dark moths were surviving and multiplying because they had become difficult to see. The tide has shifted: it had become an asset to be dark colored and a liability to be light colored. The initially small number of dark-colored moths had survived to reproduce and eventually dominate the diminishing number of light-colored moths in the population. Predictable genetic mechanisms had brought about a relatively swift change in the population of pepper moths.

This change in the population of pepper moths offered a natural laboratory to study genetics. Numerous questions arise among young science students who hear about the plight of the pepper moths. How long did it take? Would it happen more quickly in some environments than in others? If the factories stopped polluting, and the rain washed away the soot, would the light-colored moths make a comeback? If so, how long would it take? Would it be possible to eliminate one or the other type of moth so that it would never make a comeback? Does the rate of gene mutation favor one type of moth over the other? For years, science teachers have used the pepper moth to demonstrate important population genetic principles. The computer simulation displayed in Figures 4.4 to 4.6 permits learners to study the plight of the pepper moth as if it were happening in the present and perhaps better understand the principles and processes involved.

Note that it is possible to understand what happened to the pepper moths without using the computer simulation. Many of the readers of this book, for example, have read about these events or have seen them depicted in a film. But the computer simulation allows the learners to use these events as a laboratory. They are able to reconstruct "reality" several different times during a single laboratory session—to manipulate an independent variable and to observe its effect on the de-

MOTHS

In determining the number of moths in a population which will be light or dark colored, the computer considers these four factors:

1) The number of light and dark moths in the previous generation.

2. The likelihood that light or dark colored moths will be eaten by predators. This will vary in different environments.

3) The genotype which produces that color (whether the trait is dominant or recessive).

4) The probability that mutation will occur.

Press (Return) to begin?

Figure 4.4. An introductory screen from MOTHS, a simulation of the rise and fall of the pepper moth in England at the time of the Industrial Revolution. This screen demonstrates guidance to help learners learn from the simulation. (From D. Luncsford, R. Rivers, and E. Vockell, *MOTHS: The Evolution of the Pepper Moth*, West Lafayette, Indiana: Diversified Educational Enterprises, 1983.)

pendent variable. This lets learners participate more actively and draw conclusions in a different fashion than would be possible without the simulation.

Figures 4.7 to 4.9 introduce another simulation of natural events, in which the learner is allowed to manipulate any of five different independent variables and to observe the effect of this manipulation on the populations of deer and wolves in a natural environment.

How many light-colored moths are there? Pick from the range 10 to 100000.   3000

How many dark-colored moths are there? Pick from the range 10 to 100000.   1000

These are the types of environments:

1. Rural (trees are light in color)
2. Urban (trees are gray in color)
3. Industrial (trees are dark in color)

Which environment do you want? (1, 2, or 3) 3

Figure 4.5. The screen on which the learner enters values for the variables in MOTHS.

YEAR	#Light Moths	#Dark Moths
1	2593 (70%)	1087 (30%)
2	2214 (65)	1171 (35)
3	2190 (60)	1465 (40)
4	1818 (54)	1544 (46)
5	1743 (48)	1887 (52)
6	1397 (42)	1942 (58)
7	1290 (36)	2316 (64)
8	994 (30)	2323 (70)
9	881 (25)	2701 (75)
10	765 (20)	3103 (80)
11	555 (16)	3003 (84)
12	463 (12)	3379 (88)
13	324 (9)	3210 (91)
14	261 (7)	3555 (93)

```
          Press (E) to Change Environment
          Press (C) to Continue or (S) to Stop
```

Figure 4.6. Tabular output from MOTHS. (The learner can also receive the same output on a graph.) The learner can use these data to test hypotheses formulated in conjunction with accompanying work sheets. The learner can see the data for additional years or replicate the experiment. The program contains random factors in its equations, and so identical entries in Figure 4.5 will lead to variations in Figure 4.6.

```
This program is a simulation of a predator-prey
relationship.  The prey will be deer and the
predator will be wolves.

By changing the variables of . . .

1) Deer population at time zero,
2) Wolf population at time zero,
3) Type of environment,
4) Deer killed other than by wolves,
5) Wolves killed by man,

you will be able to study the effects of these
variables on the deer and wolf populations.

          Press C to Continue
```

Figure 4.7. The introductory screen from BALANCE. (From D. Luncsford, R. Rivers, and E. Vockell, *BALANCE: A Simulation of the Predator/Prey Relationship in Nature,* West Lafayette, Indiana: Diversified Educational Enterprises, 1982.)

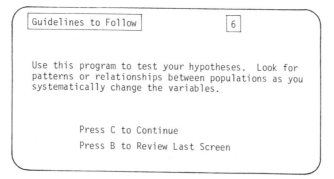

Figure 4.8. One of several guidance screens provided by BALANCE. These guidelines appear on the screen one at a time and effectively focus the learners attention in order to develop useful problem-solving strategies. Note that the learner has the option of reviewing previous screens.

YEAR	DEER POPULATION	WOLF POPULATION
0	1200	30
1	840	29
2	613	20
3	613	15
4	705	14
5	832	15
6	957	17
7	1043	19
8	1074	21
9	1042	23
10	948	24

Figure 4.9. Sample output from BALANCE. The learner has requested a "brush" environment, with no animals killed by hunting. The learner can also request graphic output.

A Matter of Convenience

In addition to making experiments possible when they would otherwise not be, the use of computer simulations also can have less dramatic but very practical benefits: (the simulation is often much more convenient and less expensive than the actual experiment is.) For example, it is possible (and it has been done for years) to have students grow plants as part of a biology course. Students can study the effect of light, for instance, by planting seeds in different light conditions and recording plant height and leaf size for several consecutive days. But what happens when a zealous janitor turns the lights off over the weekend? Or the local prankster sneaks in with scissors and clips off all the plants at ground level? If a student messes up her experiment, do you have to give her an F, or can you let her do it over while she is motivated to do so—or is there time? By simulating the growth of the plant on the computer (Figure 4.10), the whole process becomes much more easily managed. Plants may be grown once, for demonstration purposes; and thereafter their growth can be simulated on the computer.

Likewise, there are experiments conducted in science classes in which the process of setting up the experiment and cleaning up afterwards consumes much more time than the experiment itself does, for example, in examining the diffusion across cells in living tissues. The usual method is to measure how turgid (tightly inflated) a bag constructed from a membrane remains after being placed in a liquid solution for differing periods of time. This process is time-consuming, messy, and difficult to set up, and the movement of material across the membrane is difficult or impossible to observe directly. The student must generalize the observations made from the bag to living cells. But it is less expensive, less time-consuming,

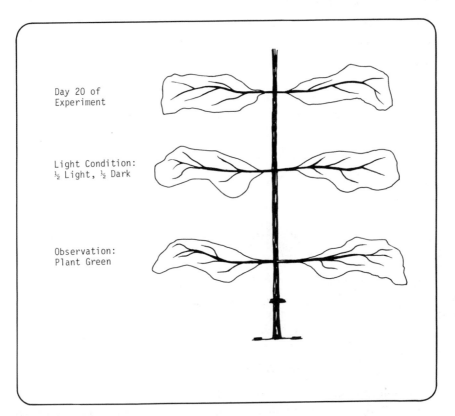

Figure 4.10. A sample output from PLANT, showing the results of growing a bean plant under conditions of half darkness and half light for twenty days. The plant started with no growth at day 0. Its growth was indicated on the screen with the passage of each day. The learner has the option of interrupting the display at any time to measure the various aspects of growth (plant size, stem size, etc.). (From D. Luncsford, R. Rivers, and E. Vockell, *PLANT: A Simulation of Plant Growth*, West Lafayette, Indiana: Diversified Educational Enterprises, 1983.)

and more direct to simulate on the computer the movement of materials across the red cell membrane. Within a short time, students can place simulated red blood cells in a variety of solutions and can make direct measurements on simulated red blood cells under these various conditions. Students can make direct associations between the changes in the simulated red blood cells and the principles of osmosis. On the other hand, students using the traditional approach with gross laboratory measurements must make at least one extra mental leap to come to the same conclusion. Figures 4.11 to 4.13 demonstrate a program that simulates this process of osmosis.

Using Simulations

Like the other instructional applications of the computer, simulations should replace ineffective and cumbersome instructional activities. They may also be used to augment other strategies that are less effective without them. Finally, it may be appropriate to use simulations to replace more expensive or time-consuming strategies when both the simulation and the other strategy are equally effective. However, such replacement should take place only when the instructor has verified that both strategies are equally effective. In any case, when using simulations, instructors should be aware of the comparative advantages and disadvantages, as pointed out in this chapter.

In addition, simulations will help learners attain their objectives most effectively if they accompany classroom work. When personal computers first started proliferating in classrooms, the computer magazines were filled with programs that pur-

```
                              OSMO


   This program presents a system with these components:


             Salt molecules
             Water molecules
             The membrane of a cell


   Within this system we can change the salt concentration
   outside the blood cell.  When we do this, something
   happens to the shape of the cell.


   As you run the program several times, look for a pattern
   and try to explain the pattern.


             Press Space Bar When Ready
```

Figure 4.11. The introductory screen from OSMO. (From D. Luncsford, R. Rivers, and E. Vockell, *OSMO: Osmosis in the Red Blood Cell*, West Lafayette, Indiana: Diversified Educational Enterprises, 1983.)

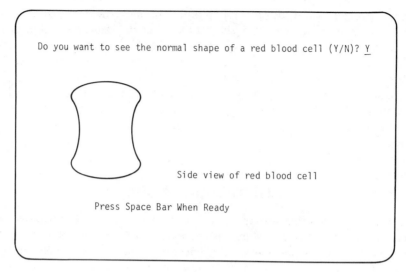

Figure 4.12. A screen from OSMO showing a normal red blood cell.

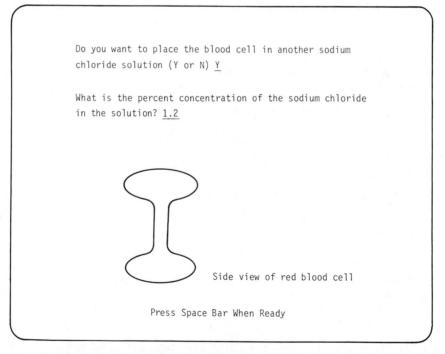

Figure 4.13. A screen from OSMO showing a red blood cell immersed in a 1.2 percent saline solution. The learner can take measurements and compare the cell with that shown in Figure 4.12.

ported to stimulate educational experiences. But the trouble with these early attempts was that they represented mere games or unadorned and isolated demonstrations of scientific principles. If teachers wanted to use these programs in their classrooms, it was up to them to fit them into their curriculum. At the present time, publishers are doing a better job of preparing simulations that can be integrated into the curriculum. For example, Figures 4.14 and 4.15 show the curricular materials that accompany BALANCE (described in Figures 4.7 to 4.9). Students who use the computer to simulate predator/prey interactions in the context of these overall objectives and guidelines are more likely to achieve educational goals than are students who approach the same simulation as an isolated game. The important point is that whether they receive such materials from publishers or develop the materials themselves, teachers should be sure to use computer simulations with other effective instructional strategies.

When students use computerized drills and tutorials, it is best for them to sit alone in front of the terminal and to interact on a one-to-one basis with the computer. This may not be equally true with simulations. Early research seems to suggest that computer simulations are better suited to small-group rather than one-to-one use. Employing small groups enables the instructor to allocate computer time as efficiently as possible. In addition, students working in small groups have an

STUDENT LABORATORY GUIDE

OBJECTIVES

After completing the BALANCE laboratory activities, you should be able to do the following.

1. Given a simulated problem and data pertinent to that problem, you should be able to identify inferences that are consistent with the data provided and which describe

    a) the effect of the environment on the predator/prey relationship,

    b) the effect of increases or decreases in the prey population on the size of the predator population,

    c) the effect of increases or decreases in the predator population on the size of the prey population, and

    d) the patterns of change in the predator and prey populations which emerge over time as any one or more of the above factors vary.

2. You should be able to apply your inferences to a given situation in such a way as to make plausible explanations for the behavior of the predator/prey populations.

3. Given a predator/prey problem, you should be able to develop an experimental design that would provide appropriate data for the solution of the problem.

Figure 4.14. The introductory page of the curriculum material that accompanies BALANCE (shown in Figures 4.7 to 4.9). By interacting with BALANCE and using these materials the learner will work toward these objectives. (Copyright © 1982 Diversified Educational Enterprises.)

```
This laboratory guide will help you investigate the
relationship between the populations of a predator (the
wolf) and a prey (the deer). The first few investigations
are designed to help you become familiar with the program
BALANCE. Use these investigations as a start. You may then
use the program to investigate on your own.

A. Balanced populations of about 2500 deer and 60 wolves in
a prairie region of Canada were divided in about half by an
oil pipeline. Half of each population was forced to move to
a forest region and the other half to a brush type region
in a valley of the Canadian Rocky Mountains.

     1. What effect did the different environments have on
     the equally divided populations? ......................
     .......................................................
     .......................................................
     .......................................................
     .......................................................

     2. Try to hypothesize or suggest a possible reason for
     any population size differences due to the different
     environments. .........................................
     .......................................................
     .......................................................
     .......................................................
     .......................................................
```

Figure 4.15. Part of the laboratory guide for BALANCE.

opportunity to interact with one another as they prepare to run the simulations and analyze the results. Such interaction encourages high-level analysis, synthesis, and evaluation.

Simulations still are merely computerized representations of theoretical models that are based on certain assumptions, and the result is necessarily an imperfect representation of reality. Table 4.1 lists the assumptions underlying the BALANCE simulation discussed earlier in this chapter. As long as the model is a reasonable representation of reality and both the instructor and the learner are aware of the assumptions and simplifications involved in the simulation, it is not likely to be misused. Serious problems arise only when these assumptions are ignored and the simulations give a false impression of reality.

One obvious solution to this problem is to use simulations based on sound assumptions. Another solution is to explain the assumptions and make sure the

Table 4.1. Some Assumptions Associated with the Equations That Formed the Basis of the BALANCE Model

Assumptions
Interaction between the deer and their food source is not considered.
Deer are the only food source of the wolf population.
The deer's deaths are caused only by wolves or humans, not by disease or old age.
The wolf population's ability to reproduce is directly proportional to the increase or decrease of the deer population.
The wolf is the ecosystem's only predator of the deer.

learners understand them. An even better solution for sophisticated learners is to withhold the list of assumptions and to ask the learners themselves to list the assumptions that they think underlie the simulation. Such learners may even be able to speculate how the simulation would change if additional or different assumptions were made. In any case, the learner's awareness that a computer can simulate reality only under the constraints of certain assumptions is an important part of computer literacy that should be encouraged.

Finally, it is important to remember that an instructor who devotes time to computer simulations is taking time away from something else. In many cases, this is a desirable trade-off, though in a few cases, it is not. For example, if students in a biology class simulate on the computer the growth of bean plants, they get precise results and can replicate the experiment as often as necessary to achieve the desired understanding. However, the teacher may decide that having the students work at the computer terminals will consume the time needed to grow the actual bean plants, and if the teacher considers it useful to have the students watch a real plant grow, the cathode ray tube alone will not provide this benefit. The solution is probably not to eliminate the computer, but rather for the teacher to use both the computer simulation and the real bean plant. One strategy is to have the entire class experiment with real plants and have small groups of students replicate the experiment and perform variations at their computer terminals.

The same combination of simulation and actual experience is useful with the osmosis experiment (Figures 4.11 to 4.13). Students who use the computer to simulate and study osmosis should first observe the processes involved in osmosis at a gross level (in pieces of carrots or potatoes, for example) before going to the cellular level (red blood cells) in the simulation. This enables them to relate what happens at the tissue level to changes at the cellular level. Students can much more easily understand the behavior of living organisms when they can make this connection. (Figure 4.16 and 4.17 show materials that accompany the osmosis simulation designed to help students understand these relationships.)

Guidelines for Good Simulations

A good computerized simulation includes three elements: (1) a sound mathematical or logical model representing some aspect of human or scientific experience, (2) a clear mode of presentation that enables the learner to interact with it, and (3) a strategy for integrating the simulation with other effective learning activities. At the present time, most of the available simulations focus on only one of these elements, and very few use all three. The following paragraphs are guidelines for carrying out each of these elements.

1. Specific strategies for developing models cannot be included in this book, as these models must be formulated in the context of a particular subject matter. This chapter briefly introduced examples from several fields but focused on examples from the biological sciences. This is because good examples are more readily available in biology than in other fields. The key point is to recognize that there are numerous assumptions. The fact that they will often be violated does not mean that a simulation should not be written. A wise strategy is to write down these

Activity #2

```
Materials Needed: potatoes
                  10% salt (NaCl) solution
                  distilled water
                  3 petri dishes
                  paper towel
                  cork borer
                  triple beam balance
```

Procedure:

1) Make about 10-20 cylinders of potato using a cork borer.

2) Cut the cylinders into 10 mm. sections.

3) Blot dry the sections of potato with paper towel.

4) Weigh out two 10g. samples of potato sections.

5) Place the samples into separate petri dishes and cover one sample with distilled water and the other with 10% NaCl solution.

6) After 10 to 15 minutes blot the potato samples dry with paper towel and weigh.

7) Calculate weight change in the two samples if any. Record your results in the chart below.

```
-----------------------------------------------------------------
Distilled Water:
-----------------------------------------------------------------
Weight    Weight    Weight   Weight    Weight    Weight    Change
  of      of plate  before     of      of plate  after
plate     + 10g               plate    + potato
=================================================================


=================================================================
-----------------------------------------------------------------
10% Salt Solution:
-----------------------------------------------------------------
Weight    Weight    Weight   Weight    Weight    Weight    Change
  of      of plate  before     of      of plate  after
plate     + 10g               plate    + potato
=================================================================


=================================================================
```

Figure 4.16. Part of the laboratory guide for OSMO.

assumptions as early as possible and to keep them in mind both while you write the simulation and use it to teach your students.

2. The strategies for putting the theoretical model into a computer program are similar to those used for drills and tutorials. A programmer who can write good drills and has a good mathematical or logical model can usually put this algorithm into a computer program. The program should be written in a user friendly format, offering directions and other information on request. Learners should have access to all the information necessary to carry out the simulation. It is not necessary, of course, for the entire simulation to be performed on the computer, and in many

Simulation of Changes in a Red Blood Cell

Materials Needed: a small centimeter ruler

Procedure:
      The purpose of this simulated experiment is to predict the
condition of a red blood cell in a variety of environments.   After
making a prediction, you will go to the computer and actually measure
the cross-sectional diameter of a simulated red blood cell on the
computer's display screen.   You will make your measurements in
centimeters using a metric ruler.   Your measurements then must be
converted to the dimensions of a real red blood cell.
      The diameter of actual red blood cells is measured in microns.
The "normal" diameter of a red blood cell in your body is 1.4
microns.   To help you convert your centimeter measurements to
microns, the computer will display a ruler on the screen when you
first go through the simulation.   Measure the distance between any
two adjacent marks on this ruler.   We will define this distance to be
1 simunit (for simulation unit).   Record your measurement in the
space below.

                1 simunit = ... centimeters

To determine the actual size of a red blood cell in microns from your
centimeter measurements, use the following equation.

$$\text{Actual Size of Red Blood Cell (in microns)} = \frac{\text{Measured Size of Simulated Cell (in cm.)}}{\text{Length of 1 Simunit (in cm.)}}$$

      Your job will be to predict the SIZE of the blood cell in several
different concentrations of salt solution after making one or two
observations first.

      First, choose two concentrations of salt solution between 0
percent and 2 percent.   Record your choices here:

                Number 1 .... percent

                Number 2 .... percent

      Now go to the computer and enter the choices you made, one at a
time.   When the computer draws the blood cell, measure with your
ruler the cross-sectional diameter at the center of the cell.

measure ⟶

      By the way, if the screen says "hemolyzed", it means your blood
cell burst.   Record your results in the table below.

Percent Concentration of Salt Solution	Red Blood Cell Diameter (microns)
1.	1. ....
2.	2. ....

Figure 4.17. Simulation of changes in a red blood cell.

cases it makes good sense to have students carry data to and from the computer as they conduct a simulation.

3. Do not assume that learners will automatically see the connection between the simulation and other instructional activities, and so check to make sure your students are. The amount of help you need to supply can range from a simple verbal statement to a set of detailed work sheets. Exactly how you will help your students make this connection will vary according to the subject matter and your teaching strategy.

Chapter 5
The Students Take Over!

The instructional applications of the computer discussed so far have assumed that someone other than the student was controlling the learning situation. Tutorials present information in a highly structured format that relies completely on the programmer's ingenuity; drills provide a continuous series of problems that a programmer has devised; and simulations rely on a programmer who has incorporated a theoretical model and a set of assumptions into a structured format.

But exciting things can happen if you can put the learners themselves in control of the computers. Most parents and teachers grew to adulthood in an age when computers were exotic tools available only to highly trained specialists, and they therefore are often hesitant to use computers. But children are much less inhibited around computers and assume that they can master them and put them to work.

It is wise to take advantage of this interest and offer students the opportunity to take control. Needless to say, students who are inappropriately introduced to computers may feel overwhelmed or may use the computer for trivial purposes. This chapter will suggest several strategies for putting students in control of computers and for encouraging them to make maximum use of them.

Students As Programmers

One possibility is to permit the students themselves to write the drills, tutorials, and simulations discussed earlier. As you have learned by now, BASIC is not an especially difficult language to learn; indeed, many teachers in our courses have reported receiving useful help from their seventh- and eighth-grade students! And even much younger students can participate in the programming process by suggesting strategies to change existing programs and telling the teacher what changes

45

to feed into the computer. Children enjoy spotting "mistakes" that the computer makes and teaching the computer to operate correctly. This early participation in debugging and programming helps students appreciate what the computer can and cannot do, one of the most important aspects of computer literacy.

As we stated in the previous chapter, simulations are based on assumptions, and it is important that students recognize them. A useful strategy is to step beyond the recognition of existing assumptions and permit the students to introduce new ones into the simulations. Students who are able to do this will come to understand the principles on which the simulation focuses and at the same time learn important programming skills that they can generalize to new settings.

It is important that computer programming not be relegated to a separate course or hour of the day. Likewise, the computers should not be reserved solely for gifted students. The ideal situation is to encourage all learners to use the computer to help them solve problems in many areas of the curriculum, including science, social studies, language arts, music, art, and physical education.

LOGO

LOGO is an educational tool and a programming language devised through the inspiration of Seymour Papert and others under the sponsorship of the National Science Foundation. Although the concepts behind LOGO are part of the public domain, various vendors have developed specific LOGO language packages. Information about buying different versions of the LOGO language and related documentation can be found in Appendix F. The examples in this chapter use the Terrapin version of LOGO (which operates on the Apple II Plus computer), but the information can be generalized to other versions of LOGO.

Papert studied under Jean Piaget in Switzerland and also worked on artificial intelligence. LOGO combines elements from both of these sources to create an educational tool that places powerful computational resources into the hands of even very young learners. The learner can control this resource to learn science, mathematics, art, and intellectual modeling. The LOGO language is structured so that learners can easily interact with the computer at their own intellectual levels, while simultaneously being challenged to progress to higher levels.

LOGO permits and requires the learner to devise a program element by element. "Primitive" commands are combined into groups called *procedures*. These procedures can be defined as steps in other procedures, and so on, until the desired level of complexity is reached. A program may contain any number of primitive commands and procedures in any configuration, and the outputs from one procedure may be used as inputs for another procedure. This encourages the learner both to analyze the real problem and to synthesize the components in order to solve the problem.

One of the easiest ways to understand the value of LOGO is to examine "turtle geometry." Learners are shown a small triangle called a turtle in the middle of the computer screen and how simple commands can make the turtle move forward and backward, turn right and left, appear and disappear, change colors, and perform a few other operations (see Figure 5.1). After the learners have experimented

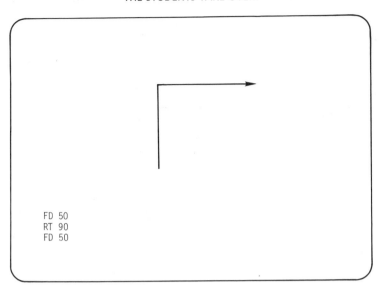

```
FD 50
RT 90
FD 50
```

Figure 5.1. The turtle has moved forward fifty units, has turned right ninety degrees, and has moved forward another fifty units.

with the turtle for a while, they learn to teach the turtle new operations based on the turtle's initial limited vocabulary of operations. For example, Figure 5.2 shows how the programmer might define the operation SQUARE for the turtle; Figure 5.3 shows how the computer would carry out this operation; and Figure 5.4 shows the result of telling the computer to repeat the operation SQUARE four times.

If this is a bit confusing to read about, it is because LOGO is designed to be experienced, not studied in a textbook. For example, when a child first tries to draw a SQUARE, the result is often something like that shown in Figure 5.5. Children who make such a mistake often spontaneously get up from their seats and walk around the room in imitation of the turtle, thus internalizing the geometry. It is easy to make up enjoyable exercises that are also educationally stimulating:

1. Ask those children who have just drawn a square to draw a triangle. Do not explain the characteristics of a triangle, but let the children discover them themselves.

```
TO SQUARE

    FD 50
    RT 90
    FD 50
    RT 90
    FD 50
    RT 90
    FD 50
```

Figure 5.2. The primitive commands used to define the new term SQUARE. Whenever the LOGO program encounters the term SQUARE, it will execute this set of primitive commands.

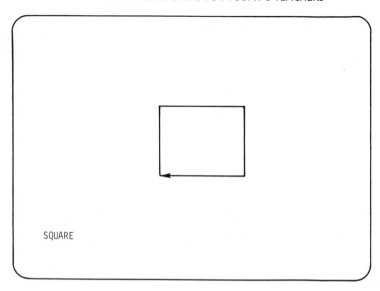

Figure 5.3. The turtle has carried out the commands designated in Figure 5.2.

   2. After the children have drawn a triangle, let them try a circle. Give no information, but just let them work it out by themselves.
   3. Let the children draw a petal on a flower. Then a whole flower. Then a
   garden. Then anything they wish to draw.

Almost all children enjoy playing with the turtle; and by doing so, they learn concepts of mathematics (especially geometry), logic, and computer programming.
Additional information regarding LOGO can be found in Abelson (1982), Watt
(1982), and Carter (1983).

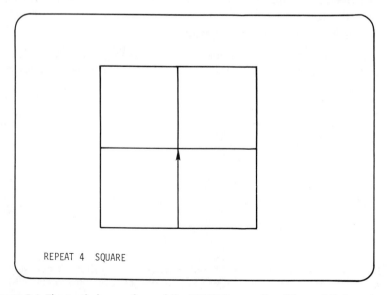

Figure 5.4. The turtle has performed the SQUARE operation (Figure 5.2) four times.

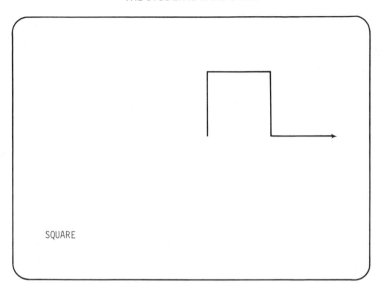

Figure 5.5. An example of an imperfect square. The learner failed to take the proper perspective at the third turn where it told the computer to turn left instead of right.

Word Processing

Think back to those days of English composition and history term papers: when you spent five hours working on a paper, what percentage of that time was spent actually thinking, as opposed to recopying, deleting, correcting, and more recopying? How many times did you think of a new way to say something but decide not to because the change would require rewriting or retyping the entire manuscript?

One of the best ways for us to grow intellectually is to state our ideas, to examine them critically, and to revise them according to this evaluation. Such a critical revision should be part of the process of composing which occurs throughout the educational curriculum. In fact, however, such revision is almost completely absent from the education of many students, because to them revision too often means the trivial recopying of old ideas.

This chapter has been revised many times, but it has been written only once, because it was composed at a microcomputer terminal using a word-processing program. If this chapter took ten hours to write, then nine of them were devoted to thinking about what we wanted to say and how to say it. Very little time was spent on the drudgery of rewriting identical thoughts. The computer can make this same contribution to the education of children who are old enough to use a computer keyboard to type on. Students can write the first draft of a manuscript at the computer, using whatever notes or other resources they would normally use. Then they can have the printer generate a triple-spaced copy of the rough draft. They can go through the rough draft, circling words, making notations, and jotting down ideas for changes. Then they can reload the original version of the manuscript from the disk on which they stored it and make revisions.

The word-processing system will provide simple strategies to enable the student to do such things as (1) locate specific words and correct spelling errors, (2) move around sentences or paragraphs within the manuscript, (3) insert new ideas, and (4) find overused expressions and make suitable replacements. The students can repeat this revision process as often as necessary. When they are satisfied with the completed product, they can instruct the printer to produce a final copy, which might be single spaced or double spaced, with the proper margins and hyphenation. If the students wish, they can even have the entire manuscript right-justified with little additional effort. If a student completes the entire process and then discovers a sensational new idea that would normally be ignored because it would require retyping the entire manuscript, they can easily make the change, and the computer can retype the manuscript while the student eats breakfast.

There are some interesting ramifications from the use of word processing by school-age children. Their papers are often a lot easier to read. Also, students can copy the work of other students by merely reproducing a disk. It is not clear, however, that this necessarily will lead to an increase in cheating, though the students who cheat may find it easier to do so. Nonetheless, teachers can resolve this problem by encouraging their students to review and edit one another's papers— processes that are easily carried out on the word-processing microcomputer.

Microcomputers currently have the capacity to look for spelling errors, and soon they will have the capacity to spot grammatical errors. Some teachers shudder at this thought. Won't students become lazy spellers and grammarians if the computer does all the work for them? Will they be able to write well without a computer? Although the concern is valid, the problem is more imagined than real. The computer does not really correct spelling errors. All it does is identify words that do not match a list in its memory. This may actually be a useful learning device, as it can direct the learner's attention to difficult words. Likewise, the computer does not really correct grammar; it merely points to anomalous usages. For example, it might flag the word *their* and print this message on the screen: "Their is an adjective meaning 'belonging to them.' Are you sure that's the word you want in this sentence?" The student might read this message and choose to replace *their* with *there, his,* or *the.* Again, such a service may be more a learning device than a crutch.

Working with Data Bases

It is possible to put a vast quantity of raw data into a data file and allow students to do something useful with them. For example, an anonymous one-hundred-item questionnaire could be circulated to a thousand students in a high school; the resulting data could be stored in a data file; and the students could analyze them. Depending on the course objectives, students could make cross-tabulations, draw graphs, or make inferences about the attitudes that underlie the responses and the factors that cause such attitudes.

Instead of using a questionnaire distributed in the school, students could have access to other sources of data. For example, an instructor could fill a data base with purely hypothetical data for the students to analyze. In addition, there are numerous sources of data available from government sources. For example, results from the 1980 census will shortly be available in a format ready for student analysis. Likewise, the raw data from many government-sponsored scientific experiments can be put in a format for computer-assisted student analysis. Students can probably benefit much more from summarizing such data themselves and drawing their own inferences than they can from looking up the same information in an almanac or encyclopedia.

In addition, students can develop their own data banks in school chemistry, biology, physics, and other science laboratories. They can do this by interfacing microcomputers with laboratory instruments regularly used in such laboratories. Special interface options exist for both the instruments and the computer. There are two advantages of using such data banks. First, students can analyze and reduce data from experiments continuously and quickly, provided that the interfacing is designed to make this possible. Second, functions not normally available with more common and less expensive laboratory equipment may be performed by the microcomputer at little or no additional cost. For example, the computer can act as a storage oscilloscope, storing several sets of data and then displaying summaries of them either singly or superimposed on one another. Likewise, a student wishing to collect data on animal behavior could have the computer monitor such variables as the revolutions of a running wheel or the range and frequency of some type of brain wave. The computer could easily analyze and correlate the data. If desired, the computer could even be programmed to introduce the independent variables (e.g., by changing the rate of reinforcement).

The amount of assistance supplied by the computer can be varied by the teacher. For some courses, it may be desirable to let the students write their own BASIC programs to analyze the data. Or students could be given programs that automatically tabulate data and draw pie graphs in various colors to accentuate important points. By selecting and varying the characteristics of tables and graphs, students learn to focus on salient information and to draw relevant inferences.

Endless Possibilities

The rapid developments in hardware and software will assure a ready supply of new ideas for classroom teachers. Developments in Computer Assisted Design (CAD) currently make it possible for an engineer, during a single work period, to simulate on a CRT screen vivid, three-dimensional representations of products that used to take a whole team of engineers several months to produce. Parents of students have access to computers that make rapid and accurate financial predictions. Exciting developments are taking place in robotics and artificial intelligence. Libraries of books, journals, and reference works are being reduced into computer-accessible formats. These developments are often frightening and sometimes threatening to teachers. In fact, many teachers rightly conclude that they themselves can happily live out their lives without knowing much about such developments. However, the students in these teachers' classrooms are not similarly overwhelmed and do not feel threatened. In addition, students cannot assume that they can live out their lives ignoring these developments. By putting students in charge of computers as early and as effectively as possible, we can give them intellectual tools to master the principles and concepts that have been the traditional goals of our educational systems, as well as an opportunity to master machines that will otherwise master them.

References

Abelson, H. "A Beginner's Guide to LOGO." *BYTE* 7 (August 1982): 88–112.

Watt, D. "LOGO in the schools." *BYTE* 7 (August 1982): 116–134.

Carter, R. "The Complete Guide to LOGO." *Classroom Computer News* 3 (April 1983).

Chapter 6
Programming in BASIC

ALTHOUGH there are many programming languages, BASIC is the language in which most commercially available instructional programs are written. For this reason, it is useful for educators to select BASIC as the programming language in which they achieve some proficiency. This chapter will introduce the fundamental concepts of BASIC programming, and subsequent chapters will help you master a moderate level of complexity in BASIC programming. Through these chapters, you should be able to understand the logic of all the programs used as examples in this book, to modify these programs to suit your own instructional needs, and, if you wish, to write your own programs at comparable levels of complexity. Most important, you will come to a clear understanding of what computers can do in education and how they do it.

These chapters will not cover everything about BASIC programming; rather, they will concentrate on the principles of BASIC that are common to all computers and that are most widely used in instructional programming. We have tried to avoid turning these chapters into a manual, but we are certain that if you understand them, you will feel comfortable using the manual that accompanies your own computer.

Finally, there are a few things that are more easily demonstrated in person that described in a book. In order to avoid excessive detail in these programming chapters, we shall assume that readers have access to a course instructor, a salesperson, a junior high computer "addict," or some other specialist who can occasionally demonstrate some of the fundamental mechanics of using the computer. For instance, we shall make no attempt to describe how to turn your computer on, how to find the return or break keys (or their equivalents), how to insert a disk or cartridge properly, how to format a disk, and the like. Problems like these are more efficiently resolved through personal interactions with a helper than through detailed explanations in a textbook.

How the Computer Works

Before we discuss any programming techniques, we shall examine the logic of a BASIC computer program, as described in Figure 6.1. A computer carries out its functions through complex patterns of electronic circuitry. There is no need, however, for the beginning programmer or interested educator to understand the principles of electronics in order to write and use instructional programs. In this book, we shall describe the computer as carrying out commands and going to different lines much as if a person were carrying out instructions. When a computer program starts to run, the computer simply goes to the first line in the program and starts to carry out the instructions it finds there. Then it continues to follow instructions until it runs out of instructions, until it is told to stop, or until an instruction is impossible to follow. Then it stops. It is as simple as that. If you read the annotated description of AGE or HELLO later in this chapter, you will see this procedure in operation.

Line Numbers

Every command in a BASIC program must be entered on a line in that program, and each of these lines must have a line number. The line numbers serve two purposes: (1) they provide a label for each line so that the computer can identify each line separately, and (2) they indicate the order in which the computer should carry out the commands. Although most computers permit more than one command to a single line, we shall assume for the moment that each command has a specific line number. For example, here is an extremely brief BASIC program:

```
100 PRINT ''HELLO.''
110 PRINT ''WHAT IS YOUR NAME?''
120 INPUT N$
130 PRINT
140 PRINT ''I'M GLAD TO MEET YOU, '';N$;''.''
150 END
```

When instructed to run this program, the computer would go to line 100, carry out the instruction there, and continue going to subsequent lines until it came to the END in line 150. (The meaning of the commands will be discussed later.) If a person named Marilyn ran this program, she would receive the following output on her screen:

```
HELLO.
WHAT IS YOUR NAME?
?MARILYN

I'M GLAD TO MEET YOU, MARILYN.
```

1. When the program starts to RUN, the computer goes to the first line
   of the program.

2. The computer tries to carry out the instruction contained on that line.

   a. If the instruction makes no sense, the computer will print an error
      message and stop.

   b. If the instruction makes sense, the computer will carry out the
      instruction.

3. If the instructions tell the computer to stop, it will stop.

4. Unless the instruction in Step 2 tells the computer to break the sequence,
   the computer will go to the next line and start over with Step 1.

5. If the instructions tell the computer to go somewhere other than the next line,
   the computer will go to the designated line and repeats Step 1.

6. If the computer runs out of lines, it will stop.

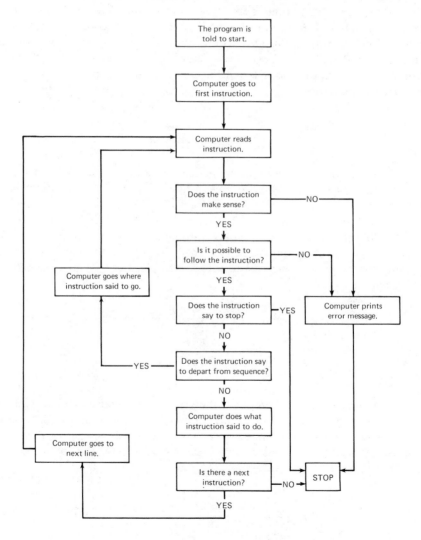

Figure 6.1. How a computer program works.

Figure 6.2.

Note that the size of the interval between adjacent line numbers is unimportant. The computer merely goes from one line to the next highest line number, and it does not matter whether the "step" between the line numbers is 1, 10, 117. For example, the program in the preceding paragraph would run exactly the same if it had the following line numbers:

```
1 PRINT ''HELLO.''
3 PRINT ''WHAT IS YOUR NAME?''
120 INPUT N$
130 PRINT
5197 PRINT ''I'M GLAD TO MEET YOU, '';N$;''.''
9650 END
```

However, most programmers prefer to number their programs in a more chronological order, as in the first example. Then why not simply use the line numbers 1 through 6 for this six-line program? The answer is that it may be necessary later to insert new lines between the existing lines, and that this can be done only if it is possible to insert a new line number between the two existing line numbers. Because it is difficult to anticipate where such insertions will be needed, most programmers leave intervals of ten between line numbers as they write their programs. Strategies for inserting lines are discussed later in this Chapter.

Putting Words on the Screen

In order to see what your computer program is doing, it is necessary to have it display the results of its activity on some output device such as a screen or printer. The following discussion will explain the use of the cathode ray (television) screen. Similar strategies are used to transmit output to other output devices. (Note: This and subsequent chapters will introduce BASIC commands as the need arises. In addition, Appendix B provides a more detailed and systematic treatment

Take this stuff and
put it on the
screen. Display every-
thing I tell you and
only what I tell you.

Figure 6.3.

of all the BASIC commands used in this book. They have been grouped together for easy reference. For further details, you may wish to consult your computer's manual for information unique to your system.)

The PRINT command tells the computer to place on the screen whatever follows the word PRINT. The computer, of course, has no idea what the symbols following PRINT mean, and so if you tell the computer to print something absurd, it will blithely carry out your orders. If the computer is told to print something enclosed in quotation marks, it will print the exact contents of what it finds within the quotation marks, including the presence or absence of blank spaces. The guidelines in Appendix B explain how to use the PRINT command.

When it encounters a PRINT command, the computer begins to place information on the screen at the current location of the *cursor*. In other words, the cursor is a visual indicator showing where the next symbol to be printed by the computer will appear. The location of the cursor is symbolized by a flashing light or some other prompt, and its movement follows certain rules. For example, on most computers, after the screen has been cleared (discussed later in this chapter), the computer will begin printing in the upper left-hand corner of the screen. If you want information to appear somewhere other than at the cursor's present location, you must first move the cursor. There are several ways to do this. For example, the TAB command works very much like the tab key on a typewriter. TAB(5) simply means that the computer should start printing five spaces in from the left margin rather than at the left margin. TAB(19) means that the computer should start in column 19.

At times, you will wish to remove information from the screen. CLS stands for "Clear the Screen," and that is exactly what the computer does when it encounters this command on the TRS-80. It eliminates whatever is on the screen and moves the cursor to the upper left-hand corner. This means that subsequent PRINT statements will start at the top of a blank screen unless the computer receives instructions to the contrary. Other computers have different methods. For example, the

Figure 6.4.

Apple   TRS-80

Figure 6.5.

equivalent command on the Apple is HOME. (The Apple programmer simply envisions the computer's "home" as being a nice, clear screen with the cursor in the upper left-hand corner.)

Variables and Variable Labels

In BASIC programming, it is possible to store pieces of information as *variables*. This means that a variable label can be assigned to the information and then used in BASIC commands to represent the information stored under that label. The term variable is used because the value can vary according to the terminal's responses or the program's instructions.

Here is an example of a very simple use of a variable in a computer program:

```
10  PRINT ''WHAT IS YOUR FIRST NUMBER?''
20  INPUT A
30  PRINT ''WHAT IS YOUR SECOND NUMBER?''
40  INPUT B
50  PRINT ''YOUR NUMBERS ADD UP TO '';A+B;''.''
```

If we ran this program, we would obtain this output:

```
WHAT IS YOUR FIRST NUMBER?
?5
WHAT IS YOUR SECOND NUMBER?
?4
YOUR NUMBERS ADD UP TO 9.
```

The computer would stop at line 20, wait for the person at the terminal to type something, and then assign the variable label A to the 5 typed in by the person at the terminal. In the same manner, B would acquire the value of 4 in line 40. (If the person at the terminal had entered different numbers, A and B would have different values.) Finally, the computer would use the current values of A and B to print the result in line 50. (The use of semicolons and the word INPUT in this program will be explained later in this chapter.)

There are two different types of variables: numeric variables and string variables. As the name implies, numeric variables refer to numbers. The variables A and B in the program in the preceding paragraph are numeric variables. The unique feature of numeric variables is that they can be treated in mathematical fashion; that is,

Figure 6.6.

they can be added, subtracted, multiplied, divided, and submitted to other mathematical operations. String variables, on the other hand, contain "strings" of symbols (usually letters or words) that cannot be treated in a mathematical fashion. The program HELLO, which will be introduced shortly, contains numerous examples of string variables.

Because the computer treats numeric and string variables differently, it must have a method for determining to which category a given piece of information belongs. It does this by attaching a dollar sign ($) to the end of all string variables and omitting the dollar sign with numeric variables. For example, the following all could be labels for string variables: A$, B$, N$, Z$, A1$, A2$; and these could be labels for numeric variables: A, B, N, Z, A1, A2.

The rules for variable labels differ according to the computer. In most cases, the label can be either a single letter (such as A or B) or a letter followed by another letter or number (such as AA or B1). The dollar sign is either added or omitted at the end of the label (such as B1 or B1$). Talking about variables in the abstract is often more difficult than understanding them or using them in actual programs. When you examine the sample programs, you will better understand these examples of variables.

The INPUT Command

The INPUT command is one means for attaching variable labels to information. Other ways to do this will be outlined in subsequent chapters. The INPUT command gives the computer the following message: "(1) Stop what you're doing. (2) Insert a question mark as a prompt to indicate that the person at the keyboard

Figure 6.7.

should do something. (3) Wait for the person at the keyboard to respond. (4) When there is a response, assign it to the variable label accompanying the word INPUT. (5) Continue where you were when you were interrupted." For example, in the sample printout on page 58, the computer (1) printed, "What is your first number?" (2) inserted the question mark on the next line, (3) waited for the respondent to enter a number, (4) assigned that number to the variable A, and then (5) continued with the next line of the program. In line 50, when the computer added A and B, it used the value of A that it had acquired in line 20 and the value of B that it had acquired in line 40. Likewise, in line 100 of HELLO, the computer will (1) stop after printing "What is your name," (2) insert the question mark after "name," (3) wait until the user enters his or her name, (4) assign this name to the label A$, and then (5) go on to lines 110 and 120 as soon as the user enters his or her name. Then in line 120 the computer will insert the user's name where the symbol A$ appears.

The Semicolon: Stringing Together PRINT Statements

When the computer finishes a PRINT statement, it normally goes to the next screen line and prints its next piece of output at the beginning of that line. However, in some cases we may want to have the computer continue on the same line rather than going to the next. For example, we may want the computer to print:

```
THE SUM OF YOUR NUMBERS IS 9.
```

rather than

```
THE SUM OF YOUR NUMBERS IS
9
```

The way to get the computer to continue printing on the same screen line is to use semicolons between the components of the PRINT statement.

In BASIC, the semicolon means to "attach" or "join" two pieces of printed output. When the computer attaches two pieces of printed output on a screen, it simply begins printing one piece of output in the space immediately following the preceding piece of output. For example, the following line instructs the computer to join three pieces of output:

```
50 PRINT ''THE SUM OF YOUR NUMBERS IS '';A+B;''.''
```

When it executes this command, the computer will print three separate pieces of output. First, it will print "The sum of your numbers is"; a number equal to the sum of A plus B (if A is equal to 5 and B is equal to 4, the computer will print 9); and then a period. Because the computer will print all three of these items in immediately adjacent spaces, they will look like one long output rather than three separate items. Because there is no semicolon after the period, the computer will print any subsequent items on the next screen line.

Sometimes when you string together outputs, you will want spaces between the words, and so you will have to insert them yourself. For example, if N$ has a value of "ED," the following line will cause the computer to print HI THERE, EDARE YOU HAPPY?

        100 PRINT ''HI THERE, '';N$; ''ARE YOU HAPPY?''

If you want the computer to insert a space after the comma and after the name, then you must supply these spaces as part of your PRINT statement. Likewise, if you want a period between the two sentences, you must include it in your PRINT statement, as in the following line:

        100 PRINT ''HI THERE, '';N$;''. ARE YOU HAPPY?''

The output ". ARE YOU HAPPY?" may look strange, but when the computer blends the three outputs into a single line, it conveys the desired message:

        HI THERE, ED. ARE YOU HAPPY?

The person reading this line on the screen will think he or she is reading a single output rather than three separate segments joined together.

In addition to blending variables into PRINT statements, the semicolon serves a useful purpose in conjunction with the INPUT statement. Remember that one of the functions of the INPUT statement is to put a question mark on the screen, at the present location of the cursor, which will usually be at the beginning of a new line. For example, you might enter these lines into the computer:

        100 PRINT ''HI THERE, '';N$;''. ARE YOU HAPPY?''
        110 INPUT A$

The computer would respond by putting the following message on the screen:

        HI THERE, ED. ARE YOU HAPPY?
        ?

Do you really want a question mark both after "happy" and at the beginning of the next line? If you are having the computer print a question, why not place the INPUT's question mark at the end of the question rather than at the beginning of the next screen line? We can do this by using a semicolon:

        100 PRINT ''HI THERE, '';N$;''. ARE YOU HAPPY'';
        110 INPUT A$

If you enter these two lines and run them, the computer will print the question with a single question mark at the end of it:

        HI THERE, ED. ARE YOU HAPPY?

This looks nicer; it also saves a line on the screen; and you may discover later that you need this extra line for additional output.

Sending the Computer to Specific Lines

IF/THEN statements enable the computer to break its normal rule of going immediately to the next command. The following is an example:

        50 IF X = 5 THEN 500

If the condition stated in the command is true (if X equals 5), then the computer will do whatever follows the word THEN (go to line 500); otherwise it will skip whatever follows THEN and will follow its normal humdrum rule of going on to the next command. (Secretly, computers probably hope that the conditions will vary once in a while.) When THEN is followed by a number, this means "GOTO" the line in the program indicated by that number. On most computers, it is also possible to insert a BASIC command (such as PRINT or GOSUB) after the word THEN (50 IF X = 5 THEN PRINT "HELLO"). In such cases, the BASIC command following THEN (PRINT "HELLO") will be executed only if the condition (X = 5) is true. Line 90 of AGE and lines 430 to 460 of HELLO are examples of typical IF/THEN statements.

GOTO statements likewise interrupt the computer's normal pattern of going to the next line. They look like this:

60 GOTO 300

Instead of going to the next command, the computer goes to the line indicated by the number following GOTO. Such GOTO staements are useful to route the computer around lines that it should not execute. For example, in AGE, the computer will print both a "right" and a "wrong" message unless it is directed around line 130 by the GOTO statement at line 120. Likewise, in HELLO, without the GOTO statement in line 590, the computer will print "It's great fun!" at line 580 and then "Sorry! I'm broke too . . ." at line 600. Line 590 eliminates this perplexing answer by sending the computer directly to line 920 after the proper message.

Ending the Program

The END statement tells the computer to stop looking for commands in the program. When it encounters this command, the computer stops running the pro-

Figure 6.8.

Figure 6.9.

gram and displays a prompt on the screen indicating that it is ready to receive further instructions. The current program, of course, is still in the computer's active memory, and so the command RUN will start the same program running again. In addition, it is possible to list the program, to make modifications in it, or to run a new program.

A computer program will stop running if it simply runs out of lines. However, it is much better to end a program with an END statement than with no more lines. When novice programmers hear that every program should end with an END statement, many of them assume that this means that the last word on the last line must be END. This may often be so, but not necessarily. The END statement can be located anywhere in the program, but the important thing is to direct the program to that line when you want it to stop running the program.

Sample Programs

Now that we have introduced the overall logic of a computer program and some fundamental concepts and commands, it will be useful to examine some programs that incorporate all the principles discussed so far. First, we shall consider a very brief program that uses these principles, and then a lengthier program. In each case, we shall offer a listing of the program, an annotated description of it, and an opportunity to modify it.

AGE

AGE is a simple program that uses all of the principles discussed in this chapter. The program assumes that it will be run in 1984 and tells the respondent what that person's age will be in the year 2000. The listing of this program is given in Figure 6.10, and a sample screen from the program appears in Figure 6.11.

```
10 CLS
20 PRINT "HI. WHAT IS YOUR NAME?"
30 INPUT N$
40 PRINT "HOW OLD ARE YOU, ";N$;
50 INPUT A
60 PRINT "HOW OLD DO YOU THINK YOU'LL BE"
70 PRINT "IN THE YEAR 2000?"
80 INPUT R
90 IF R=A+16 THEN 130
100 PRINT "I DON'T THINK SO."
110 PRINT "I THINK YOU'LL BE ";A+16;" YEARS OLD."
120 GOTO 150
130 PRINT "RIGHT!"
140 PRINT "YOU'RE PRETTY SMART."
150 END
```

Figure 6.10. A listing of AGE.

In line 10 the computer clears the screen, which eliminates any printed output that may have been on the screen and sends the cursor to the upper left-hand corner.

Line 20 instructs the computer to print a message. The programmer has included a question mark as part of this message. Line 30 is an INPUT statement which puts a question mark on the screen. This question mark appears at the current location of the cursor, which is at the beginning of a new line. (In Figure 6.11, this question mark appears immediately before the word "Bob," which was the name entered by the learner.) The computer then pauses until the person at the terminal responds and then labels the respondent's name as N$. This name is a string variable, and so it cannot be added or multiplied, even if the respondent enters a student ID number.

In line 40 the computer prints two outputs. The first is "How old are you, ".

```
HI. WHAT IS YOUR NAME?
?BOB
HOW OLD ARE YOU, BOB?15
HOW OLD DO YOU THINK YOU'LL BE
IN THE YEAR 2000?
?35
I DON'T THINK SO.
I THINK YOU'LL BE 31 YEARS OLD.
READY
>
```

Figure 6.11. A sample screen from AGE. Student responses (input) are underlined. The question marks at the beginning of the second and sixth lines were supplied as prompts by the computer when it encountered INPUT statements in the program. Likewise, the question mark at the end of the second line is a prompt, represented by the word INPUT in line 50 of Figure 6.10. The semicolon at the end of line 40 causes this prompt to appear at the end of this line. The responses to these prompts were entered by a person named Bob, who is fifteen years old and who miscalculated his projected age. The word READY is the TRS-80's reaction to an END command. The > sign is a prompt, indicating that the computer is ready to execute a new BASIC command. The rest of the lines were printed on the screen as the result of PRINT statements. Note that the lines are unnecessarily bunched together near the top of the screen. The display would be more attractive if additional PRINT commands were inserted to skip some lines.

Note that this output is followed by a space. The semicolon instructs the computer to keep printing on the same screen line, and so it prints the value of N$ (the respondent's name, which is "Bob" in Figure 6.11) in the next screen position. The final semicolon tells the computer to continue printing on the same screen line rather than to go to the next line. But because there is no further output in this PRINT statement, the computer must wait for subsequent commands so as to know what to print at this location.

Line 50 provides an INPUT statement, and so the computer puts its question mark at its present location and pauses. It then accepts an answer. This input is a numeric variable and will be used in mathematical equations in lines 90 and 110.

In lines 60 and 70 the computer prints another statement. Although this is a single sentence, the programmer found it necessary to use two separate PRINT commands, because he knew that the screen size would not be able to accommodate so many letters on a single screen line.

In line 80, the computer accepts another answer, which it classifies as R. This input is a numeric variable, and it will be used in a mathematical equation in line 90.

In line 90, the computer evaluates the answer by asking itself, "Is this answer I got in line 80 sixteen larger than the number I picked up in line 50?" If the answer is yes, the computer will digress to line 130. In that case it will never even see lines 100, 110, or 120. But if the answer is no, the computer will continue to line 100 and then to 110. (Another way to state this is to say that if the condition is true ($31 = 15 + 16$), then the computer will go to line 130. But if the condition is not true (e.g., $36 = 15 + 16$) then the computer will go to the next line (line 100).

In line 110, the computer puts three outputs on the screen. Notice that the third of these outputs includes a space before the word "years"; otherwise we would have "31years" in Figure 6.11.

Line 120 directs the computer around line 130. Without this detour line, the

Figure 6.12.

computer would print a "Right" message immediately after telling the learner that the answer was wrong.

At line 150, the computer stops looking for lines and gives a prompt to indicate that it is ready for a new command.

Modifying BASIC Programs

As the next step in your learning, you should try to modify AGE. If you can successfully modify this program, you probably understand the principles explained in this chapter. Modifying a program is a good way to find out how computer programs are put together. By modifying a program, you can see what specific parts of it accomplish. In addition, it will give you ideas for using similar programs in your own instructional settings. In order to help you modify programs, the next few pages will present important techniques.

If you know what changes you want to make, it is easy to modify a BASIC computer program. Here are some guidelines for making changes in a program:

1. Load the program you wish to modify. Guidelines for loading programs can be found in Appendix F and in your computer's manual. To verify that your program is properly loaded, type LIST and see if the appropriate lines appear on your screen. If they do not appear, check Appendix F or your manual to see what steps you still must take.

2. Using the BASIC language system on your computer, type the line number you wish to change (or add) and type the statement you want to go on the changed (or added) line. Then use whatever method your computer requires (such as pressing the enter or return key) to enter the changed (or added) line into the computer. (You can tell whether your computer is ready to receive a BASIC language command by looking for the BASIC prompt on the screen. For example, the TRS-80 displays a > when it is looking for BASIC input. Applesoft BASIC displays a].

3. To insert a line between two existing lines, use a line number that falls between the two existing numbers. The computer will automatically put the line in the correct order. It is not necessary to type such lines in a location that is physically in the right place; rather, type them when you have the BASIC prompt, and let the computer insert them. If you list the program, you will see that the lines have been inserted in the right place.

4. To eliminate a line from your program, type the line number you wish to erase and hit the enter key. You can do this at any time when you have the BASIC prompt on your screen. A major problem is that it is possible to eliminate a line *by accident.* This can occur, for example, if you start to retype a line, then change your mind and hit the return key after you type only the line number. The computer will interpret this as an attempt to erase the line, and so the line will disappear from your program. Because such errors occur quite often, some versions of BASIC (and some disk-operating systems) require you to use a DELETE command to erase lines, to help prevent accidental erasures.

5. To replace one line with a new one, it is not necessary to erase the old one first. Just enter the new line with the same number as the old one. This procedure both erases the old line and inserts the new one.

Figure 6.13.

6.   You can run your modified program as soon as you have entered the appropriate lines. But if you wish to make your modification permanent, you have to "save" the program through the proper procedures. When using floppy disks, it is usually a good idea to save a modification under a new name. Otherwise, the old program will be erased as you save your new one, and you may later wish you had the old one back. A typical procedure would be to save a modified version of DRILL as DRILL2 (and a modified version of DRILL2 as DRILL3, etc.).

7.   On many computer systems, it is also possible to modify a line without retyping it in its entirety. This is done by using the "edit mode" or by using a word-processing system. To use an editing system, you would have to consult a manual related to that system.

Figure 6.14.

Figure 6.15.

Common Errors in Modifying Programs

The following list describes common errors in modifying programs:

1.   Trying to enter new lines when your computer is at the system command level, that is, before your computer is prepared to use the BASIC language. This will result in an error message stating that you cannot do this. With some computers, such as the Apple, this problem does not occur, because the system and BASIC commands are used at the same level.

2.   Trying to enter new lines when your computer is running a BASIC program. The exact reaction will vary, depending on what program you are running, but the outcome will always be that the computer will not accept your new lines. It is necessary first to stop running a program before you can modify it. In addition to letting the program run to its natural end, there are several ways to exit from a program (e.g., pushing a break or reset key or typing control C). They vary from computer to computer.

3.   Entering new lines when the BASIC prompt appears without first loading the original program. The result is that your "new" program will consist of only the new lines. On many computers, if you save such a new program under the same name as your original program, you will erase your entire original program. This is one of the most common and most serious errors made by beginning programmers. A good way to avoid this error is to list or run the program before you modify or save it.

4.   Entering corrections on incorrectly numbered lines. This can lead to either of the following problems:

   a. The new lines may be in the wrong sequence. This may lead to the incorrect operation or nonoperation of your program.

   b. The new lines may accidentally erase old lines you wanted to keep. This will occur if you accidentally give a new line a number that you have already assigned to a previous line. Because the original line vanishes, this is often a very difficult error to track down.

5. Forgetting to save the modified program. This results in the modifications being "lost" (erased) as soon as a new program is loaded or as soon as you turn off the computer. This error occurs very frequently when a programmer modifies a program and immediately runs it to see if it works. A programmer who becomes interested in the operation of the modified program may neglect to save it in its modified form. A good way to avoid this error is to save the program (under a new name) immediately after making the modificatons and before running it.

Modifications for AGE

The present program contains a question mark at the end of line 20 plus one supplied by the INPUT statement in line 30, and so let's eliminate one of them. To do this, simply retype line 20 without the question mark but with a semicolon at the very end of the line. This will cause the INPUT question mark to appear at the end of the preceding output, giving the appearance of a question mark at the end of the sentence. The line should look like this:

```
20 PRINT ''HI. WHAT IS YOUR NAME'';
```

If you run the program now, you will get only one question mark.

Now let's modify line 140 to use the respondent's name. This is easy to do, but remember, if you want a space after the comma and a period at the end of the sentence, you will have to put them there. Retype line 140 to look like this:

```
140 PRINT ''YOU'RE PRETTY SMART, '';N$;''.''
```

Be sure to include a blank space after the comma and before the quotation mark.

Finally, let's have the computer impress the respondent at the end of the program with its vast knowledge. We will have the computer spontaneously report the respondent's year of birth. We can do this by moving the END command to a later line and inserting a new line at 150. On this new line we will insert the respondent's birth year, which we can easily calculate as 1984 minus the value of A. The new line would look like this:

```
150 PRINT ''YOU WERE BORN IN '';1984-A;'' WEREN'T
YOU?''
```

Run the program with the modification and see if it does what it is supposed to do.

Additional Modifications for AGE

Now try a few modifications on your own:

1. In lines 70 and 80, the computer still prints two question marks. Only one is necessary, and so get rid of one of them.
2. The screen is somewhat crowded. Spread things out by adding PRINT commands to skip lines on the screen (see Appendix B).

```
10 CLS
20 PRINT TAB(14); " ' H E L L O ' "
30 PRINT
40 PRINT
50 PRINT "HELLO! I AM A GENIE LOCKED INSIDE THIS COMPUTER."
60 PRINT "ALTHOUGH I CANNOT GIVE YOU THREE WISHES, I CAN"
70 PRINT "ANSWER QUESTIONS AND GIVE VALUABLE ADVICE."
80 PRINT
90 PRINT "WHAT IS YOUR NAME";
100 INPUT A$
110 PRINT
120 PRINT "HI THERE, ";A$;"."
130 PRINT "ARE YOU ENJOYING YOURSELF HERE AT THE BEAUTIFUL"
140 PRINT "CALUMET CAMPUS OF PURDUE UNIVERSITY (YES OR NO)";
150 INPUT B$
160 CLS
170 PRINT
180 IF B$="YES" THEN 260
190 IF B$="NO" THEN 310
200 PRINT B$;" IS INCOMPREHENSIBLE TO ME."
210 PRINT
220 PRINT "PLEASE ANSWER YES OR NO."
230 PRINT
240 PRINT "DO YOU LIKE IT HERE ";
250 GOTO 150
260 PRINT "I AM GLAD TO HEAR THAT.   TELL YOUR FRIENDS ABOUT US."
270 PRINT
280 PRINT "PRESS ENTER TO CONTINUE."
290 INPUT Z$
300 GOTO 340
310 PRINT " I'M SORRY TO HEAR THAT. MAYBE WE SHOULD GET TOGETHER"
320 PRINT "AND TALK ABOUT IT SOME TIME."
330 GOTO 270
340 CLS
350 PRINT "I CAN SOLVE ALL KINDS OF PROBLEMS EXCEPT THOSE"
360 PRINT "WHICH REQUIRE A LIQUID DETERGENT OR A TAX CONSULTANT."
370 PRINT
380 PRINT
390 PRINT "WHAT KIND OF PROBLEMS DO YOU HAVE? (ANSWER SEX,"
400 PRINT "HEALTH, MONEY, OR JOB.)"
410 PRINT
420 INPUT C$
430 IF C$="SEX" THEN 730
440 IF C$="HEALTH" THEN 650
450 IF C$="MONEY" THEN 600
460 IF C$="JOB" THEN 540
470 PRINT
480 PRINT "YOUR ANSWER OF  ";C$;"  IS INCOMPREHENSIBLE TO ME."
490 PRINT "IT MUST REQUIRE EITHER A LIQUID DETERGENT OR A TAX CONSULTANT."
500 PRINT
510 PRINT "PLEASE ANSWER SEX, HEALTH, MONEY, OR JOB."
520 PRINT
530 GOTO 390
540 PRINT "I CAN SYMPATHIZE WITH YOU. I HAVE TO WORK"
550 PRINT "LONG HOURS FOR LOW PAY--AND SOME OF MY BOSSES"
560 PRINT "REALLY BEAT THIS KEYBOARD. MY ADVICE TO YOU IS"
570 PRINT "TO GET A JOB TEACHING AT PURDUE UNIVERSITY."
580 PRINT "IT'S GREAT FUN!"
590 GOTO 920
600 PRINT "SORRY! I'M BROKE TOO! WHY DON'T YOU SELL"
610 PRINT "ALUMINUM SIDING BY TELEPHONE IN YOUR SPARE TIME."
620 PRINT "OR YOU COULD MARRY SOMEONE RICH OR STOP EATING"
630 PRINT "SO YOU WON'T NEED SO MUCH MONEY."
640 GOTO 920
650 PRINT "MY ADVICE TO YOU, " ;A$; " IS"
660 PRINT "          1)TAKE AN ASPIRIN."
670 PRINT "          2)DRINK PLENTY OF FLUIDS."
680 PRINT "            (ORANGE JUICE, NOT BEER)"
690 PRINT "          3)GO TO BED (ALONE)."
700 GOTO 920
710 PRINT
720 PRINT
```

Figure 6.16. The listing of HELLO (written for the TRS-80).

```
730  PRINT "IS YOUR PROBLEM TOO LITTLE OR TOO MUCH";
740   INPUT D$
750  PRINT
760  PRINT
770   IF D$="TOO MUCH" THEN 850
780  IF D$ = "TOO LITTLE"   THEN 890
790  PRINT "DON'T GET ALL SHOOK UP,   " ;A$;"!"
800   IF D$="TOO LITTLE" THEN 890
810  PRINT "JUST ANSWER THE QUESTION WITH  'TOO LITTLE' OR  'TOO MUCH'!"
820  PRINT      "              WHICH IS IT";
830  GOTO 740
840  CLS
850   PRINT "YOU CALL THAT A PROBLEM! I SHOULD HAVE SUCH PROBLEMS!"
860   PRINT "IF IT BOTHERS YOU, TAKE A COLD SHOWER OR A STATISTICS"
870   PRINT "COURSE."
880   GOTO 920
890  PRINT "WHY ARE YOU HERE, ";A$;"?"
900   PRINT "YOU SHOULD BE AT INDIANA UNIVERSITY OR BALL STATE,"
910  PRINT "WHERE THERE IS SOME REAL ACTION !"
920   PRINT
930  PRINT "ARE THERE ANY MORE PROBLEMS YOU WANT SOLVED (YES OR NO)";
940   INPUT E$
950  CLS
960   PRINT
970   IF E$="YES" THEN 1030
980   IF E$="NO" THEN 1060
990   PRINT "JUST A SIMPLE YES OR NO PLEASE."
1000  PRINT
1010  PRINT
1020   GOTO 930
1030  PRINT "WHAT KIND? (SEX, HEALTH, MONEY, JOB)"
1040   PRINT
1050   GOTO 420
1060   PRINT
1070  PRINT   "THAT WILL BE $5.00 FOR THE ADVICE, " ;A$; "."
1080   PRINT "JUST LEAVE THE MONEY ON THE TERMINAL."
1090   PRINT
1100   PRINT
1110  PRINT "IT HAS BEEN NICE TALKING TO YOU, ";A$; "."
1120   PRINT "STOP BY AGAIN SOME TIME."
1130  PRINT
1140  PRINT
1150  PRINT
1160  PRINT
1170  PRINT
1180   END
```

Figure 6.16. The listing of HELLO (written for the TRS-80). (Continued.)

3. At the end of the sequence, call the respondent by name and tell him or her how much younger (or older) he or she is than you are. Or compare his or her age to George Washington's.

HELLO

HELLO (Figure 6.16) consists almost entirely of PRINT statements, INPUT statements, and a few IF/THEN branches. It does not achieve any specific educational outcome other than introducing students to the computer. However, educators will notice that the same logic behind HELLO can be applied to writing tutorials or branching programmed instruction on the computer.

Load HELLO into your computer and run it (see Appendix F for guidelines).

Notice that HELLO forces you to respond within the framework the programmer has chosen. After you have run the program, examine the listing, by either reading the copy reproduced on these pages or loading the program and listing it at the computer terminal. You will probably want to do some of each.

You should examine HELLO to see if you can understand its logic. If you can, this will be evidence that you understand the principles discussed in this chapter. It is useful to master these principles before continuing to the next chapter. Use the "Annotated Description of HELLO" to check your own logic or to answer any questions you may have about the program.

Annotated Description of HELLO

Line 10 clears the screen, and lines 20 to 90 provide introductory information leading into the program.

Line 100 instructs the computer to stop and wait for a response (see Figure 6.17). The computer will store this response (the respondent's name) as A$ and will print the person's name whenever it encounters A$ in a PRINT statement during the program (for example, in lines 120 and 790).

Once a response has been made to the INPUT statement in line 100, the computer will continue with another series of PRINT statements, until the INPUT statement in line 150 instructs it to pause again.

Note that in line 120 there is a blank space after the comma but before the end quotation mark. If this space were not written into the PRINT statement, the computer would merge the person's name too closely with the rest of the statement:

        HI THERE, BOB.

Similar examples of such blank spaces occur in lines 200, 790, and 1110.

After clearing the screen (in line 160) the computer checks the respondent's answer. If the answer is yes, the computer will give the respondent a supportive message before going on to line 340. If the answer is no, the computer will give the respondent a more consoling message before going to line 270 and eventually

```
                     ' H E L L O '

  HELLO!  I AM A GENIE LOCKED INSIDE THIS COMPUTER.
  ALTHOUGH I CANNOT GIVE YOU THREE WISHES, I CAN
  ANSWER QUESTIONS AND GIVE VALUABLE ADVICE.

  WHAT IS YOUR NAME?JENNIFER

  HI THERE, JENNIFER.
  ARE YOU ENJOYING YOURSELF HERE AT THE BEAUTIFUL
  CALUMET CAMPUS OF PURDUE UNIVERSITY (YES OR NO)?
```

Figure 6.17. A sample screen from HELLO. The computer paused after printing WHAT IS YOUR NAME? After Jennifer gave her response, the computer presented the rest of the screen. It is now waiting for a yes or no response, after which it will clear the screen and continue.

```
I CAN SOLVE ALL KINDS OF PROBLEMS EXCEPT THOSE
WHICH REQUIRE A LIQUID DETERGENT OR A TAX CONSULTANT.


WHAT KIND OF PROBLEMS DO YOU HAVE?  (ANSWER SEX,
HEALTH, MONEY, OR JOB.)


?
```

Figure 6.18. The main branching point in HELLO.

line 340. If the respondent answers anything other than yes or no, the computer will recycle by repeating the directions to answer yes or no and then asking the question again. This recycling will continue until the computer receives a yes or no answer.

The purpose of lines 280 and 290 is to enable the computer to pause after presenting a screenful of information. Note that the computer does not even examine the input provided in line 290. After any response whatsoever, the computer proceeds immediately to line 340, where it clears the screen and continues. You may wish to delete line 290 and see how the removal of this command makes it impossible to read the output on the screen.

At line 420, the computer reaches the major branching point shown in Figure 6.18, which is similar to many encountered in tutorial programs. Depending on the input provided in line 420, the computer will branch to one of the four subroutines designated in lines 430 and 460. Note that the respondent must enter a correct spelling of one of the four alternatives presented in lines 390 to 400. Respondents who give any other response will receive the message in lines 480 to 490 and will be recycled to line 390 (see Figure 6.19). This recycling will continue until the computer receives one of the four legitimate responses.

Lines 540, 600, 650, and 730 each begin a short sequence dealing with one of the problem areas in which the computer is willing to offer advice. Each of these sequences ends with a statement saying GOTO 920. The sequence beginning at

```
YOUR ANSWER OF HEALTH IS INCOMPREHENSIBLE TO ME.
IT MUST REQUIRE EITHER A LIQUID DETERGENT OR A TAX
CONSULTANT.


PLEASE ANSWER SEX, HEALTH, MONEY, OR JOB.

?
```

Figure 6.19. The "recycling message" for improper input at the major branching point in HELLO. The computer will continue giving this message until the person at the terminal gives one of the four acceptable responses.

line 920 asks if the respondent wishes to continue. A response of yes will send the computer to line 1030 and then to the major branching point at line 420, where the computer again will branch to one of the four possible problem areas identified by the respondent. A response of no at line 940 will send the computer to line 1060, and the computer then will print a few lines and end the "counseling session."

If the respondent chooses the branch leading to line 730, then the input at line 740 will offer another opportunity to branch to either line 850 or line 890. The logic of this branch is the same as that of the overall branch.

Modifying HELLO

The following are some modifications that can be made in HELLO:

1. Have the computer use the respondent's name in lines 220 and 260. In line 220, this is easy to do. Simply change line 220 to read as follows:

```
220 PRINT ''PLEASE ANSWER YES OR NO, '';A$;''.''
```

In the revised line 220, note the extra space after the comma and the period within quotation marks after the A$. Line 260 is slightly more difficult, as the modification comes in the middle of the line. The simplest strategy would be to convert line 260 to two lines, to read as follows:

```
260 PRINT ''I AM GLAD TO HEAR THAT, '';A$;''.''
265 PRINT ''TELL YOUR FRIENDS ABOUT US.''
```

2. Allow "school" as a possible response to the question the computer asks in lines 390 to 400. First, this requires listing school as a possibility in line 400, which is easily done by changing line 400 as follows:

```
400 PRINT ''HEALTH, MONEY, SCHOOL, OR JOB.)''
```

If you are extremely perceptive, you may also have noticed that it is necessary to make similar changes in line 510 and 1030. Otherwise, the computer would be unable to recycle the respondent. Here are some correct ways to change these two lines:

```
510 PRINT ''PLEASE ANSWER SEX, HEALTH, MONEY, SCHOOL, OR JOB.

1030 PRINT ''WHAT KIND? (SEX, HEALTH, MONEY, SCHOOL, OR JOB)''
```

Next, it is necessary to allow the computer to accept school as an answer. To do this, you must branch to a new subroutine. Because this program is already quite crowded, the easiest way to do this is to put the new subroutine at the very end of the program. This can be done with the following line:

```
465 IF C$=''SCHOOL'' THEN 1200
```

Finally, it is necessary to write a clever answer in the subroutine that will start at line 1200. Perhaps you have a better idea, but the following is a possibility:

```
1200 PRINT ''A LITTLE LEARNING IS A DANGEROUS THING.''
1210 PRINT
1220 PRINT ''AND I ONCE MET A PERSON WHO LEARNED
SOMETHING IN SCHOOL.''
1230 PRINT
1240 PRINT ''SO STAY AWAY FROM SCHOOLS, '';A$;''.''
1250 PRINT ''THEY'RE DANGEROUS.''
1260 GOTO 920
```

Note that the proposed lines 1200 to 1260 consist of a series of PRINT statements followed by a recycling to line 920, which either exits the respondent from the counseling session, or recycles to line 420.

Suggested Additional Modifications for HELLO

Try making the following modifications in HELLO, which are similar to those recommended in "Modifying HELLO."

1. Program the computer to use the respondent's name in line 320.
2. Program the computer to use the respondent's name in line 390.
3. Allow some additional problem area such as sports as a possible response to the question in lines 390 and 400. (Remember that you will also have to make appropriate changes elsewhere in the program.)

Chapter 7
More BASIC Programming

THE previous chapter introduced the fundamental concepts of BASIC programming, and so this chapter will introduce several new commands and will explore two features that increase the power of the BASIC program: arrays and subroutines.

New BASIC Commands

In Chapter 6, we discussed the INPUT statement as a means for assigning values to variables, by enabling the person stationed at the computer terminal to enter the information that is assigned to a designated variable label. The LET statement, on the other hand, assigns values in the program itself, without any interaction with the person stationed at the terminal. The LET statement can be paraphrased as "Assign a value to the variable at the left of the equation by performing the mathematical or logical operation on the right of the equal sign." LET statements (like INPUT statements) are one of the easiest ways to assign values to variables. Examples of LET statements can be found in lines 10 and 350 of TRAP and in lines 580 und 760 of PIZZA. Note that the word LET may be validly omitted, as in line 580 of PIZZA.

The DIM command instructs the computer to set aside enough space in its memory for an "array" of data. (Arrays will be explained later in this chapter.) The DIM S$(16) statement in line 20 of PIZZA means "There's going to be an array of sixteen variables labeled S$(1) through S$(16) in this program. Be sure to set aside memory space for these variables." A command sometimes associated with the DIM statement is CLEAR, which sets aside a designated amount of string space in the computer's memory. Because none of the annotated programs in this book requires the use of a CLEAR statement, we shall not discuss it. But if you find

Figure 7.1.

yourself getting "Out of String Space" errors, you should refer to CLEAR in your programming manual.

The READ statement is a third means for assigning values to variables. (The other two are INPUT and LET statements.) The READ statement is always accompanied by DATA statements, which contain the values to be assigned to variables. The READ statement can be paraphrased as "Find the next value in a DATA statement, and assign that value to the variable in this READ statement." (The storage of these variables in arrays will be discussed later in this chapter.) The READ statement introduces flexibility into the program, as a user can radically alter a program simply by altering the DATA lines that the program will read.

The DATA statement contains the values to be read by the READ statement. These values may be either numbers or words ("strings"), and they follow the rules of such variables, which were outlined in Chapter 6. DATA statements may appear anywhere in the program. The first READ statement will go to the first piece of information in the first DATA statement in the program, the second to the sec-

Figure 7.2.

Figure 7.3.

ond piece of information, and so on. However, most programmers find it useful to put the DATA lines at the very end of the program or immediately after the READ statement that will read the data on that line.

The FOR/NEXT command enables the computer to repeat a command or series of commands a certain number of times. As a simple example, if you wanted to print "Hello" on five consecutive lines, you could do this with five separate PRINT statements. But you could do this more efficiently by using the following lines:

```
100 FOR I = 1 TO 5
100 PRINT ''HELLO''
120 NEXT I
```

Of course, in most programs FOR/NEXT loops accomplish something more significant than printing "Hello." For example, a common usage (as in lines 160 to 180 of PIZZA) is to use a FOR/NEXT loop to read data into an array. In addition, the FOR/NEXT loop described later in Figure 7.26 draws the map of the city in PIZZA

Figure 7.4.

Do these
next commands
12 times.

when you get
to me, go back
to him and
start over unless
you've reached
his limit.

FOR
I=1
TO
12

NEXT

Figure 7.5.

(lines 1030 to 1110). In TRAP, a FOR/NEXT loop (lines 360 to 510) sets the limit for the number of guesses the player will be permitted before being considered a loser.

The GOSUB statement is a common method for introducing subroutines, which will be examined at length later in this chapter. The GOSUB statement can be summarized as "Go out of the sequence to perform another operation, and then return to the command following this one." The GOSUB statement allows a programmer to write a series of commands a single time and yet have that series carried out many separate times during the run of the program. Line 430 of TRAP and lines 200 and 210 of PIZZA show GOSUB statements.

Make a detour.
Stop the normal
sequence and go
and do a set of
commands.

when you come
to me, go back
to him and resume
the next command.

GOSUB

RETURN

Figure 7.6.

A crucial part of many instructional programs is the random selection of a number. This is accomplished with a RND statement. RND means "select a random number." LET X = RND(12) means "select a random number between 1 and 12 and assign it to X." The format in the preceding sentence is accepted by the TRS-80 and a few other computers. The format shown in line 350 of TRAP is a more complex format, which has the advantage of being accepted by nearly all computers (including the TRS-80). Let's examine this longer format. Line 350 of TRAP states

$$\text{LET X = INT(100*RND(0))+1}$$

The term INT means "take the integer of. . . . " This command causes the computer to drop anything beyond the decimal point from the number in the succeeding parentheses. RND(0) means that the computer should select a number between 0 and 1. Therefore, line 350 of TRAP means

```
(1) Find a random number between 0 and 1.
(2) Multiply this number by 100.
(3) Take the INTeger of the result of step 2.
(4) Add 1 to the result.
(5) Assign the resulting value to X.
```

For example, assume that the computer selects as a random number the value .7645341. Let's carry this through these five steps:

```
(1) Random number = .7645341
(2) .7645341 x 100 = 76.45341
(3) Integer of 76.45341 = 76
(4) 1 + 76 = 77
(5) X = 77
```

If you think about it for a moment, this is exactly the same as the RND(100) function on the TRS-80. If you use the TRS-80 or another computer that offers the

Figure 7.7.

Figure 7.8.

simpler function, then chose the simpler method. On the other hand, if you write programs for a computer that does not offer the simpler RND function, you will have to learn the more complex formulation described in this paragraph.

The mathematical formulas in computer programs may seem complex to some readers, but they often are not as bad as they look. Figure 7.9 demonstrates the logic of using parentheses in such formulas. Note that in all such mathematical equations, the content in the inner set of parentheses is evaluated (computed) before that in the outer parentheses.

How to Use Arrays of Data

If you wanted the computer to "know" and print the names of the first ten states of the United States in alphabetical order, you could do this in the following manner, by using LET statements and PRINT statements:

```
 10 LET A$ = ''ALABAMA''
 20 LET B$ = ''ALASKA''
 30 LET C$ = ''ARIZONA''
      .
      .
      .

100 LET J$ = ''GEORGIA''

110 PRINT A$
120 PRINT B$
130 PRINT C$
      .
      .
      .

200 PRINT J$
```

Programming the computer to know and print the names of ten states in this fashion uses a total of twenty lines. The same outcome could be accomplished in

LET X = INT(100*RND(0))+1

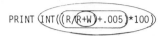

PRINT (INT(((R/R+W)+.005)*100))

Figure 7.9. The order in which mathematical computations and functions are performed. The computer finds the first end parenthesis in the line and matches that up with the nearest left parenthesis. It then finds the next set of parentheses and continues this process until all the parentheses are used up. In this diagram, each computation or function is circled to indicate the numbers or variables used in that calculation. The innermost circles are computed first.

twenty-three lines by using the following combination of READ statements, DATA statements, and PRINT statements:

```
 10  READ A$
 20  READ B$
 30  READ C$
      .
      .
      .
100  READ J$

110  PRINT A$
120  PRINT B$
130  PRINT C$
      .
      .
      .
200  PRINT J$

210  DATA ALABAMA,ALASKA,ARIZONA
220  DATA ARKANSAS,CALIFORNIA,COLORADO
230  DATA CONNECTICUT,DELAWARE,FLORIDA,GEORGIA
```

But we can shorten the process to nine lines if we use READ statements combined with a FOR/NEXT loop and DATA statements, as in the following example:

```
10  FOR I = 1 TO 10
20  READ A$ (I)
30  Next I
40  FOR I = 1 TO 10
50  PRINT A$ (I)
60  NEXT I
70  DATA ALABAMA,ALASKA,ARIZONA
80  DATA ARKANSAS,CALIFORNIA,COLORADO
90  DATA CONNECTICUT,DELAWARE,FLORIDA,GEORGIA
```

In each of these examples, the outcome was identical: the computer memorized ten names by attaching variable labels to these names and then printed each of the names. A major difference, however, is that the use of the FOR/NEXT loops permitted the computer to do this much more concisely. The difference in concise-ness would become even greater if the computer tried to deal with all fifty states.

The variables derived from the FOR/NEXT "read loop" are referred to as *sub-scripted variables,* and a set of such subscripted variables is referred to as an *array.* The variables in an array can be thought of as *boxes* or *pigeonholes* into which a computer will place information that it derives from READ statements. This pro-cess is diagrammed in Figure 7.10.

In almost every case in which the members of a set of variables are conceptually

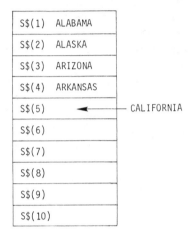

The above diagram presents the "S$ Array" as a set of
"boxes" or "pigeonholes" into which the computer will
insert information found in DATA statements. This would
be accomplished through a "READ loop" such as the one
which follows:

```
10 FOR I=1 TO 10
20 READ S$(I)
30 NEXT I
100 DATA ALABAMA,ALASKA,ARIZONA
110 DATA ARKANSAS,CALIFORNIA,COLORADO
120 DATA CONNECTICUT,DELAWARE,FLORIDA,GEORGIA
```

On the computer's first run through this READ loop, the
"I" in line 20 would have a value of "1". Therefore,
the computer would give the first piece of DATA
(ALABAMA) the label S$(1). You can picture the computer
as putting ALABAMA into the box labeled S$(1) in the
diagram. The next time the computer came to line 20,
the value of "I" would become "2," and therefore
the box labeled S$(2) would get the second piece of
DATA, which is ALASKA.

In the diagram, the computer is on its fifth run
through the loop and is assigning the fifth piece of
DATA (CALIFORNIA) to the S$(5) box. Since line 10 says
to repeat this process 10 times, the computer will
continue this process until it has assigned GEORGIA to
the S$(10) box.

Figure 7.10. How the computer reads data into arrays.

similar and will be used systematically, it is better to enter the variables as members of an array rather than as isolated single variables. The advantages of variables and an array, however, go far beyond the ease of entering data. In educational computing, the use of arrays permits the easy random selection of questions, facilitates the evaluation of learner responses for correctness, and makes it possible to do such things as print lists and check responses for correctness of spelling. Chapter 8 will present examples of each of these uses of arrays. In each case, if you try to visualize performing the same task without arrays, you will find that the task is exceedingly cumbersome.

You may want to ask a question about a random item from a longer list of similar items. Once the variables have been read into an array, this is an extremely simple task. All the computer must do is select a number at random and then choose the item from the array that corresponds to that number. Figure 7.11 demonstrates the computer's capacity to do this.

Once the computer has selected the item from an array about which to ask a question, it is often quite easy to select a correct answer from a similar array and to use this correct answer to evaluate the learner's response. This is demonstrated in Figure 7.12. The strategy demonstrated in Figure 7.12 will work, of course, only if the data are entered into the respective arrays in exactly the correct order. It is important, therefore, to enter data into arrays in such a way as to eliminate errors in the order of the data. Figure 7.13 shows a useful strategy to facilitate proofreading of the order of data entry.

```
10 FOR I = 1 TO 10
20 READ S$(I)
30 NEXT I
40 LET X = RND(10)
50 PRINT "WHAT IS THE CAPITAL OF ";S$(X);
60 INPUT A$
70 END
100 DATA ALABAMA,ALASKA,ARIZONA
110 DATA ARKANSAS,CALIFORNIA,COLORADO
120 DATA CONNECTICUT,DELAWARE,FLORIDA,GEORGIA
```

The above "program" would simply print the question and pause for a response. It has not been programmed to do anything with the response it receives in line 60. To do that, it would have to "know" the answers and compare the learner's input to the known answer. This is what happens in Figures 7.12 and 7.13.

Also note that the computer will randomly select a number between 1 and 10 each time it encounters line 40. When numbers are chosen at random in this way, there is one chance in 10 that the exact same number will be chosen on an immediately subsequent occasion. This means that if a player would receive ten questions, chances are that the computer would offer some states several times rather than each state only once. If you want to keep the computer from making such repetitive choices, you have to build this into the program. The guidelines on "eliminating duplications" suggest a good strategy to accomplish this. The program CAPS does not have such a mechanism, but BEHMOD does.

Figure 7.11. How the computer can randomly select an item from an array in its memory.

```
10 FOR I = 1 TO 10
20 READ S$(I),C$(I)
30 NEXT I
40 LET X=RND(10)
50 PRINT "WHAT IS THE CAPITAL OF ";S$(X);
60 INPUT A$
70 IF A$ = C$(X) THEN 90
80 PRINT "WRONG. THE CORRECT ANSWER IS ";C$(X);"."
85 GOTO 95
90 PRINT "RIGHT! GOOD JOB."
95 END
100 DATA ALABAMA,MONTGOMERY,ALASKA,JUNEAU
110 DATA ARIZONA, PHOENIX,ARKANSAS,LITTLE ROCK
120 DATA CALIFORNIA,SACRAMENTO,COLORADO,DENVER
130 DATA CONNECTICUT,HARTFORD,DELAWARE,DOVER
140 DATA FLORIDA,TALLAHASSEE,GEORGIA,ATLANTA
```

In the above program, the computer selects a random
number in line 40. If the computer selects the number
9, for example, then in line 50 it will print S$(9),
which is FLORIDA, as part of the question. Then when it
evaluates the correct answer in line 70, the computer
will compare A$ to C$(9), which is TALLAHASSEE.

For this process to work properly, it is essential that
FLORIDA be the ninth S$(I) that the computer reads and
that TALLAHASSEE be the ninth C$(I) it reads. If this
is not the case, then the computer will make
"mistakes." For example, if the programmer would have
accidentally omitted the word DOVER in line 130, then
the computer would have read FLORIDA as C$(8),
TALLAHASSEE as S$(9), and GEORGIA as C$(9). Thus the
"misinformed" computer would think that Georgia was the
capital of Tallahassee!

Because entering data into arrays in the proper order
is so crucial, this process is further elaborated in
Figure 7.13.

Figure 7.12. Modification of Figure 4.13 to enable the computer to evaluate answers for correctness.

Data entered into arrays can be used in many ways. For example, Figure 7.14 shows that it is possible to list the names in an array in either a single column or in two columns. In every case, the use of arrays makes such tasks less cumbersome, and as the number of variables in a list increases, the task becomes more complex without the availability of arrays.

The program PIZZA at the end of this chapter demonstrates the use of an array to draw the map of a city. The programs CAPS in Chapter 8 and FOOTBALL in Chapter 10 exemplify the use of arrays to select questions at random in educational drills. Likewise, the program BEHMOD in Chapter 11 shows the flexibility of arrays as part of a "universal drill." In BEHMOD, the program's content can be changed to almost any subject, simply by altering the content of the DATA statements that the computer will read into the arrays.

The arrays discussed thus far have been one-dimensional arrays, but there are also two-dimensional arrays, which are even more useful. Two-dimensional arrays consist of a variable name followed by two subscripts within parentheses. They can be envisioned as a matrix or chart with each member of the array being assigned one set of coordinates in the chart, as shown in Figure 7.15. Thus, in Figure

```
10 FOR I = 1 TO 10
15 READ S$(I)
20 NEXT I
25 FOR I = 1 TO 10
30 READ C$(I)
35 NEXT I
      .
      .
      .
100 DATA ALABAMA,ALASKA,ARIZONA
110 DATA ARKANSAS,CALIFORNIA,COLORADO
120 DATA CONNECTICUT,DELAWARE,FLORIDA,GEORGIA
130 DATA MONTGOMERY,JUNEAU,PHOENIX
140 DATA LITTLE ROCK,SACRAMENTO,DENVER
150 DATA HARTFORD,DOVER,TALLAHASSEE,ATLANTA
```

The above program would accurately enter the DATA
necessary for the program described in Figure 7.12.   It
employs two consecutive FOR/NEXT loops: one to read the
names of the states and one to read the names of the
capitals. Therefore, the first three DATA lines contain
the ten states and the next three the capitals. The
following program would accomplish the same thing:

```
10 FOR I = 1 TO 10
20 READ S$(I),C$(I)
30 NEXT I
      .
      .
      .
100 DATA ALABAMA,MONTGOMERY
110 DATA ALASKA,JUNEAU
120 DATA ARIZONA,PHOENIX
130 DATA ARKANSAS,LITTLE ROCK
140 DATA CALIFORNIA,SACRAMENTO
150 DATA COLORADO,DENVER
160 DATA CONNECTICUT,HARTFORD
170 DATA DELAWARE,DOVER
180 DATA FLORIDA,TALLAHASSEE
190 DATA GEORGIA,ATLANTA
```

This second program uses only one FOR/NEXT loop, and
this in itself is an advantage. However, the primary
advantage lies in the fact that it is much easier for
the programmer to proofread the program—to make sure
that all the data are included in the right order. This
advantage would become even more important if the
program became more complex by including data on all
fifty states.

Figure 7.13. Strategies for making sure that the data are read in the right order.

7.15 T$(1,2) would be G. W. Carver Museum, T$(9,1) would be Disney World, and so forth. To read data into a two-dimensional array, it is necessary to use *nested loops*. Likewise, printing information from a two-dimensional matrix also often requires nested loops, and selecting an item for a question or answer from a two-dimensional array requires choosing two random numbers rather than a single random number.

It is also possible to have arrays with more than two dimensions, but these are difficult to conceptualize, and so we shall not discuss them here.

When you use arrays it is often necessary to "dimension" the arrays ahead of time. Simply stated, this means that you have to prepare enough "boxes" or "pigeonholes" to receive the information you plan to read into the array. You can do

The following lines could be inserted into the program
in Figures 7.11 to 7.13 to produce a list of all ten states:

```
200 FOR I = 1 TO 10
210 PRINT S$(I)
220 NEXT I
```

The above lines would list all ten states in a single
column. If you preferred to have the list in two
columns, you could use the following lines:

```
200 FOR I = 1 TO 5
210 PRINT S$(I);TAB(30);S$(I+5)
220 NEXT I
```

This second format would list the first five in
alphabetical order in the first column and the final
five in the second column.

The first format would use ten lines on the screen.
Although the use of ten lines may be acceptable for a
short list of ten states, a programmer would have to
use two or even three columns for all fifty states. You
may wish to try your hand at the lines needed for a
three column list.

No matter how many columns you choose, the printing of
such lists is much easier when data are stored in
arrays.

Figure 7.14. Printing lists of DATA read into arrays.

this with a DIM statement at the beginning of your program. DIM statements tell
the computer to set aside enough space in its memory to receive the information
that you will later send to it. Some computers (including the Apple and the TRS-
80) automatically assign ten spaces for a one-dimensional array and one hundred
(ten-by-ten) spaces for a two-dimensional array, and therefore it may not really be
necessary to use DIM statements when your arrays will be smaller than ten or ten-
by-ten arrays. However, for larger arrays, DIM statements are essential.

The labels assigned to arrays follow the same rules as do the labels assigned to
other variables. This means that if the contents of an array will be "words" (letters
or symbols—"strings"—rather than numbers), the label must be accompanied by
a dollar sign. On the other hand, if the contents of the array will be numbers (that
is, if the contents will be subjected to mathematical operations), the label must
not be accompanied by a dollar sign.

As line 400 of FOOTBALL demonstrates, it is often necessary to combine within
a single FOR/NEXT loop both one-dimensional and two-dimensional and numeric
and string arrays.

How to Use Subroutines

A subroutine is best described as a smaller program that is executed many times
during a larger overall program. If a set of commands is to be carried out repeatedly, it is considerably simpler to write the set of commands a single time and to
instruct the computer on several separate occasions to perform this one set of

T$(1,1) HELEN KELLER'S BIRTHPLACE	T$(1,2) G.W. CARVER MUSEUM
T$(2,1) GLACIER BAY NAT'L MONUMENT	T$(2,2) SEAL FUR ROOKERIES ON PRIBILOF ISLAND
T$(3,1) METEOR CRATER	T$(3,2) PETRIFIED FOREST
T$(4,1) THE ONLY U.S. DIAMOND MINE	T$(4,2) BLANCHARD CAVERNS
T$(5,1) BRISTLECONE PINES	T$(5,2) YOSEMITE NAT'L PARK
T$(6,1) MT. EVANS	T$(6,2) ROCKY MOUNTAINS NATIONAL PARK
T$(7,1) WINCHESTER GUN MUSEUM	T$(7,2) YALE UNIVERSITY
T$(8,1) THE OLDEST PROTESTANT CHURCH STILL IN USE IN U.S.	T$(8,2) HAGLEY MUSEUM
T$(9,1) DISNEY WORLD	T$(9,2) KENNEDY SPACE CENTER
T$(10,1) SITE OF THE FIRST GOLD RUSH IN U.S.	T$(10,2) OKEFENOKEE SWAMP

The above is an example of a two-dimensional array. This "T$ Array" focuses on tourist attractions, and the array coordinates with the states and capitals arrays in Figures 7.11 to 7.13.

A two-dimensional array can be viewed as a set of "boxes" with a number of "compartments" within each box. The "address" (subscript) identifies both the box and the compartment. For example, YALE UNIVERSITY is located in Box 7 Compartment 2 of the T$ Array. Likewise, the address of DISNEY WORLD is T$(9,1).

Note that if DATA are entered in the right order, it will be easy to match up a tourist attraction with its state. For example, once it knows that DISNEY WORLD is T$(9,1), the computer can automatically match this with S$(9), which is the label it would have given to FLORIDA in Figure 7.10.

Figure 7.15. An example of a two-dimensional array. (This array would be labeled T$(10,2) in the DIM statement.)

commands than it is to write the same set of commands several different times. The use of subroutines provides substantial savings in both programming time and the amount of memory space that the computer will need to store and run the program.

Many of the situations in which subroutines are useful are obvious. If you are writing a program and notice that the same operation will have to be performed repeatedly, then you should use a subroutine. In other situations, it requires a bit of ingenuity to structure a program so that the operations become identical and several can be performed using subroutines.

In all cases, subroutines must necessarily be isolated from the rest of the program. In other words, they have to be designed so that the program will not automatically enter the subroutine by any procedure other than by being "sent" to that subroutine. This means that the program must be written so that the subroutine cannot be entered in the normal course of events as the computer simply

```
100 PRINT "BEFORE YOU RUN THIS PROGRAM,"
110 PRINT "BE SURE YOU HAVE PAPER AND PENCIL HANDY."
120 PRINT
130 PRINT "ARE YOU READY TO CONTINUE (YES OR NO)";
140 INPUT A$
150 CLS
160 IF A$ = "YES" THEN 200
170 IF A$ = "NO" THEN 9000
180 PRINT "ANSWER YES OR NO, PLEASE."
190 GOTO 130
200 PRINT "THE COMPUTER WILL PRESENT ONE PROBLEM"
210 PRINT "AT A TIME FOR YOU TO ANSWER."
220 PRINT
230 PRINT "IF YOUR ANSWER IS CORRECT,"
240 PRINT "THE COMPUTER WILL GIVE A MORE DIFFICULT PROBLEM."
250 PRINT
260 PRINT "IF YOUR ANSWER IS INCORRECT,"
270 PRINT "THE COMPUTER WILL GIVE YOU ANOTHER"
280 PRINT "QUESTION OF ABOUT EQUAL DIFFICULTY."
290 PRINT
300 PRINT "ARE YOU READY TO CONTINUE (YES OR NO)";
310 INPUT A$
320 CLS
330 IF A$ = "YES" THEN 400
340 IF A$ = "NO" THEN 9000
350 PRINT "ANSWER YES OR NO, PLEASE."
360 GOTO 300
400 PRINT "IF YOU WANT TO STOP THE PROGRAM,"
410 PRINT "ENTER THE LETTER Q (FOR QUIT)"
420 PRINT "IN RESPONSE TO ANY QUESTION."
430 PRINT
440 PRINT "ARE YOU READY TO CONTINUE (YES OR NO)";
450 INPUT A$
460 CLS
470 IF A$ = "YES" THEN 400
480 IF A$ = "NO" THEN 9000
490 PRINT "ANSWER YES OR NO, PLEASE."
500 GOTO 440
      .
      .
      .
9000 END
```

Figure 7.16. A needlessly cumbersome part of a program that can be improved by using subroutines.

progresses from one line to the next in the program. Therefore, in every case the first line of a subroutine should be immediately preceeded by a "detour line," such as GOTO, IF, or END.

In many cases, a simple restructuring of a program allows the programmer to replace more cumbersome lines with subroutines. For example, Figure 7.16 shows an example of an unnecessarily cumbersome program that can be greatly shortened and made more efficient by using subroutines, as in Figure 7.17. The programmer was able to convert Figure 7.16 to Figure 7.17 by simply using the same term for the response throughout the entire program and then treating this response through a subroutine. In a few cases, it is not possible to use the same variables throughout the entire program, but in such cases it is often possible to make up additional variables to introduce subroutines into part of the program. An example of the use of such an additional variable is shown in Figure 7.18.

There are several ways to introduce subroutines into a computer program. One of the most common is by using the GOSUB command. The GOSUB command

```
100 PRINT "BEFORE YOU RUN THIS PROGRAM,"
110 PRINT "BE SURE YOU HAVE PAPER AND PENCIL HANDY."
120 GOSUB 900
200 PRINT "THE COMPUTER WILL PRESENT ONE PROBLEM"
210 PRINT "AT A TIME FOR YOU TO ANSWER."
220 PRINT
230 PRINT "IF YOUR ANSWER IS CORRECT,"
240 PRINT "THE COMPUTER WILL GIVE A MORE DIFFICULT PROBLEM."
250 PRINT
260 PRINT "IF YOUR ANSWER IS INCORRECT,"
270 PRINT "THE COMPUTER WILL GIVE YOU ANOTHER"
280 PRINT "QUESTION OF ABOUT EQUAL DIFFICULTY."
290 GOSUB 900
400 PRINT "IF YOU WANT TO STOP THE PROGRAM,"
410 PRINT "ENTER THE LETTER Q (FOR QUIT)"
420 PRINT "IN RESPONSE TO ANY QUESTION."
430 GOSUB 900
      .
      .
      .
900 PRINT
910 PRINT "ARE YOU READY TO CONTINUE (YES OR NO)";
920 INPUT A$
930 CLS
940 IF A$ = "YES" THEN 970
950 IF A$ = "NO" THEN 9000
960 PRINT "ANSWER YES OR NO, PLEASE."
965 GOTO 910
970 RETURN
      .
      .
      .
9000 END
```

Figure 7.17. A revision that incorporates subroutines into the program in Figure 7.16.

instructs the computer to go to a designated line and to continue processing commands from subsequent lines until it encounters a RETURN command, at which time it will return to the command immediately following the GOSUB command that sent it to the subroutine. It is possible, of course, to have subroutines within subroutines, and in such cases each RETURN statement sends the computer back to the command immediately following the most recent GOSUB command.

The ON GOSUB statement is a variation of the GOSUB statement. It is really a combination of several IF/THEN statements combined with GOSUB statements, as is shown in Figure 7.19. When a computer encounters an ON GOSUB statement, it is "sent" to the first line of the relevant subroutine and processes the commands there until it encounters a RETURN statement. At that time it goes back to the line immediately following the ON GOSUB line. In Figure 7.19, for example, the computer returns to line 590 after completing its subroutine.

Both GOSUB and ON GOSUB statements can be used only when the computer is supposed to return to the next line after completing the subroutine. In certain cases, however, the programmer will want the computer to perform a subroutine and then to return to some line other than after the one that directed it to the subroutine. In such cases, it is often desirable to use a GOTO statement (or its equivalent) instead of a GOSUB. In these instances, the RETURN statement is replaced with another GOTO statement or perhaps an ON GOTO statement. Examples of such GOTO subroutines can be found in CAPS (line 1140) and in FOOTBALL (line 230).

```
400 PRINT "WHAT TYPE OF COLLEGE WOULD YOU"
410 PRINT "LIKE TO ATTEND";
420 INPUT C$
425 LET A$=C$
430 GOSUB 1000
440 PRINT "WHAT IS THE HIGHEST DEGREE"
450 PRINT "YOU WISH TO ATTAIN";
460 INPUT D$
465 LET A$=D$
470 GOSUB 1000
480 PRINT "IN WHAT SUBJECT WOULD YOU"
490 PRINT "LIKE TO MAJOR";
500 INPUT M$
505 LET A$=M$
510 GOSUB 1000
520 PRINT "IN WHAT SUBJECT WOLD YOU"
530 PRINT "LIKE TO MINOR";
540 INPUT N$
545 LET A$=N$
550 GOSUB 1000
    .
    .
    .
1000 IF A$="HELP" THEN 4000
1010 IF A$="QUIT" THEN 5000
1020 IF A$="START" THEN 6000
1030 IF A$="MENU" THEN 7000
1040 IF A$="LIST" THEN 8000
1050 RETURN
```

Since the programmer plans to use each of the inputs
later in the program, it is impossible to use A$ in the
INPUT statements. (Doing so would immediately erase the
previous input value.) Therefore, the programmer
converts each input to the additional variable of A$
just long enough to run it through the subroutine. This
temporary value is erased as soon as the next input is
attached to A$, but by then the programmer has used the
subroutine to accomplish the desired purpose of
checking to see if the input matched the key words.

Figure 7.18. An example of a minor restructuring that enables the computer to use subroutines.

TRAP

TRAP was described with sample screens in Chapter 3. It consists of LET statements, PRINT statements, two INPUT statements, and a few loops. Although this program is a game, it can be educationally useful, as it requires learners to apply addition, subtraction, division, and estimation skills in order to narrow the range and eventually guess the computer's number.

You can examine a listing of TRAP either by reading the listing (Figure 7.20) or by loading the program and listing it at the computer terminal after you have run it. You will probably want to do some of each.

Annotated Description of TRAP

In the first line, the programmer establishes G as the number of guesses that will be permitted (ten guesses).

Line 20 clears the screen, and line 30 introduces the game.

```
500 PRINT "WHICH PROGRAM DO YOU WANT"
510 PRINT TAB(5);"1. STATE CAPITALS."
520 PRINT TAB(5);"2. STATE ABBREVIATIONS."
530 PRINT TAB(5);"3. STATE NICKNAMES."
540 PRINT TAB(6);"4. STATE BIRDS."
550 PRINT
560 PRINT "ENTER A NUMBER BETWEEN 1 AND 4."
570 INPUT A
580 ON A GOSUB 1000,1050,1100,1150
590 LET X=RND(50)
    .
    .
    .
```

In the above program, the variable A receives a value
in line 570. The computer then is sent to a subroutine
in line 580. The subroutine to which it will go depends
on the value of A. For example, a learner who wanted
state abbreviations would have entered a "2," and
therefore the computer would go to the second
subroutine in line 580. In this case, the computer
would go to line 1050. (The subroutines are not
included in the above lines.) When the computer reached
the word RETURN in that subroutine, it would return to
line 590 and continue with the rest of the program.

Figure 7.19. An example of an ON GOSUB subroutine.

Line 40 introduces a short sequence that enables a respondent to skip the instructions (by going immediately to line 350) if he or she already knows how to play the game.

Question: As the program is written, what will happen if the player enters the letter N in response to the question regarding instructions? Will the computer:

1. Skip to line 350, omitting the instructions?

2. Tell the player that the response of N was unacceptable and ask for another response?

3. Give the instructions anyway?

Answer: Note that the question asked what the computer *will* do, not what it *should* be programmed to do. The answer is that it would give the instructions anyway. As the program is currently written, the only way the instructions will be omitted is if the player enters the correct spelling of the word *no.* In fact, either of the other two options would provide a more user friendly program, but additional lines would have to be added to achieve this friendliness.

Lines 80 through 340 give the instructions. These are straightforward PRINT statements, interrupted by an INPUT statement that makes the computer stop long enough for the respondent to read one screenful of information before proceeding to another.

In line 350, the computer randomly selects x, the number the respondent is going to try to guess. This line is written in a format compatible with many non-TRS-80 computers, though the TRS-80 accepts LET X = RND(N) to do the same thing. Note that line 350 is a LET statement, in which the word LET has been validly omitted.

Lines 360 to 510 represent a loop in which the respondent makes successive guesses to try to determine the number the computer has chosen. The computer

```
10 LET G=10
20 CLS
30 PRINT "THE NAME OF THIS GAME IS 'TRAP'"
40 PRINT "WOULD YOU LIKE INSTRUCTIONS?    (YES OR NO)";
50 INPUT Z$
60 CLS
70 IF Z$="NO" THEN 350
80 PRINT "I AM THINKING OF A NUMBER BETWEEN 1 AND 100."
90 PRINT
100 PRINT "TRY TO GUESS MY NUMBER."
110 PRINT
120 PRINT "ON EACH GUESS, ENTER 2 NUMBERS,"
130 PRINT "TRYING TO TRAP MY NUMBER BETWEEN YOUR TWO NUMBERS."
140 PRINT
150 PRINT "I WILL TELL YOU IF YOU HAVE TRAPPED MY NUMBER,"
160 PRINT "IF MY NUMBER IS LARGER THAN YOUR TWO NUMBERS,"
170 PRINT "OR IF MY NUMBER IS SMALLER THAN YOUR TWO NUMBERS."
180 PRINT
190 PRINT
200 PRINT "ARE YOU READY TO CONTINUE (PRESS ENTER)";
210 INPUT A$
220 CLS
230 PRINT "TYPE IN THE FIRST TRAP NUMBER OF YOUR GUESS"
240 PRINT "AND PRESS THE ENTER KEY."
250 PRINT "WHEN ?? APPEARS, TYPE IN THE SECOND TRAP NUMBER"
260 PRINT "OF YOUR GUESS AND PRESS THE ENTER KEY FOR CLUES."
270 PRINT
280 PRINT "       **** NOTE ****   "
290  PRINT "IF YOU WANT TO GUESS ONE SINGLE NUMBER, TYPE"
300  PRINT "YOUR GUESS FOR BOTH YOUR TRAP NUMBERS."
310  PRINT
320  PRINT "YOU GET ";G;" GUESSES TO GET MY NUMBER."
330 PRINT
340 PRINT "GOOD LUCK"
350  X=INT(100*RND(0))+1
360  FOR Q=1 TO G
370  PRINT
380  PRINT "GUESS #";Q;
390  INPUT A,B
400  IF A<>B THEN 420
410  IF X=A THEN 580
420  IF A<=B THEN 440
430  GOSUB 540
440  IF X<A THEN 480
450  IF X<=B THEN 500
460  PRINT "MY NUMBER IS LARGER THAN YOUR TRAP NUMBERS."
470  GOTO 510
480  PRINT "MY NUMBER IS SMALLER THAN YOUR TRAP NUMBERS."
490  GOTO 510
500  PRINT "YOU HAVE TRAPPED MY NUMBER."
510  NEXT Q
520  PRINT "SORRY, THAT'S"; G;" GUESSES. THE NUMBER WAS";X;"."
530  GOTO 590
540 LET R=A
550 LET A=B
560 LET B=R
570  RETURN
580  PRINT "YOU GOT IT!!!"
590  PRINT
600  PRINT "TRY AGAIN?   (YES OR NO)";
610  INPUT T$
620  IF T$="NO" THEN 650
630 CLS
640  GOTO 350
650  END
 10 CLS
 20 PRINT TAB(14); " ' H E L L O ' "
 30 PRINT
 40 PRINT
 50 PRINT "HELLO! I AM A GENIE LOCKED INSIDE THIS COMPUTER."
 60  PRINT "ALTHOUGH I CANNOT GIVE YOU THREE WISHES, I CAN"
```

Figure 7.20. The listing of TRAP (written for the TRS-80).

```
70   PRINT "ANSWER QUESTIONS AND GIVE VALUABLE ADVICE."
80   PRINT
90  PRINT "WHAT IS YOUR NAME";
100   INPUT A$
110   PRINT
120  PRINT "HI THERE, ";A$;"."
130   PRINT "ARE YOU ENJOYING YOURSELF HERE AT THE BEAUTIFUL"
140  PRINT "CALUMET CAMPUS OF PURDUE UNIVERSITY (YES OR NO)";
150  INPUT B$
160  CLS
170   PRINT
180   IF B$="YES" THEN 260
190   IF B$="NO" THEN 310
200  PRINT B$;" IS INCOMPREHENSIBLE TO ME."
210  PRINT
220  PRINT "PLEASE ANSWER YES OR NO."
230  PRINT
240  PRINT "DO YOU LIKE IT HERE ";
250   GOTO 150
260   PRINT "I AM GLAD TO HEAR THAT.   TELL YOUR FRIENDS ABOUT
     US."
270  PRINT
280  PRINT "PRESS ENTER TO CONTINUE."
290  INPUT Z$
300   GOTO 340
310  PRINT " I'M SORRY TO HEAR THAT. MAYBE WE SHOULD GET
     TOGETHER"
320   PRINT "AND TALK ABOUT IT SOME TIME."
330  GOTO 270
340  CLS
350   PRINT "I CAN SOLVE ALL KINDS OF PROBLEMS EXCEPT THOSE"
360   PRINT "WHICH REQUIRE A LIQUID DETERGENT OR A TAX
     CONSULTANT."
370  PRINT
380  PRINT
390  PRINT "WHAT KIND OF PROBLEMS DO YOU HAVE? (ANSWER SEX,"
400   PRINT "HEALTH, MONEY, OR JOB.)"
410  PRINT
420   INPUT C$
430   IF C$="SEX" THEN 730
440   IF C$="HEALTH" THEN 650
450   IF C$="MONEY" THEN 600
460   IF C$="JOB" THEN 540
470  PRINT
480  PRINT "YOUR ANSWER OF   ";C$;"   IS INCOMPREHENSIBLE TO ME."
490  PRINT "IT MUST REQUIRE EITHER A LIQUID DETERGENT OR A TAX
     CONSULTANT."
500  PRINT
510  PRINT "PLEASE ANSWER SEX, HEALTH, MONEY, OR JOB."
520   PRINT
530   GOTO 390
540   PRINT "I CAN SYMPATHIZE WITH YOU. I HAVE TO WORK"
550   PRINT "LONG HOURS FOR LOW PAY--AND SOME OF MY BOSSES"
560   PRINT "REALLY BEAT THIS KEYBOARD. MY ADVICE TO YOU IS"
570  PRINT "TO GET A JOB TEACHING AT PURDUE UNIVERSITY."
580  PRINT "IT'S GREAT FUN!"
590   GOTO 920
600  PRINT "SORRY! I'M BROKE TOO! WHY DON'T YOU SELL"
610   PRINT "ALUMINUM SIDING BY TELEPHONE IN YOUR SPARE TIME."
620   PRINT "OR YOU COULD MARRY SOMEONE RICH OR STOP EATING"
630  PRINT "SO YOU WON'T NEED SO MUCH MONEY."
640   GOTO 920
650  PRINT "MY ADVICE TO YOU, ";A$; " IS"
660   PRINT "            1)TAKE AN ASPIRIN."
670   PRINT "            2)DRINK PLENTY OF FLUIDS."
680   PRINT "             (ORANGE JUICE, NOT BEER)"
690   PRINT "            3)GO TO BED (ALONE)."
700   GOTO 920
710  PRINT
720  PRINT
730  PRINT "IS YOUR PROBLEM TOO LITTLE OR TOO MUCH";
```

Figure 7.20. The listing of TRAP (written for the TRS-80). (Continued.)

```
740   INPUT D$
750 PRINT
760 PRINT
770   IF D$="TOO MUCH" THEN 850
780 IF D$ = "TOO LITTLE"  THEN 890
790 PRINT "DON'T GET ALL SHOOK UP,   " ;A$;"!"
800  IF D$="TOO LITTLE" THEN 890
810 PRINT "JUST ANSWER THE QUESTION WITH  'TOO LITTLE'  OR  'TOO
    MUCH'!"
820 PRINT       "            WHICH IS IT";
830 GOTO 740
840 CLS
850   PRINT "YOU CALL THAT A PROBLEM! I SHOULD HAVE SUCH
    PROBLEMS!"
860   PRINT "IF IT BOTHERS YOU, TAKE A COLD SHOWER OR A
    STATISTICS"
870   PRINT "COURSE."
880   GOTO 920
890 PRINT "WHY ARE YOU HERE, ";A$;"?"
900  PRINT "YOU SHOULD BE AT INDIANA UNIVERSITY OR BALL STATE,"
910 PRINT "WHERE THERE IS SOME REAL ACTION !"
920   PRINT
930 PRINT "ARE THERE ANY MORE PROBLEMS YOU WANT SOLVED (YES OR
    NO)";
940   INPUT E$
950 CLS
960   PRINT
970   IF E$="YES" THEN 1030
980   IF E$="NO" THEN 1060
990   PRINT "JUST A SIMPLE YES OR NO PLEASE."
1000 PRINT
1010 PRINT
1020   GOTO 930
1030 PRINT "WHAT KIND? (SEX, HEALTH, MONEY, JOB)"
1040   PRINT
1050   GOTO 420
1060   PRINT
1070 PRINT   "THAT WILL BE $5.00 FOR THE ADVICE, " ;A$; "."
1080   PRINT "JUST LEAVE THE MONEY ON THE TERMINAL."
1090   PRINT
1100   PRINT
1110   PRINT "IT HAS BEEN NICE TALKING TO YOU, ";A$; "."
1120   PRINT "STOP BY AGAIN SOME TIME."
1130 PRINT
1140 PRINT
1150 PRINT
1160 PRINT
1170 PRINT
1180   END
```

Figure 7.20. The listing of TRAP (written for the TRS-80). (Continued.)

labels each guess Q, and Q becomes one number higher each time the computer reaches line 510. When Q reaches 11 (that is, when it exceeds 10), the computer goes on to line 520 and tells the respondent that he or she has used too many guesses. Note that because the value of G is 10, the command "FOR Q = 1 TO G" actually means "FOR Q = 1 TO 10."

Let's examine the loop in lines 360 to 510 closely. The computer accepts two numbers as the trap numbers in line 390. Then at line 400 the computer checks to see if they both are the same number. According to the rules in lines 290 to 300, if both numbers were the same, this would mean that the respondent was trying to guess the exact number. If this happens to be the case, the computer will check in line 410 to see if the guess is correct. If it is correct, the computer will give a "correct message" in line 580 and ask if the respondent wants to play again.

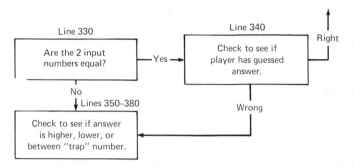

Figure 7.21. The overall strategy of evaluating the trap numbers in lines 330 to 380 of TRAP.

If the respondent is not trying to make an "official guess" or if the guess is wrong, the computer will branch to lines 460, 480, or 500 to tell the respondent whether the chosen number is above, below, or between the trap numbers. This process is shown in Figure 7.21.

At line 430 the computer is sent to a subroutine that begins at line 540. Note that it will go to this subroutine only if A (the first number the respondent entered) is larger than B (the second number). (If A is less than or equal to B, line 420 will tell the computer to skip line 430, and therefore the computer will miss the GOSUB 540 statement.) The purpose of this subroutine is to reverse the numbers—to make A the smaller number and B the larger number—in the event that the respondent entered them in the opposite order. This reversal is necessary because the computer expects them to be in that order when it evaluates them in lines 440 and 450. This strategy for reversing the numbers is shown in Figure 7.22.

In line 440, the computer checks to see if the number it has selected is smaller than the lower trap number. If so, it will give the message in line 480. If not, then

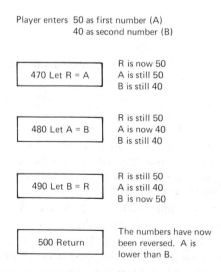

Figure 7.22. The logic of the subroutine in lines 470 to 500 of TRAP.

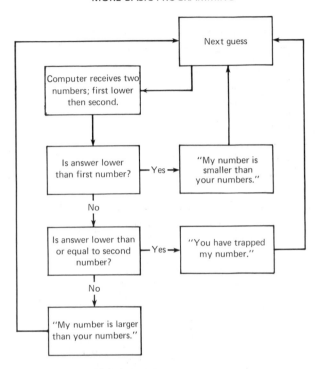

Figure 7.23. The logic of the incorrect-guess messages in TRAP.

it will continue to line 450, where it will check to see if the number it has selected is smaller than the larger number entered by the respondent. If so, it will provide the message in line 500. If neither of these conditions is true, the computer will arrive at line 460 and notify the respondent that the number is larger than the trap numbers. The logic behind these messages is described in Figure 7.23.

Each of these three possible messages is followed by a GOTO 510 command, which sends the computer to the end of the loop. At that point the computer either continues the loop (if the limit has not yet been reached) or continues to line 520. The logic of this entire loop is diagrammed in Figure 7.24.

Both winners and losers eventually arrive at line 600, where they get a chance to try again. If they say no, they will exit by going to the end at line 650. If they say anything other than no, the program will continue by going to line 350, where the whole cycle (after the directions) will start over again.

Modifying TRAP

There are several modifications that can easily be made to make TRAP function in a slightly different manner. Try the following:

1. Give the player fifteen guesses rather than ten. To do this, merely change line 10 to read

```
10 LET G = 15
```

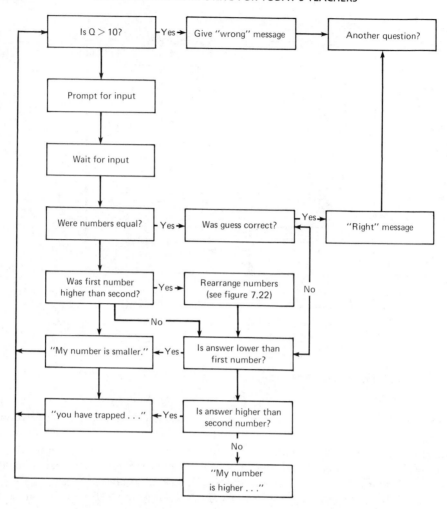

Figure 7.24. The logic of the FOR/NEXT loop in lines 290 to 440 of TRAP.

2. Change the range of numbers to 1 and 1,000 instead of the present range of 1 and 100. To do this, merely change line 350 to read

```
350 LET X = INT(1000*RND(0)) + 1
```

3. Many players get confused when they are required to enter two numbers at the same time at line 320. Let's change this by requesting one trap number first and then the other. The following lines will do the trick:

```
382 PRINT ''ENTER YOUR TRAP NUMBERS ONE AT A TIME.''
384 PRINT
386 PRINT ''WHAT IS YOUR FIRST TRAP NUMBER?''
388 INPUT A
390 PRINT ''WHAT IS YOUR SECOND TRAP NUMBER?''
392 INPUT B
```

Additional Modifications for TRAP

The following are some more modifications you can use to make TRAP function slightly differently:

1. Set up the program so that the computer will select a number between 1 and 500.
2. Have the computer obtain the player's name. Then have the computer greet the player by name and use the player's name correctly in lines 200, 320, and 500.
3. Add an "error trap" after line 70 to accommodate responses other than no.

PIZZA

PIZZA is a disguised drill, which was described in Chapter 3. Children who run PIZZA think they are playing a game, but in fact they are repeatedly solving problems involving geometric coordinates.

PIZZA (Figure 7.25) has the following major components: (1) PRINT lines to instruct the player, (2) a READ loop to store data in an array, (3) the random selection of a name of a "customer," (4) a mathematical formula to designate the correct answer, (5) a subroutine to draw a map of the city where the potential customers live, and (6) feedback mechanisms to evaluate and respond to the learner's response.

How PIZZA Works

Rather than giving a line-by-line annotation of PIZZA, we will focus on specific questions regarding how PIZZA carries out its functions. Some of these questions may seem extremely simple, whereas others may seem exceedingly complex. You may wish to focus on those topics which are of interest to you and to skip over those which are of less interest.

Question 1: How does the computer learn the player's name?
Answer: Lines 30 to 50 print a greeting message on the screen, and line 60 makes the computer pause and wait for the player to enter his or her name. This name (N$) will be used to refer to the player throughout the game.

Question 2: How does the computer learn the names which it prints on the map?
Answer: In lines 160 to 180, the computer memorizes the sixteen letters of the alphabet that will represent the names of the pizza customers. The data for this memorization process are contained in line 190. It is actually more common for such DATA lines to be near the end of the program, although it is perfectly acceptable to put them right after the READ statements, as in this example. The awkward order of the letters of the alphabet was necessary in order to make the letters appear in the desired order on the map in lines 990 to 1140.

Question 3: How does the computer draw the map of the city?
Answer: After the pause subroutine at line 200, the computer draws its first map of the city. If the map were to be drawn only once, the lines to draw it would have been

```
10 CLS
20 DIM S$(16)
30  PRINT "PIZZA DELIVERY GAME"
40  PRINT
50  PRINT "WHAT IS YOUR FIRST NAME";
60  INPUT N$
70 CLS
80  PRINT
90 PRINT "HI, ";N$;"."
100 PRINT
110  PRINT "IN THIS GAME YOU ARE TO TAKE ORDERS FOR PIZZA.
120 PRINT "THEN YOU ARE TO TELL A DELIVERY BOY WHERE TO"
130 PRINT "DELIVER THE ORDERED PIZZAS."
140  PRINT
150  PRINT
160  FOR I=1 TO 16
170  READ S$(I)
180  NEXT I
190 DATA M,N,O,P,I,J,K,L,E,F,G,H,A,B,C,D
200 GOSUB 930
210 GOSUB 990
220  PRINT "THE ABOVE IS A MAP OF THE HOMES WHERE"
230  PRINT "YOU ARE TO SEND PIZZAS."
240 GOSUB 930
250  PRINT "YOUR JOB IS TO GIVE A TRUCK DRIVER"
260  PRINT "THE LOCATION OR COORDINATES OF THE"
270  PRINT "HOME ORDERING THE PIZZA."
280  PRINT
290 PRINT "DO YOU NEED MORE INSTRUCTIONS (YES OR NO)";
300  INPUT A$
310 CLS
320  IF A$="YES" THEN 360
330  IF A$="NO" THEN 580
340 PRINT "ANSWER YES OR NO, PLEASE."
350  GOTO 290
360  PRINT
370  PRINT "SOMEBODY WILL ASK FOR A PIZZA TO BE"
380  PRINT "DELIVERED. THEN YOU WILL TELL THE DELIVERY BOY"
390  PRINT "WHERE TO DELIVER THE PIZZA."
400 GOSUB 930
410 GOSUB 990
420 PRINT "FOR EXAMPLE:"
430 PRINT "THIS IS J. PLEASE SEND A PIZZA.
440  PRINT
450  PRINT "DRIVER, J LIVES AT"
460  PRINT
470  PRINT "YOUR ANSWER WOULD BE 2,3";
480  PRINT TAB(45);"UNDERSTAND";
490  INPUT A$
500 CLS
510  IF A$="YES" THEN 540
520  PRINT "THIS JOB IS TOO DIFFICULT FOR YOU.   THANKS ANYWAY."
530  GOTO 920
540  PRINT "GOOD.   YOU ARE NOW READY TO START TAKING ORDERS."
550  PRINT
560  PRINT "GOOD LUCK!!"
570 GOSUB 930
580  S=INT(RND(0)*16+1)
590 GOSUB 990
600 PRINT "MAMA PAPINO'S PIZZA.   PEPPERONI ";N$;" SPEAKING."
610  PRINT
620 PRINT "THIS IS ";S$(S);". PLEASE SEND ME A PIZZA."
630  PRINT
640 PRINT "NOW TELL THE DRIVER WHERE ";S$(S);" LIVES, ";N$;"."
650  PRINT
660  INPUT A1,A2
670 GOSUB 970
680  IF A1>4 THEN 710
690  IF A2>4 THEN 710
700  GOTO 760
710 PRINT "YOUR NUMBER WAS GREAT FOR THE TACO BUSINESS,"
```

Figure 7.25. The listing of PIZZA (written for the TRS-80).

```
720 PRINT "BUT TOO HIGH FOR US. cHOOSE AGAIN."
730 PRINT
740 GOSUB 990
750 GOTO 640
760 LET T=A1+(4-A2)*4
770  IF T=S THEN 830
780  PRINT "THIS IS ";S$(T);".   I DID NOT ORDER A PIZZA."
790  PRINT "I LIVE AT";A1;",";A2
800  PRINT
810 GOSUB 990
820  GOTO 640
830 PRINT "MAMA PAPINO'S  PIZZA, THIS IS ";S$(S);"."
840 PRINT "THANKS FOR THE PIZZA."
850  PRINU
860 PRINT "DO YOU WANT TO DELIVER MORE PIZZAS?"
870  INPUT A$
880 CLS
890  IF A$="YES" THEN 580
900  PRINT
910 PRINT "O.K. ";N$;", SEE YOU LATER!"
920  END
930 PRINT
940 PRINT
950 PRINT "ARE YOU READY TO CONTINUE (PRESS ENTER)";
960 INPUT A$
970 CLS
980 RETURN
990 PRINT "MAP OF THE CITY"
1000  PRINT
1010 PRINT "-------1---2---3---4------"
1020 LET K=4
1030 FOR I=1 TO 16 STEP 4
1040 PRINT K;
1050 PRINT "    ";S$(I);
1060 PRINT "    ";S$(I+1);
1070 PRINT "    ";S$(I+2);
1080 PRINT "    ";S$(I+3);
1090 PRINT "    ";K
1100 K=K-1
1110  NEXT I
1120 PRINT "-------1---2---3---4------"
1130  PRINT
1140 RETURN
```

Figure 7.25. The listing of PIZZA (written for the TRS-80). (Continued.)

inserted at line 210. But because the map will be drawn several times throughout the course of the program, the programmer has written it as a subroutine that he or she can call at will.

The map subroutine is a fairly complex set of commands. You should not feel discouraged if you look at them and conclude that you are unable or unwilling to write such a complex subroutine. However, these lines demonstrate the effective use of a loop to accomplish a useful task. You may wish to examine this subroutine to see the application of many of the principles discussed earlier in this chapter. In addition, after you examine this subroutine, you will understand how computer programs are easily able to perform apparently complex tasks repeatedly within a run of a program. You will also discover that you can make interesting modifications in the map, even if you don't feel capable of writing the subroutine by yourself.

To understand how the 990 subroutine draws the map of the city, run the program and get the map on the screen of your computer. Then examine the following annotation of the map subroutine. The process is also summarized in Figure 7.26.

Lines 990 to 1010 are easy to understand. The K in line 1020 is a counter which will range between 4 and 1 and is used in lines 1040 and 1090 to print a number in the left-

```
Line           New Value        Printed Output
990                             ------1---2---3---4------
1000           K=4
1010           I=1
1020                            4
1030-1070                              M   N   O   P   4
1080           K=3
1090           I=2
1020                            3
1030-1070                              I   J   K   L   3
1080           K=2
1090           I=3
1020                            2
1030-1070                              E   F   G   H   2
1080           K=1
1090           I=4
1020                            1
1030-1070                              A   B   C   D   1
1090           I=5
1100                            -------1---2---3---4------
1110                                          (blank line)
1120              RETURN
```

Figure 7.26. Summary of the map loop.

hand and right-hand margins of the map. Because K has an initial value of 4, (line 1020), the first time the computer encounters line 1040 or 1090, it will print a 4. Each time the computer prints a line of the map, it will encounter line 1110, in which the value of K decreases by 1. Therefore, on subsequent arrivals at line 1040 and 1090, the computer will print 3, 2, and 1 in the margins.

After printing the number in the left margin, the programmer wants the computer to print the names of the potential customers. These are the letters from A to P that the computer has previously stored in the S$(I) array. Therefore, as the computer proceeds from line 1040 to line 1090, it prints a line number (actually a coordinate) in the left margin, four consecutive names separated by spaces, and then the line number again. Note that all the PRINT statements from line 1040 to line 1090 have been joined by semicolons, which caused each subsequent entry to be printed in the immediately adjacent space. Line 1090 breaks this sequence by omitting the semicolon after the K. This omission of the semicolon can be interpreted as "Finish this line with spaces and then start the next PRINT statement on the following line."

The computer repeats the sequence from 1030 to 1110 four times. After leaving the FOR/NEXT loop, the computer prints the final line of the map at line 1120, skips a line, and returns to the line immediately following the GOSUB statement that sent it to this subroutine. Note that the programmer had to plan the map carefully to make it look presentable.

Question 4: How does the programmer make some of the instructions optional?
Answer: After the first printing of the map, the computer returns to line 220 and prints some instructions related to the map, and then at line 290 it asks if the player needs more instructions. One answer gets the player more instructions, whereas the other gets an order for a pizza.

Question 5: How does the computer select a customer to purchase a pizza?
Answer: In line 580, the computer selects a random number between 1 and 16 to designate one of the sixteen names memorized in line 170. The computer then simulates a conversation in which a customer calls N$ (the player) and orders a pizza. As part of this conversation, the customer gives the randomly selected name at line 620. Then at line 660 the computer pauses to let the player enter the coordinates of the address where he or she thinks the customer lives.

Question 6: How does the computer know the correct address of the customer?

Answer: Line 760 contains a mathematical formula that represents the address of the customer, by reducing the input coordinates to a single number between 1 and 16. The programmer would have to understand this formula in order to write the program, of course, but as a reader you can afford to ignore it if you wish. The important thing is that the formula works.

Question 7: How does the computer know whether the learner has entered the correct coordinates?

Answer: Line 770 compares the player's estimated location of the customer with the actual number selected in line 580. If they match, the player will get a correct message in lines 830 to 850 and is offered a chance to deliver more pizzas. But if the player's answer is wrong, the computer will go to line 780, where the person who really lives at the address that the player entered calls to state that he or she had not ordered a pizza. This is realistic but nonpunitive feedback. The player is then instructed to deliver the pizza to the correct address.

Suggested Modifications for PIZZA

The following are suggested modifications for PIZZA:

1. Have the computer call the player by name in line 540.
2. Have the computer clear the screen and print a new copy of the map if the player gives an answer which is "too high" at line 720.
3. Change the map to contain people's first names instead of letters of the alphabet. You will have to use short names (Ed, Mary, Jane, etc.) in order to make them fit in the confined space. In addition, you will have to alter lines 1010 and 1120 to line up with the greater number of letters on each line of the map. Finally, if the names contain varying numbers of letters, it will be necessary to make adjustments for such variations. It may be easiest to choose all names with the same number of letters. When you make this modification, you are likely to make mistakes. For example, the names may appear in a strange order or the map may have a jagged appearance. When this happens, try to figure out why the mistake occurred, and then correct the error in your revised program.

Chapter 8
CAPS: An Integration of Basic Principles

CAPS is a computerized drill that takes advantage of many of the features that a computer can make available to drill on factual information. It uses three pieces of information (state, capital, and abbreviation) and combines them in several different drill formats:

1. The player can study either capitals or abbreviations.
2. In both the capitals and the abbreviation games, the player can choose as a prompt from the computer either the name of the state or the capital or abbreviation.
3. The computer can give the player a state data list for an individual state or for all states.
4. The computer automatically corrects the spelling of the names of the states. It requires the correct spelling of the state name, and if the player misspells it, the computer will notify the player of this error and allow him or her to see a list of the correct spellings of all states. Errors in spelling do not count against the player's total score.
5. On request, the computer will offer a list of all the states.
6. The computer provides immediate feedback after each response. In addition, it keeps track of correct and incorrect answers for the final feedback at the end of the game.
7. The questions are randomly selected, and therefore everyone who uses the drill will receive different sets of questions, and so will those who perform the drill more than once.

Because CAPS treats its material so comprehensively, it is necessarily a somewhat complex program. Numerous loops and subroutines are necessary to provide feedback to the player and to direct the computer into the channels dictated by the player's responses. Nevertheless, it can be valuable to examine a program at this level of complexity, as once you understand the logic of the program, you will be able to see how the computer can be used in many analogous learning situations.

Some theorists in computerized education decry the use of computers for such "trivial purposes" as drills like this one. They maintain that computers should be dedicated to "higher" goals, such as simulations and problem solving, and that CAI drills turn computers into "glorified flashcards." If this is true, then it is worth noting that the computer does make a pretty good flashcard. Where else can you find a set of flashcards that presents information, with endless patience, to learners who can digest the information and respond at their own pace and repeat the drill as often as they desire? In addition, a drill like CAPS keeps accurate records on the person using the drill and provides supplemental information (such as the list of the states) at exactly the time the learner needs it to make a response.

The strategies used in CAPS can be applied to a variety of learning situations in which drill on factual information is important. Such drills need not stifle creativity; indeed, teachers who let students use computers for drilling on factual or remedial information can spend more time stimulating creativity and answering questions that they would never be able to if they had to conduct these drills.

How CAPS Works

A listing of CAPS is shown in Figure 8.1, and Figure 8.2 diagrams the overall strategy of the program. This section will present several sets of questions and answers regarding how CAPS carries out its functions. This format will enable you to focus on those topics and strategies that are of greatest interest to you.

Question 1: This program contains several lines with more than one command per line. How does this work?

Answer: These multiple-command lines (e.g., line 50) are created by joining the commands with a colon. The colon tells the computer to look for the next command on the same line instead of on the next line. You should refer to your manual to determine how such multiple commands can be helpful to you on your own computer.

Line 240 offers another example of multiple commands on a single line. This line differs from the previous example of multiple commands because it begins with an IF command. When there are multiple commands on an IF line, the IF condition will apply to all the commands on the line. For example, in line 240, there are three commands after the word THEN. If C falls between 1 and 3, the computer will execute none of these commands but will simply continue to line 250. If C falls below 1 or above 3, however, the computer will execute all three of these commands before returning to line 170. CAPS contains several other examples of multiple commands on IF lines (e.g., lines 350 and 1220).

Question 2: How does the computer learn the names of the states, the abbreviations, and the capitals?

Answer: The computer reads the data on the states into its memory at lines 140 and 160. The computer does this by examining each DATA statement in the order in which they are presented, starting at line 1620. (The DIM statement in line 40 previously reserved space for the arrays of states, abbreviations, and capitals.) Notice that each of the

```
5 RANDOM
10 REM   WRITTEN BY EDWARD AND MARC VOCKELL
20 REM FEBRUARY 8, 1982
30 REM   ALL RIGHTS RESERVED
40 DIM S$(60),A$(50),C$(50)
45 REM *** THE FOLLOWING LINES GIVE A TITLE PAGE.
50 CLS:PRINT:PRINT:PRINT:PRINT TAB(17);"CAPITALS AND
   ABBREVIATIONS"
60 PRINT TAB(20);"OF THE UNITED STATES"
70 PRINT:PRINT TAB(28);"BY"
80 PRINT TAB(20);"ED AND MARC VOCKELL"
90 PRINT TAB(19);"(ALL RIGHTS RESERVED)"
100 PRINT:PRINT TAB(13);"ARE YOU READY TO START (PRESS ENTER)";
110 INPUT A$
120 CLS
130 PRINT TAB(20);"ONE MOMENT PLEASE."
140 FOR I=1 TO 50
150 READ S$(I),A$(I),C$(I)
160 NEXT I
170 CLS:PRINT "WHICH GAME DO YOU WANT TO PLAY?"
180 PRINT "1. STATE CAPITALS"
190 PRINT "2. STATE ABBREVIATIONS"
200 PRINT "3. STATE DATA LIST"
210 PRINT:PRINT "ENTER THE NUMBER OF THE GAME YOU CHOOSE."
220 PRINT "WHAT NUMBER DO YOU WANT";
230 INPUT C
240 IF C>3 OR C<1 THEN PRINT:PRINT "CHOOSE EITHER 1, 2, OR 3,
    PLEASE.":GOTO 180
250 CLS
260 GOTO 270
270 LET K1=1:R=0
275 REM *** BRANCHING POINT TO SPECIFIC DRILLS.
280 ON C GOTO 290, 460, 1060
285 REM *** THE FOLLOWING LINES PRESENT THE STATE CAPITALS
    GAME.
290 GOSUB 790
300 GOSUB 920
310 IF C$="B" THEN 390
320 PRINT:PRINT:PRINT
330 PRINT "WHAT IS THE CAPITAL OF ";S$(N);
340 INPUT R$:CLS
350 IF R$=C$(N) GOSUB 1460 :GOTO 300
355 REM *** THE FOLLOWING LINE PERMITS A VARIANT SPELLING OF
    ST. PAUL.
360 IF N=23 AND R$="SAINT PAUL" GOSUB 1460 :GOTO 300
370 PRINT:PRINT:PRINT "WRONG. ";C$(N);" IS THE CAPITAL OF
    ";S$(N);"."
380 GOSUB 1480 :GOTO 300
390 PRINT:PRINT
400 PRINT C$(N);" IS THE CAPITAL OF WHAT STATE";
410 INPUT R$:CLS
420 GOTO 710
430 IF R$=S$(N) GOSUB 1460 :GOTO 300
440 PRINT:PRINT "WRONG. ";C$(N);" IS THE CAPITAL OF ";S$(N);"."
450 GOSUB 1480 :GOTO 300
455 REM *** THE FOLLOWING LINES PRESENT THE STATE ABBREVIATIONS
    DRILL.
460 GOSUB 930
470 GOSUB 920
480 IF C$="B" THEN 570
490 PRINT:PRINT:PRINT
500 PRINT "WHAT IS THE OFFICIAL ABBREVIATION FOR ";S$(N);
510 INPUT R$
520 CLS
530 IF R$=A$(N) GOSUB 1460 :GOTO 470
540 PRINT:PRINT:PRINT
550 PRINT "WRONG. ";A$(N);" IS THE ABBREVIATION FOR ";S$(N);"."
560 GOSUB 1480 :GOTO 470
570 PRINT:PRINT:PRINT
580 PRINT A$(N);" IS THE OFFICIAL ABBREVIATION FOR WHAT STATE";
590 INPUT R$
```

Figure 8.1. The listing of CAPS (written for the TRS-80).

```
600 CLS:GOTO 710
610 IF R$=S$(N) GOSUB 1460 :GOTO 470
620 PRINT:PRINT:PRINT
630 PRINT "WRONG. ";A$(N);" IS THE ABBREVIATION FOR ";S$(N);"."
640 PRINT:PRINT
650 GOSUB 1480 :GOTO 470
655 REM *** THE FOLLOWING LINES PRESENT THE LIST OF THE STATES.
660 LET R$=""
670 FOR I=1 TO 13
680 PRINT
    S$(I);TAB(15);S$(I+13);TAB(30);S$(I+26);TAB(45);S$(I+39)
690 NEXT I
700 PRINT:ON C GOTO 400, 580, 1300
710 IF R$="LIST" THEN 660
715 REM *** THE FOLLOWING LINES VERIFY THAT THE LEARNER HAS
    ENTERED THE CORRECT SPELLING OF ONE OF THE STATES.
720 FOR I=1 TO 50
730 IF R$=S$(I) THEN 780
740 NEXT I
750 PRINT:PRINT R$;" IS NOT A CORRECT SPELLING OF ONE OF THE
    STATES."
760 PRINT:PRINT "EITHER ENTER A CORRECT SPELLING OR TYPE THE
    WORD LIST."
770 ON C GOTO 400, 580, 1300
780 ON C GOTO 430, 610, 1340
790 PRINT "THERE ARE TWO FORMS OF THE STATE CAPITAL GAME."
800 PRINT
810 PRINT "YOU CAN EITHER:"
820 PRINT TAB(10);"A. NAME THE CAPITAL WHEN THE COMPUTER"
830 PRINT TAB(13);"GIVES THE STATE, OR"
840 PRINT
850 PRINT TAB(10);"B. NAME THE STATE WHEN THE COMPUTER
860 PRINT TAB(13);"GIVES THE NAME OF THE CAPITAL."
870 PRINT
880 PRINT "WHICH DO YOU WANT (ENTER A OR B);"
890 INPUT C$
900 CLS
910 RETURN
920 LET N=RND(50):RETURN
930 PRINT "THERE ARE TWO WAYS TO PLAY THE ABBREVIATION GAME."
940 PRINT
950 PRINT "YOU CAN EITHER:"
960 PRINT TAB(10);"A. GIVE THE ABBREVIATION WHEN THE COMPUTER"
970 PRINT TAB(13);"GIVES THE STATE, OR"
980 PRINT
990 PRINT TAB(10);"B. GIVE THE STATE WHEN THE COMPUTER"
1000 PRINT TAB(13);"GIVES THE ABBREVIATION"
1010 PRINT
1020 PRINT "WHICH ONE DO YOU WANT (ENTER A OR B)";
1030 INPUT C$
1040 CLS
1050 RETURN
1055 REM *** THE FOLLOWING LINES PRESENT THE STATE DATA LIST.
1060 PRINT TAB(23);"STATE DATA LIST"
1070 PRINT:PRINT "DO YOU WANT"
1080 PRINT TAB(5);"1. THE CAPITALS AND ABBREVIATIONS"
1090 PRINT TAB(8);"FOR ALL 50 STATES, OR"
1100 PRINT:PRINT TAB(5);"2. DATA ON A SPECIFIC STATE";
1110 INPUT A
1120 CLS
1130 IF A<1 OR A>2 THEN PRINT:PRINT "CHOOSE 1 OR 2,
     PLEASE.":GOTO 1070
1140 IF A=2 THEN 1300
1150 LET F=1
1160 PRINT " STATE";TAB(15);"ABBREVIATION";TAB(32);"CAPITAL"
1170 PRINT
1180 FOR I=F TO F+9
1190 PRINT S$(I);TAB(20);A$(I);TAB(30);C$(I)
1200 NEXT I
1210 F=F+10
1220 IF F<50 THEN PRINT:PRINT "ARE YOU READY TO CONTINUE (PRESS
     ENTER)";:INPUT R$:CLS:GOTO 1160
```

Figure 8.1. The listing of CAPS (written for the TRS-80). (Continued.)

```
1230 PRINT:PRINT "DO YOU WISH TO"
1240 PRINT TAB(5);"1. CONTINUE"
1250 PRINT TAB(5);"2. STOP";
1260 INPUT A
1270 CLS
1280 IF A>2 OR A<1 THEN CLS:PRINT "CHOOSE EITHER 1 OR 2,
     PLEASE.":GOTO 1230
1290 ON A GOTO 170  ,1600
1300 PRINT:PRINT "FOR WHICH STATE DO YOU WISH TO SEE DATA";
1310 INPUT R$
1320 CLS
1330 GOTO 710
1340 FOR I=1 TO 50
1350 IF R$=S$(I) THEN 1370
1360 NEXT I
1370 CLS:PRINT S$(I)
1380 PRINT:PRINT "OFFICIAL ABBREVIATION: ";A$(I)
1390 PRINT:PRINT "STATE CAPITAL: ";C$(I)
1400 PRINT:PRINT "DO YOU WANT DATA ON ANOTHER STATE";
1410 INPUT R$
1420 IF R$="YES" OR R$="Y" THEN 1300
1430 IF R$="NO" OR R$="N" THEN 1230
1440 PRINT "ANSWER YES OR NO, PLEASE."
1450 GOTO 1410
1460 PRINT:PRINT:PRINT "RIGHT."
1470 R=R+1
1480 PRINT:PRINT "WOULD YOU LIKE ANOTHER QUESTION";
1490 INPUT A$
1500 CLS
1510 IF A$="YES" OR A$="Y" THEN 1540
1520 IF A$="NO" OR A$="N" THEN 1590
1530 GOTO 1480
1540 K1=K1+1:RETURN
1550 PRINT:PRINT "ARE YOU READY TO CONTINUE (PRESS ENTER)";
1560 INPUT A$
1570 CLS:RETURN
1580 NEXT I
1590 PRINT:PRINT "YOU GOT";R;" RIGHT OUT OF ";K1;" QUESTIONS."
1600 PRINT:PRINT "PLAY AGAIN SOME TIME!"
1610 PRINT:END
1620 DATA ALABAMA,AL,MONTGOMERY
1630 DATA ALASKA,AK,JUNEAU
1640 DATA ARIZONA,AZ,PHOENIX
1650 DATA ARKANSAS,AR,LITTLE ROCK
1660 DATA CALIFORNIA,CA,SACRAMENTO
1670 DATA COLORADO,CO,DENVER
1680 DATA CONNECTICUT,CT,HARTFORD
1690 DATA DELAWARE,DE,DOVER
1700 DATA FLORIDA,FL,TALLAHASSEE
1710 DATA GEORGIA,GA,ATLANTA
1720 DATA HAWAII,HI,HONOLULU
1730 DATA IDAHO,ID,BOISE
1740 DATA ILLINOIS,IL,SPRINGFIELD
1750 DATA INDIANA,IN,INDIANAPOLIS
1760 DATA IOWA,IA,DES MOINES
1770 DATA KANSAS,KS,TOPEKA
1780 DATA KENTUCKY,KY,FRANKFORT
1790 DATA LOUISIANA,LA,BATON ROUGE
1800 DATA MAINE,ME,AUGUSTA
1810 DATA MARYLAND,MD,ANNAPOLIS
1820 DATA MASSACHUSETTS,MA,BOSTON
1830 DATA MICHIGAN,MI,LANSING
1840 DATA MINNESOTA,MN,ST. PAUL
1850 DATA MISSISSIPPI,MS,JACKSON
1860 DATA MISSOURI,MO,JEFFERSON CITY
1870 DATA MONTANA,MT,HELENA
1880 DATA NEBRASKA,NE,LINCOLN
1890 DATA NEVADA,NV,CARSON CITY
1900 DATA NEW HAMPSHIRE,NH,CONCORD
1910 DATA NEW JERSEY,NJ,TRENTON
1920 DATA NEW MEXICO,NM,SANTA FE
```

Figure 8.1. The listing of CAPS (written for the TRS-80). (Continued.)

```
1930 DATA NEW YORK,NY,ALBANY
1940 DATA NORTH CAROLINA,NC,RALEIGH
1950 DATA NORTH DAKOTA,ND,BISMARCK
1960 DATA OHIO,OH,COLUMBUS
1970 DATA OKLAHOMA,OK,OKLAHOMA CITY
1980 DATA OREGON,OR,SALEM
1990 DATA PENNSYLVANIA,PA,HARRISBURG
2000 DATA RHODE ISLAND,RI,PROVIDENCE
2010 DATA SOUTH CAROLINA,SC,COLUMBIA
2020 DATA SOUTH DAKOTA,SD,PIERRE
2030 DATA TENNESSEE,TN,NASHVILLE
2040 DATA TEXAS,TX,AUSTIN
2050 DATA UTAH,UT,SALT LAKE CITY
2060 DATA VERMONT,VT,MONTPELIER
2070 DATA VIRGINIA,VA,RICHMOND
2080 DATA WASHINGTON,WA,OLYMPIA
2090 DATA WEST VIRGINIA,WV,CHARLESTON
2100 DATA WISCONSIN,WI,MADISON
2110 DATA WYOMING,WY,CHEYENNE
```

Figure 8.1. The listing of CAPS (written for the TRS-80). (Continued.)

DATA lines contains the name of a state, an official abbreviation, and its capital. The computer reads the first piece of data (Alabama) and classifies that as S$(1) in its memory. Then it reads the second piece of data (AL) and classifies that as A$(1). Next it reads the third piece of data (Montgomery) and classifies that as C$(1). It repeats this process fifty times, eventually "memorizing" the entire set of data. The computer is applying the strategy described later in the discussion of arrays.

While the computer reads the data, the words "One Moment Please" appear on the screen. This user friendly strategy is discussed as part of BEHMOD in Chapter 11.

Question 3: The computer provides three major variations of CAPS (Capitals, Abbreviations, and the State Data List). How does it branch to these variations?
Answer: Line 170 begins the PRINT sequence which presents on the screen the three versions of the program from which the player can choose. The player makes a choice in line 230, and then line 280 branches the player to the selected version of CAPS.

Within each of the major branches, additional branches occur. For example, in line 290, a player who selects the State Capital Game is sent to a subroutine which gives a choice of two versions of this drill. The player chooses one in line 890, and then the computer returns to line 300.

Question 4: What if the player enters a number higher than 3 as his/her choice of game?
Answer: Line 240 makes sure the response in 230 was valid before continuing. An improper answer (such as a 4) would get the learner recycled to the branching point at line 230.

Question 5: How does the computer select the state about which it will ask questions?
Answer: From line 300, the computer goes to a very short subroutine at line 920 in which it selects a number between 1 and 50. This number identifies the state about which the computer will ask questions. The reason this is written as a subroutine is because the exact same operation is required in both the capitals and the abbreviations drills, and the programmer has found it convenient to write it only once rather than repeating it within each version. In addition, if the programmer may want to add additional features (such as eliminating the possibility that the same state will be used twice in a row), this could easily be accomplished in this subroutine. See BEHMOD in Chapter 11 for an example of this application.

Question 6: How does the computer know whether or not the player has selected the right answer?

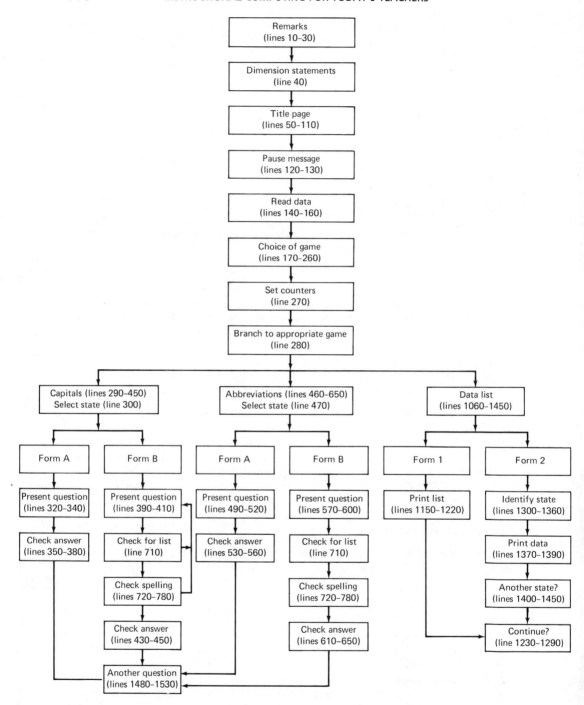

Figure 8.2. The logic of CAPS.

Answer: The computer asks for the capital of a state at line 330. The state mentioned in this question will be the one whose subscript in the State Array matches the random number that the computer chose in the subroutine at line 920. The computer then pauses to accept the player's answer at line 340 and labels this as R$. Then at line 350, the computer checks to see if the player's answer corresponds to the name of the capital with the same subscript in the Capital Array. Nearly identical strategies are incorporated into the other drills within CAPS.

Question 7: What happens if the player gets the answer right?

Answer: If the player's answer matches the appropriate item in the array, the player will receive a "right" message in the subroutine beginning at line 1460; the right-answer counter (R) will increase by one; and the player will get a chance (in line 1480) to request another question.

Question 8: One of the capitals (St. Paul) has two different correct spellings. How does the computer deal with the variant spelling?

Answer: The computer has memorized one correct spelling for each state. If the player's answer does not match the name of the capital of the designated state, the computer will go to line 360. At this point, it will make one further check before proclaiming the player to be in error. There is only one state (Minnesota) whose capital has two spellings. The computer, therefore, will check to see if that state was chosen; and if so, it will check to see if the player entered the variant spelling. Finally, if the player still has not achieved a match, the computer will give a "wrong" message at line 370.

Question 9: What happens if the player gives a wrong answer?

Answer: The computer gives the correct answer and then sends the player to a subroutine providing an opportunity for another question. Note that this subroutine is actually the second half of the subroutine to which the player would have gone for a right answer. The player who is wrong merely skips lines 1460 and 1470 and goes directly to line 1480. Before the player gets a new question, the question counter (K1) will increase by one at line 1540.

Question 10: In the variations where the player tries to name a state, the player is permitted to request a list. How is this list presented?

Answer: After the player gives an answer in line 410, line 420 sends the computer to a subroutine at line 710 to see if the player entered the word *list* as the answer. If the response was *list,* the computer will proceed to provide a list of the states in lines 660 to 690 and then will return to evaluate the answer the player gave after seeing the list.

The logic of the list routine is diagrammed in Figure 8.3. Note that the computer actually prints *fifty-two* states. This occurs because it was necessary to use thirteen lines, and there are only fifty states. Therefore, when the computer prints the twelfth line of the list, it prints S$(12), S$(25), S$(38), and S$(51). Also note that in line 40, the DIM statement had reserved fifty-two spaces for states, but the loop at lines 140 to 160 reads only fifty states into this array. S$(51) and S$(52) were established as blank spaces in line 40, and because nothing ever happened to change their status, they are still blank spaces when the computer prints them in line 680. Naive learners who think they see only fifty states are unaware that they are looking at two blank states at the end of the list! If the DIM statement had reserved only fifty spaces for state names in line 40, an error message would have been explained when the computer tried to run line 680.

Question 11: How does the computer check for the correct spelling of a state?

Answer: If the player's response is anything other than *list,* the computer will continue with the 710 routine by checking the spelling of the entry in the loop at lines 720 to 740. A correct spelling is operationally defined as a response which matches one of the

The computer goes through the loop 13 times, printing one of
the following lines on each trip through the loop:

Screen Col. 1	Screen Col. 15	Screen Col. 30	Screen Col. 45
S$(1)	S$(14)	S$(27)	S$(40)
S$(2)	S$(15)	S$(28)	S$(41)
S$(3)	S$(16)	S$(29)	S$(42)
S$(4)	S$(17)	S$(30)	S$(43)
S$(5)	S$(18)	S$(31)	S$(44)
S$(6)	S$(19)	S$(32)	S$(45)
S$(7)	S$(20)	S$(33)	S$(46)
S$(8)	S$(21)	S$(34)	S$(47)
S$(9)	S$(22)	S$(35)	S$(48)
S$(10)	S$(23)	S$(36)	S$(49)
S$(11)	S$(24)	S$(37)	S$(50)
S$(12)	S$(25)	S$(38)	S$(51)
S$(13)	S$(26)	S$(39)	S$(52)

Each time the computer goes through the loop, it prints S$(I),
S$(I+13), S$(I+26), and S$(I+39) at the designated TAB positions.
Note that on the twelfth time through the loop, the computer will
print S$(51) and on the thirteenth, S$(52). Although these
"states" do not exist on the North American continent, they do
exist as blank spaces in the S$(I) array. Therefore, the computer
will print black spaces in the locations designated for these
variables.

Figure 8.3. The logic of the list routine in CAPS.

items stored in the S$(I) array. If the player's entry matches any of the items stored in that array, the computer will go to the end of the loop at line 780 and continue evaluating the answer at line 430. But if the computer goes through the entire S$(I) array without a match, when it reaches line 750, it will notify the player that the spelling was incorrect and then will restate the question in line 400. The logic of this spelling correction strategy is described in Figure 8.4.

Notice that the computer entered this subroutine at line 710 with a GOTO command rather than a GOSUB command, and therefore, will return from the subroutine with an ON GOTO statement rather than a RETURN statement. This combination of commands was necessary because the point to which the computer will return after the subroutine will vary according to the subprogram (capitals, abbreviations, or data list) that the player is running and the results of the spelling analysis during the subroutine.

Question 12: The computer provides a list of states, but not a list of capitals. Why this difference?

Answer: The difference is based upon pedagogical (not programming) problems. Providing the list really turns the drill into a large-scale multiple choice test. Choosing from a list requires slightly different skills than inventing an answer on one's own. The programmer felt that since there are only fifty states and most of the learners would know the names of all fifty, providing the list would serve as a useful reminder without providing an inappropriate clue. However, when it comes to capitals, there is not a small list of possible choices. It is not appropriate to supply a list of *the* fifty capitals and to ask which one belongs to a particular state. To take an example, if the computer asks for the capital of Kentucky, the learner might inaccurately think that Louisville or Lexington is the correct answer. If the list of the fifty capitals were provided, these inaccurate answers would not even appear on it; and so the task would be modified for that learner. Rather than being required to think of the name of the capital of Kentucky, the learner would now be required merely to decide which of the fifty cities on the list is located in Kentucky. This is why the programmer decided *not* to provide a list of capitals. The

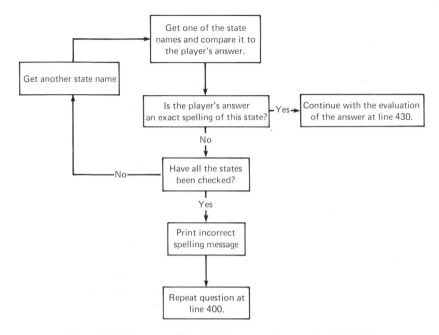

Figure 8.4. The logic of the spelling correction routine in CAPS.

programmer employed similar logic in his decision not to display a list of the possible abbreviations in that subversion of CAPS.

Question 13: The computer corrects spelling errors for states, but not for cities. Why this difference?

Answer: The logic here is the same as in the previous question. The computer defines an inaccurate spelling as a failure to match any items on a list. The capital of Kentucky is spelled *Frankfort.* Using the logic of the spelling correction routine (question 11), therefore, the computer would consider both *Louisville* and *Frankfert* to be incorrect spellings. The programmer considered this to be intolerable, and so he decided to omit the spelling correction for the capitals.

Note that the programmer could have solved the problem differently. One alternate strategy would have been to have the computer memorize a second list of cities. The cities on this second list would include likely mistakes such as Louisville, Lexington, Los Angeles, San Francisco, and other cities which are likely to be mistaken for capitals. This additional set of cities could then be used for both the list in question 12 and for the spelling correction. However, the programmer decided that this additional effort was unnecessary for his present concerns.

Question 14: How does the player exit from the program?

Answer: When a player stops performing either the capitals or the abbreviations drill (by answering "no" in line 1490), the computer goes to line 1590, where it provides feedback and ends the program.

Question 15: How does the State Data List work?

Answer: If a player chooses the State Data List in line 230, then line 280 will direct the computer to the sequence beginning at line 1060. Here the computer gives the player a choice of seeing all the data on all fifty states (lines 1150 to 1220) or looking at the data on a specific state (lines 1300 to 1450). This leads to the additional complication that

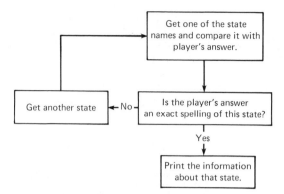

Figure 8.5. The logic of the state recognition routine in CAPS.

the computer must "recognize" the name of a state (in lines 1340 to 1360) and then match the subscript with the appropriate subscript for the information that it has memorized in its arrays. The logic of this recognition process is explained in Figure 8.5. Note the similarity of this logic to that of the spelling correction in Figure 8.4. The player who has examined the State Data List (in either version) eventually gets a chance (lines 1230 to 1270) to try one of the other two versions of CAPS.

Inside the Mind of the Computer: A Trip Through CAPS

By this time you have probably loaded and run CAPS, have examined its listing, and understand its major strategies. To make sure, you may wish to take a run through the program (Figure 8.6). Your examination of Figure 8.6 will be most fruitful if you examine it at a computer terminal while you run CAPS and if you refer frequently to the complete listing of CAPS in this chapter.

What If . . .

Readers who wish to do so should be coming to an understanding of the fundamental strategies of instructional computer programming by this time. A good way to verify this is to hypothesize about what would happen if the computer program were changed. If a programmer made a designated change to the program, would it still run? Would it stop and print an error message? Would it run but present crazy results? Or would everything be perfectly normal?

The following are some questions about specific lines in CAPS. See if you can predict what would happen if these changes were made. In each case, assume that *only that one change* would be made and that the rest of the program would remain exactly as it was presented. Record your prediction, and then check your hypothesis by either entering the change into the program and running it or by looking at the answers at the end of this chapter.

Lines	Computer's Thoughts
40	Set aside storage space in the arrays.
50-110	Print the Title Page.
140-160	Read the data and store it in the arrays.
170-230	Get the player's choice of games. (ASSUME THAT THE PLAYER ENTERS "2".) Remember that C = 2.
240	Make sure the choice was valid.
270	Set the Question Counter at 1 and the Right Answer Counter at 0
280	"On 2 GOTO line 460."
460	Detour temporarily to line 930.
930-1050	Give the player instructions about the two variations of the game. Get the player's choice. (ASSUME THAT THE PLAYER ENTERS "B".) Remember that C$ = "B". Then return to the command immediately after the GOSUB in line 460.
470	Detour temporarily to line 920.
920	Select a random number between 1 and 50 and then return to line 480. (ASSUME THAT THE COMPUTER SELECTS "15" AS ITS RANDOM NUMBER.) Remember that N = 15
480	Since C$ is equal to "B" GOTO line 570.
570	Skip three lines.
580-600	Print "IA is the official abbreviation for what state?" Pause and wait for the player to give an answer at the keyboard. (ASSUME THAT THE PLAYER ENTERS "IOWA".) Remember that R$ = "Iowa". Then clear the screen and GOTO line 710.
710	If R$="LIST" . . . It's not; so I can skip the rest of this line.
720-740	R$ is not equal to "Alabama" or "Alaska" or any of the first fourteen values of S$(I), but it is equal to "Iowa". Therefore I'll GOTO line 780.
780	"On 2 GOTO line 610."
610	If "Iowa" is equal to "Iowa" . . . This condition is true, so I'll detour to line 1460.
1460-1530	Print "Right." Add 1 to the Right Answer Counter (0 + 1 = 1). Find out if the player wants another question. (ASSUME THAT THE PLAYER ANSWERS "YES".) Add 1 to the Question Counter (1 + 1 = 2). Then go back to finish line 610.
610	GOTO line 470.
470	Get another random number from the subroutine at line 920. (ASSUME THAT THE COMPUTER SELECTS "46".) Remember that N = 46.
480	Since C$ = "B" GOTO line 570.
570-600	Skip three lines and print "VA is the official abbreviation for what state?" Wait for an

Figure 8.6. A run through CAPS inside the mind of the computer.

answer. (ASSUME THAT THE PLAYER ANSWERS VERGINIA —WHICH IS AN INCORRECT SPELLING OF VIRGINIA.) Remember that R$ = "VERGINIA". Then clear the screen and GOTO line 710.

710 If R$ = "LIST" . . . It's not; so I can skip the rest of this line.

720-740 "Verginia" is not equal to "Alabama", "Alaska", or any of the fifty values of S$(I), so there's no reason to GOTO line 780. I'll GOTO line 750 instead.

750-760 Print "Verginia is not the correct spelling of any of the states. Either enter a correct spelling or type the word LIST."

770 On 2 GOTO line 580.

580-600 Print "VA is the official abbreviation for what state?" Wait for an answer. (ASSUME THAT THE PLAYER ANSWERS "VIRGINIA".) Remember that R$ = "VIRGINIA". Clear the screen and GOTO line 710.

710 If R$ = "LIST" . . . It's not; and so I can skip the rest of this line.

720-740 "Virginia" is not equal to any of the first 45 values of S$(I), but it is equal to S$(46). Therefore I'll GOTO line 780.

780 On 2 GOTO line 610.

610 If "Virginia" is equal to "Virginia" (It is) take a detour to line 1460.

1460-1530 Print "Right." Add 1 to the Right Answer Counter (1 + 1 = 2). Find out whether the player wants another question. (ASSUME THAT THE PLAYER ANSWERS "NO".) "No" means to GOTO line 1590.

1590-1610 Search memory to recall the values of R and K1. Print "You got 2 right out of 2 questions. Play again some time." Then print READY and the BASIC prompt on the screen.

Figure 8.6. A run through CAPS inside the mind of the computer. (Continued.)

If you are trying to give this chapter a merely casual reading, you are likely to have trouble with these questions. In most cases, they will require you to make a close examination of the program listing in order to arrive at the correct answers.

QUESTIONS:

1. What would happen if we replaced A$(50) in line 40 with A$(60)?
2. What if we replaced A$(50) in line 40 with A$(40)?
3. What if we omitted line 240?
4. What would happen if we changed line 140 to read FOR I = 1 TO 60?
5. What if we changed line 140 to read FOR I = 1 TO 40?
6. What would happen if we omitted R = 0 from line 270?
7. What would happen if we omitted line 300?
8. What would happen if we omitted line 320?

9. What would happen if line 330 concluded with S$(I) instead of S$(N)? (This is a hard question!)
10. How many of the fifty states would be eliminated from the list if line 670 read FOR I = 1 TO 12? Which states would be omitted? (This also is a hard question.)
11. What would happen if line 710 were *completely* omitted? (This is a *very tricky* question.)
12. What would happen if we omitted line 1210?
13. What would happen if we omitted line 1750?
14. What would happen if we spelled the capital of Idaho "Boisy" in line 1730?
15. What would happen if we put a comma *after* Springfield in line 1740?
16. What would happen if we typed line 1750 *twice*? (Assume that the line number and contents of the line are identical both times.)

ANSWERS:

1. This would "waste" some of the computer's memory space, by reserving an unnecessary ten spaces in an array for nonexistent abbreviations. Other than that, however, there would be no adverse impact on the program's actual operation.
2. This would cause an error message when the computer made its forty-first READ loop at line 150. The computer would try to store the abbreviation of the forty-first state and would discover that only forty boxes had been reserved in the A$(I) array. The computer then would stop the run of the program and print an error message.
3. The omission of line 240 would cause no problems, *as long as the player running the program entered a number between 1 and 3 at line 330.* However, if, for example, the player entered a 5, this would cause a problem (error message and termination of the program) at line 280.
4. This would cause an error message in line 150. The computer would try to read the fifty-first state and would discover that no DATA lines had been provided.
5. Believe it or not, this would cause an error message at line 330 *the first time the computer randomly selected a number above 40 in line 920!* The computer would break no rules by ignoring the final ten lines of DATA during the 140 to 160 READ loop. The problem would occur only when it tried to print a nonexistent S$(N) in line 330. (There are several places in the program where this same error message would occur if the computer happened to come to one of them before reaching line 330.)
6. This would cause no problems in this program. This command merely re-sets the value of R to zero, and as the program is written, there is no possible way for the computer to come to this line without R's already being set at zero. In the present form of this program, therefore, this command is superfluous.
7. Omitting line 300 would result in an error message at line 330, at which the computer would try to print the nonexistent N$(0). The subroutine at line 920 is where the computer chooses the random state.

8. The computer would simply print line 330 at the very top of the screen rather than three lines down from the top.

9. The computer would take the most recent value of "I" and would try to print the state with the corresponding number in the array. The current value of "I" was assigned at the end of the READ loop in line 160. The way the TRS-80 works, "I" would have the value of 51 at this point. Because the S$(I) array has fifty-two boxes (line 40), the computer would not print an error message but, rather, would print the contents of the fifty-first box as part of the question in line 330 or 500. In other words, it would show a blank space every time it encountered this line. On a few other computers, the value of "I" at the end of the READ loop would be 50. In such cases, the computer would ask about Wyoming every time it came to line 330 or 500.

10. This alteration would eliminate the last two states in alphabetical order (Wisconsin and Wyoming).

11. If line 710 were completely omitted, the result would be an error message at line 420 (or 600 or 1330). At 420, for example, the computer would receive an impossible instruction to go to a nonexistent line.

12. The computer would endlessly repeat the list of the first ten states in alphabetical order.

13. This would cause an error message in line 150. On its fiftieth run through this loop, the computer would be looking for the fiftieth DATA line and would find it missing.

14. This would cause no difficulty to the computer, but it would cause it to insist that "Boisy" is the correct spelling of the capital of Idaho. This would anger or frustrate the learner and the citizens of Idaho.

15. Everything would be fine until the end of the computer's thirteenth run through the READ loop at lines 140 through 160. Then the computer would look for a piece of data after the comma. It would find one, of course, but it would find a blank space (which is a valid piece of data). The computer would therefore read S$(14) as " ", A$(14) as "Indiana," C$(14) as "IN," S$(15) as "Indianapolis," and so forth. The computer would print no error but just produce nonsensical output whenever line 920 selected a number higher than 13.

16. This would cause no problem whatsoever. In theory, you replaced line 1750 with an identical line 1750, but as far as the computer is concerned, only the most recent line exists.

Chapter 9
Writing the Actual Program

WE have now examined the tutorials, drills, simulations, and higher level applications of computers in education. We also discussed many of the important commands and strategies in BASIC programming in the context of sample programs. Now let's try to put these ideas together. If *you* wanted to write an instructional program in the BASIC language, what steps should you take?

A good instructional program has both good content and good programming. The content consists of the information, concepts, and principles to be incorporated into the program and the order in which this information is arranged for presentation. No matter how well written a computer program may be, if the content is inaccurate, misleading, or arranged in a pedagogically ineffective sequence, the resulting instructional program will be ineffective.

This chapter, of course, cannot focus on the content of the program, as it will vary widely from application to application. Rather, this chapter will assume that you have good content to fit into a computer program and will outline the steps that will help you write a good program to present the content: first, the plan of the overall program; second, strategies for making information appear on the screen as you want it to; and third, some important considerations in providing user friendliness.

Guidelines for Planning Programs

The following guidelines will help you create sound programs:

1. Decide what you want the computer to do, and make a fairly detailed plan before you start writing any lines of the program. At various points throughout this book, we have used flowcharts to indicate the logic of a program or of part of a

program. If you feel comfortable with such flowcharts, use them. At the very least, write an outline of the major steps in your program. It is often wise to develop a plan for both the overall program and any complex part. For example, Figure 8.2 showed the overall plan of CAPS, and Figure 8.4 zeroed in on a specific aspect of the program.

2. Whenever possible or appropriate, use subroutines to achieve the goals of your program. There is no reason to enter identical or similar sets of lines twenty-five separate times into the computer if you can instead simply enter the set once and then send the computer to that subroutine whenever it is appropriate. The use of subroutines saves typing effort on your part when you write the program and saves memory space in the computer when the program is run. In addition, the use of subroutines often makes it much easier to modify or expand a program later. In many cases, you will send the computer to the subroutine with a GOSUB statement, but it is also possible to use other approaches (see Subroutine Guidelines, Chapter 7).

3. Program the computer to respond to all possible responses. Failure to do this will cause the program either to go to a wrong subsequent step or to come to an abrupt stop. In the sample program HELLO, for example, the computer will accept absolutely any response the learner gives. If the response is one that the computer is programmed to handle, it will act upon it; otherwise it will recycle the learner to provide the input it desires.

In its original format, the sample program TRAP violated this third guideline, as the player received the instructions by spelling no incorrectly. The overall logic for enabling the computer to react to all possible responses is diagrammed in Figure 9.1. The best examples of the application of this logic can be seen in HELLO and its accompanying annotation (Chapter 6).

4. Provide variations on different runs through the same drill, by using arrays and randomly selecting items with the RND function. Fit the items into the struc-

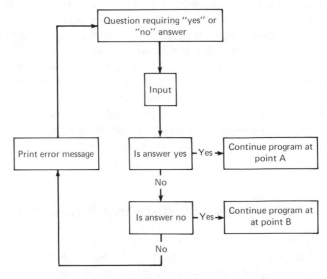

Figure 9.1. The logic of forcing a yes or no answer to a question.

ture discussed in guideline 5. If your program does not use arrays from which items will be randomly drawn, use some other mathematical model to provide a different set of problems on subsequent runs of the drill.

5. Devise a structured format for the drills and their questions and answers. Use natural wording and correct grammar. For example, each of the following is a structured format for asking a drill question:

```
100 PRINT ''WHAT IS THE CAPITAL OF '';S$(X);
200 PRINT ''WHAT WORD MEANS THE SAME THING AS''
210 PRINT W$(X);
300 PRINT ''WHAT IS THE SUM OF '';A;'' PLUS '';B;
```

In each case, the computer will simply insert a randomly chosen word or number into the format. The answer is then chosen from a corresponding array or through mathematical calculation.

In developing your structure, avoid unnecessary clues. For example, if you use the term *take away* in all your subtraction problems, this may give the learners a clue that will enable them to solve problems they do not really understand. Sometimes you may wish to devise several alternative formats to avoid such clues. For example, each of the following questions involves subtraction:

a. Joan needed eighteen ounces of chocolate chips to make cookies, but she had only twelve ounces. How many more ounces did she need?

b. Bill had read fifty-four pages of his book. The book had 281 pages. How many pages did Bill still have to read?

c. Mary had five little lambs. Old MacDonald had ten little lambs. Who had more? How many more?

d. A new basketball costs $9.95. Ted has saved $5.47. How much more does Ted have to save before he can buy the basketball?

e. A new car costs $6,955. The Smiths have saved $4,565. How much will they have to borrow to pay for the car?

Because subtraction is used in so many settings, the computer could supply problems in all of these settings, by being programmed to choose any of these (or other) formats at random; to insert names, objects, and numbers at random; and to ask drill questions without giving context clues.

The following excerpt from a program presents subtraction problems without the unnecessary clue provided by the words *take away* in subtraction word problems:

```
100 PRINT ''JOHNNY HAD '';X;'' OBJECTS.''
110 LET A=INT (4*RND(0)+1)
120 ON A GOTO 130, 140, 150, 160
130 PRINT ''SOMEBODY TOOK '';Y;'' AWAY.'':GOTO 200
140 PRINT ''HE GAVE '';Y;'' TO BILLY.'':GOTO 200
150 PRINT ''HE LOST '';Y;'' OF THEM.'':GOTO 200
160 PRINT ''HE ATE '';Y;'' OF THEM.'':GOTO 200
200 PRINT ''HOW MANY DID JOHNNY HAVE THEN'';
210 INPUT R
```

The logic of this subroutine is shown in Figure 9.2. Note that in this example the pattern can be further concealed by adding additional variables as part of the string. For example, line 100 could be revised to read:

```
100 PRINT P$(P);'' HAD '';X;'' '';T$(T);''.''
```

Before executing line 100, the computer would select a person from the P$(P)

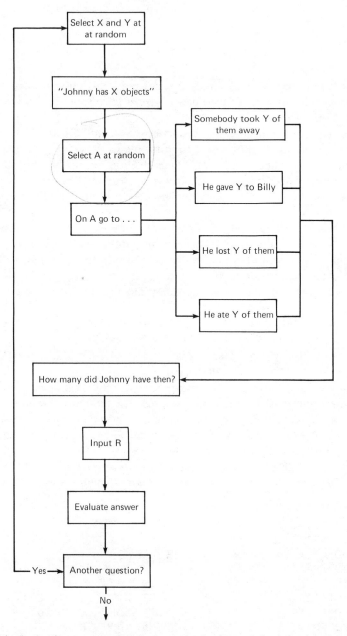

Figure 9.2. The logic of a program designed to vary the format of subtraction word problems.

array, a random number X to indicate the initial number of objects, and an object from the T$(T) array. By making the proper insertions, a programmer with a little ingenuity can randomly generate a seemingly endless variety of word problems free from stereotypical and unnecessary clues.

6. With drills, allow the learner to ask for lists or guidelines as needed. Do everything possible to allow the learner access to all information necessary to answer the question (see User Friendliness Guidelines later in this chapter.)

7. In drills, provide an appropriate computer reaction to all possible solutions the learner could give. Do you really want to give a "wrong" message for all answers that do not precisely match the one in the computer's memory, or do you want to adjust for certain types of errors? How do you want to respond to alternative or incorrect spellings? What if the learner rounds a number in a different way than the computer does? What if the learner enters a dollar sign when none is anticipated? It is often possible and desirable to program the computer to anticipate and deal with such difficulties. The spelling correction described in CAPS (Chapter 8) and the VAL module (Appendix C) are good examples of attempts to deal with such difficulties.

8. Look for predictable errors and provide feedback specifically related to these errors. Some errors are not easy to predict, and therefore feedback for these errors must necessarily be vague. For example, the program BEHMOD might ask, "What term refers to the systematic withholding of the reinforcers that previously maintained a behavior?" If the learner replies, "Obliteration," the computer will not recognize this word and will simply respond, "Wrong. Extinction is the term that refers to the systematic withholding of the reinforcers that previously maintained a behavior." But if the learner replies, "Satiation," the computer will recognize this word and can therefore offer this additional feedback: "Satiation refers to the technique of letting a behavior occur until it loses its reinforcing value" (see the discussion of BEHMOD in Chapter 11). Because learners, immediately after making the mistake, are likely to wonder about the difference between the two terms, it is advantageous for the computer to identify the exact nature of the misunderstanding. Careful programming can make this possible.

Likewise, in an arithmetic drill, it is useful to be able to say to a learner, "Wrong. You added when you should have subtracted. The correct answer is 89." Figures 9.3 and 9.4 show how such specific feedback can be incorporated into a program. The program described in Figure 9.3 is able to identify three predictable errors:

    a. The learner may add instead of subtract. This error is easy to spot, as the learner will have entered the sum rather than the difference.

    b. The learner may forget to borrow during the subtracting process. In two-digit subtraction, this will cause the result to be exactly ten higher than it should be.

    c. The learner may make a minor error in calculation. This is operationally defined as being within two of the actual answer.

Because of how these lines are written, the computer will respond to *every* error with the word *wrong* and the correct answer. In addition, for *some* errors (the ones it has been programmed to identify), the computer will provide more specific feedback.

9. To give proper feedback at the end of drills, it is necessary to record the

number of correct and incorrect responses made by the learner. This is easily done by including "counters" immediately after the computer evaluates the correctness of the responses. A right-answer counter can be inserted at line 275 in Figure 9.3, for example, and a wrong answer counter at line 195:

$$195 \text{ LET } W = W + 1$$
$$275 \text{ LET } R = R + 1$$

Such counters can be reset to zero during any new run of the program. (Examples of such counters occur in CAPS, BEHMOD, and FOOTBALL.)

10. In drills, it is necessary to provide learners with feedback about the accuracy of each answer, and in most cases this feedback should be given immediately after the learner's response. This feedback can be the same for every correct response; it can vary on a random basis; or it can vary based on the number of correct responses (either overall or consecutively). Figure 9.5 describes some lines that can be added to CAPS in order to have it give more supportive reinforcement after every five consecutive correct responses. The same type of reinforcement can be inserted into any program containing a right-answer counter.

11. With drills, it is also possible to have the computer compile a list of specific errors to be provided at the end of the program. In a vocabulary drill, for example, you could do this by putting missed words into an "error array" as soon as they have been identified and then printing the error array at the end of the program.

12. Allow the learner to exit from the program. It is frustrating to be stuck in the middle of a drill and not know when it will end. A good strategy is to give a question number with each item and to permit the learner to terminate the drill after each question, by typing a designated number or letter. Likewise, a learner should be permitted to enter a special command that will terminate a tutorial. Ideally, the learner should be able to return automatically to the same point on a later session with the same tutorial.

13. After exiting from a drill, the learner should be told the number of right and wrong answers, which can also be converted into a percentage of correct answers.

```
100 PRINT N$(X);" HAD ";A;" PIECES OF CANDY."
110 PRINT "HE GAVE ";B;" OF THEM TO ";N$(Y);"."
120 PRINT "HOW MANY PIECES OF CANDY DID ";N$(X);" HAVE THEN?"
130 INPUT R
140 IF R=A-B THEN 270
145 PRINT "WRONG."
150 IF R=A+B THEN 200
160 IF R=A+B+10 THEN 220
170 IF R<A-B-2 THEN 240
180 IF R>A-B+2 THEN 240
190 GOTO 250
200 PRINT "YOU ADDED WHEN YOU SHOULD HAVE SUBTRACTED."
210 GOTO 250
220 PRINT "IT LOOKS LIKE YOU FORGOT TO BORROW!"
230 GOTO 250
240 PRINT "VERY CLOSE!"
250 PRINT "THE CORRECT ANSWER WAS ";A-B;"."
260 GOTO 300
270 PRINT "RIGHT! GOOD ANSWER."
300 END
```

Figure 9.3. A part of a program to give feedback for specific types of errors. These lines assume the existence of additional lines to introduce the problem, to read variables into arrays, and to select numbers at random for the problem.

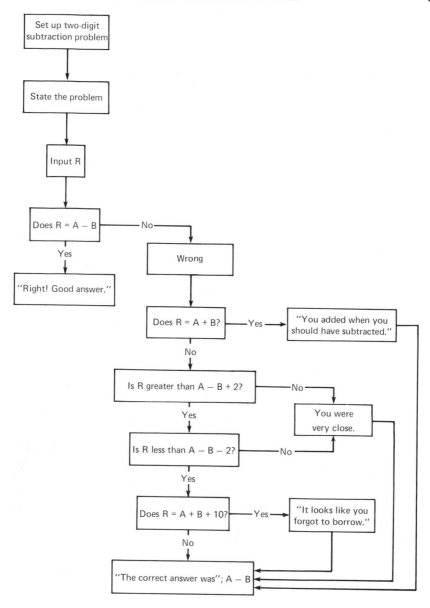

Figure 9.4. The logic of the program listed in Figure 9.3.

If desired, this information can be stored in a data file to provide feedback to parents or teachers.

14. In many cases, the same set of data can be used for more than one drill. In CAPS, for instance, while using the same set of data, the learner can either be given a state and be asked to name a capital or be given a capital and be asked to name the state. Once a program is written to offer one or the other of these drills, it requires the addition of only a few extra lines to enable the program to do the other drill. In CAPS, the student chooses in line 330 and receives one or the other

```
9001 GOSUB 9100
   .
   .
   .
9100 LET R=R+1
9110 IF R=5 THEN PRINT "VERY GOOD JOB!":GOTO 1477
9120 IF R=10 THEN PRINT "WAY TO GO!":GOTO 1477
9130 IF R=15 THEN PRINT "FANTASTIC JOB!":GOTO 1477
9140 IF R=20 THEN PRINT "EXCELLENT WORK!":GOTO 1477
9150 IF R=25 THEN PRINT "YOU'RE GETTING A LOT RIGHT!"
9160 IF R=30 THEN PRINT "SUPER JOB!"
9170 PRINT "THAT MAKES ";R;" RIGHT ANSWERS"
9180 PRINT "OUT OF ";K1;" QUESTIONS."
9190 RETURN
```

If the above lines were inserted into CAPS, the
computer would tell the learner how many questions
he/she had answered correctly after every correct
response (lines 9170-9180). In addition, after the
fifth, tenth, fifteenth, twentieth, twenty-fifth,
and thirtieth correct responses the computer would
provide the indicated form of praise (lines 9110
to 9160).

The programmer could obviously expand the number
of reinforcers. Also note that the programmer had
to use a subroutine because there was no room to
insert these lines between lines 9001 and 9002 of
the original program. A better idea would have
been to leave sufficient room and insert them in
the proper sequence. The unnecessary subroutine
would make the program more difficult to read and
modify on future occasions.

Figure 9.5. A modification of CAPS to provide intermittent reinforcement after every fifth correct response.

drill based on his or her response. It is equally possible for the computer to make this selection, and FOOTBALL (Chapter 10) is a good example of the computer's randomly choosing one of eight drills for each separate question it will ask. The logic (used in FOOTBALL) of having the computer randomly select the format for a question is described in Figure 9.6. As you can see, this logic is almost exactly the same as that used to vary the subtraction format in Figure 9.2.

15. In addition, once a drill is written with one set of questions and a corresponding answer for each question, it is often possible (and desirable) to add another answer from a different category for each of the questions. The result can be another useful drill, created with very little additional effort. In fact, in many cases it is possible to use the strategy described in the previous paragraph to flip-flop the questions and answers in such a way as to come up with more than one additional drill, by adding only a single set of additional data. For example, by adding nicknames to the state and capitals in the program CAPS, the programmer can offer the wide range of drills in Figure 9.7.

In some cases, it is possible to find matched sets of data in many categories. For example, by using several categories (and sufficient computer memory), CAPS can evolve into the program AMERICA, shown in Figure 9.8. Such a combination of data results not only in many isolated drills, created with very little additional effort, but also in the possibility of combining information into a larger, different drill, as shown in Figure 9.9.

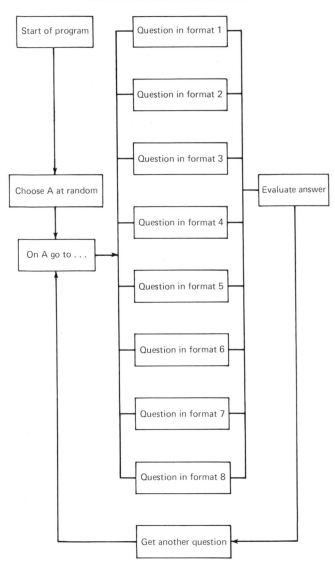

Figure 9.6. The logic of having the computer select one of eight question formats, as in the program FOOTBALL.

Putting Words on the Screen

In nearly every program you write, the format of the program's words on the screen will be important. Words and numbers can be presented in such a way as to confuse and overwhelm a person or in such a way as to enable the person to learn effectively. The following guidelines will help you use the computer screen efficiently:

1. Use PRINT statements to put words, sentences, and numbers on the screen. Follow the guidelines in Chapter 6.

```
What is the capital of Ohio?

Of what state is Columbus the capital?

What is the nickname of Ohio?

What state is nicknamed the Buckeye state?

What is the capital of the Buckeye state?

What is the nickname of the state whose capital is
Columbus?
```

In addition, it is possible to provide feedback and follow-up questions as follows:

```
Computer question: What is the capital of Ohio?
Learner answer: Cincinnati.
Computer response: No, Columbus is the capital of the
    Buckeye state.

Computer question: What state is nicknamed the Buckeye
    state?
Learner answer: Iowa.
Computer response: Wrong.  Here's a hint: the capital of
    the Buckeye state is Columbus.  Now try to name the
    state.
```

Figure 9.7. The variety of questions that can be asked about Ohio if the name of a state, its capital, and its nickname are included as DATA.

2. To skip lines, use PRINT statements followed by nothing after the word PRINT. Remember that you have a whole screen to work with and that there is no reason to squeeze your entire text onto the first few lines at the top of the screen.

3. To indent words toward the right across the screen, either use several blank spaces inside quotation marks or use the TAB command.

4. If you want the computer's next output to be on the subsequent screen line, simply go on to the next command after your PRINT command. However, if you

```
WHICH GAME DO YOU WANT TO PLAY?

 1. STATE CAPITALS          11. MAJOR CITIES
 2. STATE ABBREVIATIONS     12. PLACES OF INTEREST
 3. STATE MOTTOES           13. STATE NICKNAMES
 4. STATE BIRDS             14. NAME THAT STATE!
 5. STATE FLOWERS           15. STATE DATA LIST
 6. STATE TREES
 7. STATE SONGS
 8. FAMOUS NATIVES
 9. GEOGRAPHICAL FEATURES
10. STATE LOCATIONS

ENTER THE NUMBER OF THE GAME YOU CHOOSE.
WHAT NUMBER DO YOU WANT?
```

Figure 9.8. The main branching point in the program AMERICA, which is simply CAPS with many more data on each state.

```
                        NAME THAT STATE!

        THE COMPUTER WILL SELECT A STATE AT RANDOM.

        YOUR JOB IS TO GUESS THE NAME OF THE STATE
        FROM THE CLUES THE COMPUTER GIVES YOU.

        YOU START WITH 10 POINTS ON EACH ATTEMPT.
        EVERY TIME YOU FAIL TO GUESS CORRECTLY IN RESPONSE
        TO A CLUE, YOU LOSE A POINT.

        AFTER TEN CLUES, THE COMPUTER WILL GIVE YOU THE ANSWER.

        ARE YOU READY TO CONTINUE (PRESS ENTER)?
            "
            "
            "
        MAMMOUTH CAVE CAN BE FOUND IN THIS STATE.
            "
            "
            "
        THIS STATE IS NICKNAMED THE BLUEGRASS STATE.
            "
            "
            "
```

Figure 9.9. The first few lines from NAME THAT STATE, which is option 14 in AMERICA (Figure 9.8).

want the computer's next output to come on the *same* line (immediately after what you have just told the computer to print), use a semicolon. Note the following:

a. It is possible to string together a large number of outputs in this fashion, and when strung together on the screen, the several outputs will look like one long output.

b. An INPUT statement automatically supplies a question mark as a prompt to tell the user to enter something while the computer pauses. Therefore, if you end a question with a semicolon outside the quotation marks and put the INPUT command on the next line, this will make the computer pause immediately after the question mark.

c. Because the INPUT command supplies this question mark, you often may wish to print a question followed by a semicolon immediately before your INPUT statement. This eliminates unsightly and unnecessary question marks on separate lines. For example,

```
100 PRINT ''ARE YOU READY TO CONTINUE (PRESS ENTER)'';
110 INPUT A$
```

will present this output on the screen:

```
        ARE YOU READY TO CONTINUE (PRESS ENTER)?
```

The preceding output makes more sense than this alternative output:

```
        PRESS ENTER TO CONTINUE.
        ?
```

d. When you string outputs together, if you want spaces between items in your series, *you* will have to supply them; the computer will not put them in for you. Examples of inserting such spaces have appeared in nearly all the sample programs.

5. If you wish to print more information than will fit on a single screen, you will need to make the computer pause to give the reader time to read the information. Otherwise, some of the earlier information will move off the top of the screen to make room for the next PRINT lines. There are two widely used ways to make the computer pause:

a. Print a desired number of lines, and then have the computer "waste some time" before continuing. For example, you might use the following lines:

```
100 FOR I = 1 to 1000
110 NEXT I
```

When executing these lines, the computer does nothing but "count" to one thousand. While the computer is counting, the person at the terminal can read the words currently on the screen. To make the pause longer, increase the one thousand to a higher number.

b. Insert an INPUT statement, which will place a question mark on the screen and pause to wait for the person at the terminal to respond. This strategy is used in several of the sample programs.

The first strategy has the advantage that the pace is determined by the programmer instead of by the learner. But in many cases, this can be a disadvantage if the predetermined pace is not suitable for the learner. The second strategy enables the learner to control the pace, but in this case the learner may press the key without really reading the information. One compromise is to use the first strategy in combination with the second: after the computer has "counted" to one thousand, give the learner the option of continuing, by pressing the proper key.

In most cases, the programmer clears the screen (CLS) before presenting more lines of information.

6. Use the CLS (or equivalent) command to eliminate from the screen that information that is no longer needed. *But remember:* Once you clear the screen, the words that have been cleared are no longer available to the person looking at the terminal. This means that if you clear the screen and then tell the user that his or her answer is wrong, the user cannot look back at the question to figure out the mistake.

7. In general, use the screen to focus attention where you want it. Break down information into smaller packages and present it clearly on the screen.

Common Errors in Putting Words on the Screen:

Common errors in putting words on the screen are the following:

1. Clearing the screen so quickly that the reader cannot possibly read what is on it.

2. Clearing from the screen information that the user will need later. (Sometimes you can resolve this problem by restating some of the information after the screen has been cleared or by giving the learner the option of returning to a previous screen.)

3. Allowing the screen to become cluttered by failing to clear information that is no longer useful.

4. Writing confusing sentences. Watch your grammar and spelling.

5. Using only a restricted area (such as the very top) of the screen rather than the entire screen.

6. Trying to print variables that have not been assigned a value. If you try to print a numeric variable that has no value, the computer will print a zero. If you try to print a string variable that has no value, the computer will print a blank (which is invisible).

7. Forgetting to include the semicolon between the outputs that you wish to string together or putting the semicolon in the wrong place (such as inside the quotation marks).

8. Having words truncated in the middle because a string is too long and has exceeded the screen's capacity. The wraparound routine described in Module 3 of Appendix C can help resolve this problem.

User Friendliness

User friendliness refers to the ease with which the learner can interact with the mechanics of the computer. The learner should be able to decide easily what kind of input to give to the computer and, when errors occur, to be able to decide easily how to correct them. The following are programming techniques that can be used to enhance the user friendliness of instructional programs:

1. List possible answers, rules, and guidelines for solving problems when the learner requests them. CAPS (Chapter 8) follows this guideline by listing the possible states after the computer gives the abbreviation or the name of the capital. Note, however, that in the same program the computer does *not* list the capitals when it gives the state. This is because the list of states would be an improper clue. A student who believes that Houston is the capital of Texas will realize his or her mistake after seeing that Austin, but not Houston, is on the list of capitals. You should determine whether a list of possible answers is desirable and then supply the list if it will be beneficial.

2. It is also a good idea to allow the learner to respond while looking at the list, rather than finding the answer, returning to the program, and only then entering the answer. CAPS, FOOTBALL, and BEHMOD all demonstrate strategies for accomplishing this.

3. Allow the learner to review important parts of the tutorial whenever it is appropriate to do so. This can often be done by building in a subroutine after each learner input. If the learner has asked to review certain materials, then that information should be displayed on the screen before the learner is permitted to continue to the next step. If the learner makes no such request, the subroutine should verify this, and the learner should proceed immediately to the next step. One useful subroutine to insert this way is the "Help" routine, described in Chapter 2.

4. Give the learner the option of reviewing the screen just before the one cur-

rently being viewed, by pressing a designated key. This helps the student review an idea that was lost or that was not attended to until the current screen called for it. You can usually do this by using looping strategies.

5. Accept alternative input. For example, you may wish to accept either "Y" or "yes" for an affirmative answer. The following line would do this:

```
100 IF A$=''YES'' OR A$=''Y'' THEN 500
```

Another way to achieve a similar outcome would be to use the following line:

```
100 IF LEFT$(A$,1)=''Y'' THEN 500
```

Both of these lines will accept both yes and "Y" as acceptable responses. They differ in that the second will also accept "yess" or "yeess," as well as "yesterday" or "yataghan."

CAPS and FOOTBALL use similar strategies for dealing with variant spellings of the names of cities and with more than one correct answer to a question.

6. Put the information on the screen in such a way as to allow the learner to focus on the learning task, free from worrying about how to work the computer.

The preceding guidelines focused on positive ways of increasing user friendliness; yet, research indicates that when adults are asked to recall their best and worst teachers, they find it much easier to remember the things that their bad teachers did than the things that their good teachers did. Thus it seems likely that a similar phenomenon will occur when learners use computers: bad points may stand out better than good points may. This means that one of the best ways to make a program user friendly is to discover those aspects that are annoying or unfriendly and eliminate them.

The following is a short (and partial) list of some of the things that militate against user friendliness:

1. The computer may simply stop running or "break" when the learner enters faulty input. It is much more desirable to explain briefly what the error was or what kind of input should have been provided and then give the learner the opportunity to enter proper input.
2. The computer may recycle the learner by continually responding with a simple "?" to faulty input. Again, more specific information should be given so that the learner can correct the error.
3. The learner may encounter technical messages that he or she probably will not understand, such as "Syntax error in line 3030." It is more constructive to offer simply stated, grammatically coherent sentences that instruct the learner what to do next.
4. A learner reaches the absolute apotheosis of frustration when he or she has patiently and correctly entered several answers and suddenly realizes that a rash push of a key has resulted in a wrong answer that invalidates the entire process. Prevent this frustration by permitting the learner to alter an erroneous response after it has been made.
5. Sometimes the computer presents on the screen messages that make no sense whatsoever. For instance, what would you make of a message that states: "Wrong. The correct answer is $1.52, not $1.52." We have found this type of paradoxical message in several of the programs that our students

have written. This particular error occurred because the program was not looking for the dollar sign at the point of INPUT but had inserted one during the PRINT statement. Thus $1.52 only *seems* to be equal to "$1.52," but "1.52" with a dollar sign printed in front of it certainly looks like "$1.52"! The way to eliminate such errors is to be aware of the possibility of confusion and to write the program in such a way as to eliminate it.

In summary, user friendliness requires that the programmer spend more time in writing the program in order to reduce the user's effort in using the program.

Debugging: Eliminating Errors from Programs

The following are examples of problems or "bugs" in computer programs:

John banged his hands on the table in despair. "That does it! I'm dropping the course and throwing the computer away. This stupid thing simply won't work!"

Beth leaned back in the chair and smiled contentedly. She was waiting for the computer to save the modifications she had just inserted into the program. *Now* it would run perfectly. As soon as the computer indicated it was ready, she typed run and gleefully watched her program appear on the screen, step by step, gliding through the well-written program. Her smile broadened as the frame that had required two hours of work and fourteen lines of modification came and went. No error at all. But then her smile turned to a gasp of disbelief as the very next frame registered SYNTAX ERROR IN LINE 1415!

"Eureka! That's it!" shouted Bill, as he clapped his hands and jumped out of bed at two o'clock in the morning. Bill's wife rolled over and mumbled, "Are you leaving me or what?" "No," replied Bill, "I've just figured out what was wrong with my program," and he raced off to his computer in the spare bedroom to give it one more shot.

Mrs. Hicks felt a gentle tug on her sleeve. "The computer says something's wrong," said Kristin. Mrs. Hicks smiled. "Such a naive kid. Four million kids have run that program, and there hasn't been a single problem." So Mrs. Hicks was astonished when she looked at the screen. SUBSCRIPT OUT OF RANGE IN LINE 2014. "Who's been messing with my subscripts?!", she shouted.

Each of the teachers or programmers in the preceding anecdotes had a problem with a "bug" in their computer program. A "bug" is an inexplicable difficulty that causes something in a program to go wrong. The process of eliminating such errors and making the program function correctly is referred to as *debugging*. In most cases, programmers find that they spend about ten times as much time and effort debugging their programs as they did writing the original programs.

Errors in computer programs can be divided into those errors that cause the program to fail to run, and those that permit the program to run but to run improperly. In addition, errors can enter a program when the program is first being written and when the program is being modified. Thus, even if you have no intention of writing programs from scratch, you should know how to debug programs so that you can modify them to suit your own educational purposes.

Language Errors: Interpreting Error Messages

When you make certain types of programming errors, the result will be that your command will make no sense to the computer. For example, you might spell a command incorrectly, and therefore the computer would not recognize the command. Or you might tell the computer to print the fifty-first item in an array that contains only fifty items. Or you might instruct the computer to read fifty pieces of data when you have included only ten on the DATA lines. In each of these cases the computer will not be able to carry out a sensible instruction. When these errors occur, the computer stops its run of the program and states the nature of the error it has encountered. Errors of this sort are referred to as *language errors*.

The error message printed by the computer is often a great help in correcting a language error. A summary of language error messages and steps to correct them are shown in Table 9.1. Although Table 9.1 focuses on the TRS-80 and Apple computers, similar error messages and strategies for overcoming these errors are available on all computers.

An examination of this table indicates that the error messages on these two systems are similar. In general, most computers that use BASIC have a similar set of error messages. Likewise, the strategies for correcting or avoiding the language errors are almost identical on the two systems. Note that this is not a comprehensive list of error messages and how to treat them. You should consult the manual of your specific computer for more detailed information. In addition, computers may differ significantly in the helpfulness of their error messages: some systems enable the programmer to identify the difficulty much more easily than do other systems. Note too that it is not always possible to correct language errors by simply altering the line on which the computer says that the language error occurs. For example, when an error message indicates an inappropriate subscript, it is often the outcome of an error somewhere else in the program in which the magnitude of the subscript was erroneously determined. An example of such an error is shown in Figure 9.10. In such cases, of course, the best strategy is not to change the line on which the computer pointed out the error but, rather, to locate the real error and make a correction there.

Logical Errors: The Trace Function

In many cases, a program can be entirely free of language errors and still produce no output or produce incorrect output. This is because the program contains logical errors. The computer is receiving instructions that it can understand but that are not the instructions necessary to meet the program's intended objectives. The strategy for eliminating logical errors relies not on the interpretation of error messages but, rather, on a careful logical analysis of the program.

The most common way to deal with logical errors is to obtain a listing of the program, either on the screen or on a printer, and to examine the logic of the lines in the program. Such an examination will often lead to the discovery of the error, which can be corrected by adding, deleting, or altering commands at the proper places in the program.

In addition, most computers have a *trace function*. When the TRACE is turned

Table 9.1. Some Common TRS-80 Error Messages, Their Apple Equivalents, and Steps to Correct Them

Error Message	Apple Equivalent	Explanation	Steps to Correct Error	Note
NEXT WITHOUT FOR	NEXT WITHOUT FOR ERROR	A NEXT statement occurs without a corresponding FOR statement, or the variable in a NEXT statement does not match the corresponding FOR that is still in effect.	(1) Add a FOR statement in the proper location or delete the NEXT statement. (2) Check the variables in the FOR and NEXT statements to make sure they match. (3) If a nested loop is used, make sure that the NEXT statements are not reversed in relation to the FOR statements.	This message can also occur as the result of an inaccurate GOTO (or equivalent) line. For example, if the GOTO line mistakenly sends the computer into the middle of the FOR/NEXT loop rather than to the beginning, this error message will result. In such cases, the solution is to correct the GOTO message.
SYNTAX ERROR	SYNTAX ERROR	Indicates incorrect punctuation, missing parentheses in an expression, incorrect spelling of a command (e.g., PRIT for PRINT), or invalid characters including blanks) in a line.	Simply locate and correct the offending syntax. (These are frequently typographical errors.)	Some excellent operating systems give more specific information regarding syntax errors (e.g., they indicate which word is unrecognized).
RETURN WITHOUT GOSUB	RETURN WITHOUT GOSUB	The computer has encountered a RETURN statement without first encountering a corresponding GOSUB statement. (This error	Either make sure that a GOSUB statement is inserted at a point where it will be executed before the RETURN, or remove the unwanted RETURN.	This error often occurs because the computer gets into a subroutine by mistake (e.g., by continuing to the next line of the program). Such

Table 9.1. Some Common TRS-80 Error Messages, Their Apple Equivalents, and Steps to Correct Them (con't)

Error Message	Apple Equivalent	Explanation	Steps to Correct Error	Note
		often will result when the programmer has confused GOTO with GOSUB.)	Often this means replacing the RETURN with GOTO (or equivalent) command.	mistakes are eliminated by correctly isolating the subroutines with GOTO (or equivalent) commands immediately before the subroutines.
OUT OF DATA	OUT OF DATA ERROR	Because there were not a sufficient number of entries on the DATA lines, the computer was unable to execute a READ statement. Such an error results when a DATA statement is missing or when all the DATA statements have already been executed. It is the common result of miscounting the number of elements in the DATA statements.	(1) Check DATA statements to make sure that all are present. (2) Count the number of entries in your DATA statements and make sure that the total is not smaller than that required by your READ statements. (3) If your program requires the repeated reading of the same set of DATA, make sure that the RESTORE statements are in the right place.	
ILLEGAL FUNCTION CALL	ILLEGAL QUANTITY ERROR	The computer attempted to execute a math or string function but found that the equation included an illegitimate parameter. A typical example of illegitimate parameters is a negative term in an array subscript or in the square root function.		This error often results from a miscalculation somewhere other than where the error is actually identified by the computer.

OVERFLOW	OVERFLOW ERROR	The size of a number put into or calculated by the computer is too large to be represented by the computer. (This error often occurs when functions are not executed in a logically correct order.)	Correct or limit calculations performed by the computer to within permissible limits.	There is no such thing as underflow. Extremely small numbers should be rounded to zero.
OUT OF MEMORY	OUT OF MEMORY ERROR	All memory available to the computer has been used. This may occur because of (1) the length of the program, (2) very large arrays, (3) a large number of nested FOR/NEXT loops or complex subroutines, (4) complex expressions containing nested parentheses, or (5) a large number of DATA statements.	(1) Reduce the number of DATA statements (and the size of the program) by placing the data in files. (2)Reduce the complexity of the program by simplifying complex expressions, loops, and arrays. (3) Cut programs into subprograms and chain them together for execution.	
UNDEFINED LINE	UNDEFINED STATEMENT ERROR	A GOTO, GOSUB, or THEN statement refers to a line number that does not exist.	Identify the correct spot to which you want the program to branch, and then make sure that the line number cited in the GOTO statement matches the line number assigned to the statement to which you want the program to branch.	

Table 9.1 Some Common TRS-80 Error Messages, Their Apple Equivalents, and Steps to Correct Them (con't)

Error Message	Apple Equivalent	Explanation	Steps to Correct Error	Note
SUBSCRIPT OUT OF RANGE	BAD SUBSCRIPT ERROR	The computer has attempted to assign an element to an array indicated by a subscript beyond the range defined by the DIM statement or permitted by default. This would occur, for example, if there were a negative subscript or if the computer tried to READ an eleventh piece of DATA into an array dimensioned to receive only ten.	(1) Make sure the DIM statements for all variables match or exceed the number of elements that will actually be assigned to those arrays. (2) Make sure that you have not accidentally allowed a READ or PRINT loop to get beyond the limit you intended. (For example, in two-column PRINT loops, remember that you must print blank spaces that must also be represented in the array.) (3) Make sure that the commands that assign the subscripts to the arrays are written correctly.	
REDIMENSIONED ARRAY	REDIM'D ARRAY ERROR	The computer encountered a DIM statement for an array that had already been dimensioned either explicitly or by default (i.e., by prior use in the program).	(1) It is good practice to DIM all arrays at the beginning of the program, where you can easily verify that each is used only once. (2) Make sure that you do not use the same label for both a one-dimensional and a two-dimensional array.	

DIVISION BY ZERO	DIVISION BY ZERO ERROR	The computer attempted to use a denominator of zero, which is mathematically undefined.	(1) Do not permit division to take place when the denominator is zero. (2) Make sure that your denominator contains only variables that have been previously defined. (Undefined variables have a default value of zero on their first usage.) (3) Remember that very small values may round off to zero and result in this error message.	If you accidentally leave a space in the wrong place when typing a mathematical function—such as INT(X) —the computer will recognize this as a variable rather than as a function and will assign a value of zero to this "variable." The result will be this error message.
TYPE MISMATCH	TYPE MISMATCH ERROR	The computer was looking for a string variable and found a numeric variable, or it was looking for a numeric variable and found a string variable. Such mismatches can be found in INPUT statements, LET statements, IF statements, or in any other situation in which the nature of the variable is important.	(1) Be sure that string characters are assigned to string variables. (2) Do not attempt to perform mathematical operations on string variables. (3) In IF and LET statements, be sure that the variables on both sides of the equation match correctly.	

Table 9.1.   Some Common TRS-80 Error Messages, Their Apple Equivalents, and Steps to Correct Them (con't)

Error Message	Apple Equivalent	Explanation	Steps to Correct Error	Note
OUT OF STRING SPACE	(None. The Apple system allocates enough string space to operate any reasonable program.)	The computer allocates a specific amount of space to store string variables in its main memory. This message means that you have attempted to store more strings than the computer can handle.	Place a CLEAR N (N is some value, such as one thousand) at the beginning of your program. If the problem persists, increase the value of N. (Note that this solution also reduces the amount of memory space available for the rest of the program.)	
STRING TOO LONG	STRING TOO LONG ERROR	An attempt has been made to create a string that exceeds 255 characters.	Break strings into segments of no more than 255 characters in length.	
CAN'T CONTINUE	CAN'T CONTINUE ERROR	An attempt has been made to continue execution of a program when (1) no program exists in the computer's main memory; (2) an error has occurred in the program execution; or (3) lines have been added, deleted, or altered since the program was interrupted. Any of these steps will make the CONT statement ineffectual.	Rerun the program. If there is no program, reload it.	

REDO

REENTER

The user has attempted to enter a string variable when the computer was expecting a numeric variable.

Enter the correct type of data or change the INPUT statement so that the computer can anticipate the type of data the user will actually enter. This problem can be minimized by giving the user clear instructions regarding what kind of data to enter and how to react when this message occurs.

```
100 DIM S$(20)
    .
    .
    .
200 FOR I=1 TO 20
210 READ S$(I)
220 NEXT I
    .
    .
    .
300 LET X=RND(50)
310 PRINT "WHAT IS THE DEFINITION OF";S$(X);
    .
    .
    .
```

Figure 9.10. An example of a language error in which the actual error is not in the designated line. In this example, the computer will print a "SUBSCRIPT OUT OF RANGE" error at line 310 any time the computer selects a random number higher than 20 at line 300. This will happen because the computer will realize that it cannot print a nonexistent member of an array. The way to correct this error is to change line 300, by selecting a number between 1 and 20, or to change lines 100 and 200 to increase the size and contents of the array to a range of 1 to 50.

on, the computer will print on the screen each line number as it executes the command on that line during its run through the program. By examining this listing of lines, it is possible to see whether the computer is actually doing what you tried to program it to do. It is also possible to examine the lines encountered by the computer immediately before it makes an error. For example, an examination of such a listing might indicate that the computer is omitting an entire subroutine or that an operation is being performed only once rather than the expected ten times. When such discrepancies occur, they occur for a reason, and by examining the TRACE listing, it is possible to pinpoint and correct the error.

The trace function can be turned on and off at will. (You will not want to leave it on permanently, as the listing of lines clutters up the screen.) On the TRS-80, the command TRON turns the trace function on, and the command TROFF turns it off. On the Apple, the command TRACE turns it on, and the command NOTRACE turns it off. You should refer to the manual to determine how to use this helpful function on other computers.

Examining the Output

In many cases, of course, it is possible to ascertain the nature of a logical error simply by looking at what the computer prints on the screen and reasoning how this improper output could have been produced. For example, if a computer omits a space between sentences, it should be simple enough to find the place in the program where the computer prints those sentences and to look at the logic of the program to see if the program was designed to supply the needed space. Likewise, if the computer is supposed to select a new term to define on each run of the program but is actually selecting the same term each time, then it should be simple enough to discover that part of the program at which the terms are selected and then look for errors in programming logic at that point.

In some cases, however, it is not so simple to identify the source of errors.

Sometimes an error will occur only under certain circumstances, and the program will function correctly under all other conditions. For example, errors may occur only when a certain random number is selected or only when a correct answer is given immediately after a previous incorrect answer. In such cases, the debugging strategy is the same as in the simpler cases, only less visible. The programmer must formulate a hypothesis about what the various variables in the program should be doing at a given time and then check to see if they in fact do. The strategies described in the following paragraphs will help make this task easier.

Reading the Mind of the Computer

One useful strategy is to find out what the computer is "thinking" at specific points in the program. For example, if line 210 of your program is supposed to establish a new value for the variable K, then you should be able to read the computer's mind when it runs through line 210 to see if the value really changes correctly. (Of course, you can use the trace function to verify that the computer actually does run line 210.) There are three ways to do this:

1. Insert additional lines into the program (for example, at line 209 or 211 or both) in which you print on the screen important values (in this case, the value of K and related variables). Such lines can later be removed from the program.
2. Interrupt the program with a STOP command at an important point (at line 209 or 211 or both). Then when the computer gives its BASIC prompt, type PRINT and the name of the important variables on the screen. The computer will respond by printing on the screen the current value of the variables you have requested. When you use this procedure, it is possible to continue the program by typing CONT, as long as you have made no changes in the program.
3. Do whatever is necessary, according to your manual (such as pressing the break or reset key), to interrupt the program when the error seems to be occurring. Then have the computer print the correct values, as in Step 2. There are disadvantages with this procedure, as compared with Step 2, because it is somewhat less precise in getting the computer to stop at the right place. However, it has the advantage that the programmer can interrupt the program several times without inserting a large number of STOP commands.

The following are some examples of useful strategies for reading the computer's mind to identify errors:

1. If you are not certain whether the computer is reading all the data, interrupt the program after the DATA lines have been read, and have the computer print the last piece of data. This strategy also permits you to see whether you entered all the desired DATA lines without laboriously proofreading each entry. For example, if you are reading data on the fifty states and establish that S$(I), stands for the names of the states and then if you interrupt the program and type PRINT S$(50), the computer should print Wyoming on the screen. If it does not (for example, if it prints Wisconsin or Cheyenne or nothing), this will indicate that there is something wrong with either your

READ loop or the DATA lines. But if the computer prints Wyoming during your interruption but does not correctly print the name of the state during the actual run of the program, then you know that you should be looking for an error somewhere other than in the READ loop or the DATA lines. Such logic can help you narrow the field of possible errors and find the right place for remediation.

2. If you are being penalized for wrong answers when you are certain you are putting in correct ones, then have the computer print the correct answer and the learner's response during an interruption immediately after the negative feedback. For example, if A$ stands for the learner's answer and S$(X) for the correct answer, then have the computer print both A$ and S$(X). If they do not match, then you will know that you should look for an error in the way that one or the other of these variables has been identified and stored. On the other hand, if they do match, it will indicate that there is a logical error in your feedback procedure.

3. In many cases you may want the computer to execute a certain command only when a given variable has a particular value. A good strategy in this case is to insert an additional command to print the value of that variable immediately before to the relevant IF/THEN statement. If the value of the variable is *not* what you expected it to be, then this will indicate that you should look for the error at that point of the program that that variable received its value, rather than in the IF/THEN statement or in the subsequent lines. If the value *is* what you expect it to be, then this will indicate that there is something faulty in either the IF/THEN statement itself or in the lines to which the program is directed by the IF/THEN statement.

Bugs are the most annoying part of programming. Computers do, in fact, sometimes make errors, but they are exceedingly rare. In almost every case that one of your programs malfunctions, the computer is being overly logical—carrying out an instruction that you never intended to give. With care and patience, you can learn to avoid making errors and to discover and correct the errors that you do make.

Closing Comment

If you understand the principles discussed up to this point, you should be capable of writing effective instructional drills. More importantly, you should be able to modify existing drills that you receive from commercial sources or from the public domain. By doing so, you can tailor these programs to your own educational needs, and you should find the guidelines in Appendix B and many of the modules in Appendix C to be helpful.

Note, however, that we have not tried to cover all the principles of programming but have discussed only those principles necessary to understand the programs used in this text as samples. That represents a formidable supply of programming principles. But as your needs and interests expand, you will certainly need information beyond what is presented here. We believe that if you have understood these fundamentals, you can branch out to use the additional sources (such as manuals and consultants) that will become available to you.

Finally, never assume that a program is "finished" the first time that you have gotten it to run successfully. Always assume that you will have to "debug" the program based on the feedback you will get when you let your target audience start running the program. This will probably lead to the discovery of additional bugs. Only when the learners report that the program contains all the necessary steps in the logically correct order, can you conclude that the program is finished (at least until someone notices another bug).

Chapter 10
FOOTBALL: A Case Study

THE program FOOTBALL was designed to meet the special needs of a nine-year-old learning-disabled child named Paul, who was classified in his school system as "communication disordered."

Paul needed drill and practice on such language-related skills as categorization (concept development), alphabetization, and vocabulary development. He was also below his grade level in such social studies skills as map reading and knowledge of the cities and states of his country. In mathematics, Paul was slightly above grade level in computational skills but slightly below grade level in his ability to apply these skills to actual problem solutions.

Paul had recently become interested in professional football and so watched football on television and spent a lot of time playing with football trading cards. Although this activity was prompted more by a desire to be like his thirteen-year-old brother than by an actual love for the sport, Paul's interest in football was real. He enjoyed knowing the names and nicknames of each team and wanted to learn as much as he could about his new sport.

Paul spontaneously started to use his interest in football to develop his own language skills. He did this by asking questions about the football cards and teams, and the members of his family responded by answering these questions and prompting him with more. At this point Paul was typical of many young children who are motivated to enhance their learning skills in a way that would be impossible in a less interesting classroom setting. Experienced teachers often take advantage of such opportunities. Knowing this, Paul's father wrote FOOTBALL to join Paul's interests to his academic needs.

This computer program started as a very simple drill that allowed Paul to match the teams' nicknames with their home cities. When it became clear that Paul's interest in football could be used as a basis for helping him develop several academic skills, the program expanded into its present version. Although the present program focuses on professional football teams, as seasons and interests change, it should be easy to adapt the program to basketball, baseball, or hockey, simply by altering the DATA statements and a few lines in the program. Likewise, there is no reason that the program has to stick to professional sports: it could be modified to focus on college, high school, or Little League sports. Of course, a strategy similar to this could use hobbies or interests other than sports to motivate learning academic skills.

How FOOTBALL Works

The program (Figure 10.1) is not presented here exactly as it evolved. It has been "cleaned up." The present line numbers, the order of the subroutines, and the inclusion of REM statements make the program easier to apply to your own needs. The overall logic of the program is diagrammed in Figure 10.2. Note that FOOTBALL is written for an Apple computer, whereas previous sample programs were written for the TRS-80.

The following questions focus on important concepts demonstrated in FOOT-BALL.

Question 1. The computer appears to be able to "recognize" individual learners and even to base its questions on this recognition. How does this happen?
Answer: Lines 110 and 120 obtain the name of the person running the program. The player's name is important for two reasons: (1) experience showed that Paul (like most young children) responded better when the computer seemed to "know" him, and (2) the subroutine at line 2400 enabled the computer to assign varying levels of difficulty to persons that it "knew." The logic of this subroutine is described in Figure 10.3. This subroutine makes it possible for other learners to use the program at an appropriate level of difficulty. More immediately it allowed both Paul and his thirteen-year-old brother to play the same game. Paul got only questions that he was likely to be able to answer, and his brother received more difficult ones. This provided a "modeling effect": seeing his brother involved in the program helped nurture Paul's interest.

Question 2: The program contains questions at different levels of complexity. Yet these were introduced to Paul in gradual stages as he became ready for them. How was the programmer able to carry out this gradual increase in complexity?
Answer: By changing the value of L in line 170 or in the 2400 subroutine, the programmer could offer gradually more difficult tasks for Paul as he showed himself ready to deal with them. Originally, the value of L had been permanently set at 8. The 2400 subroutine was added after Paul's first encounter with the program. At that time he enjoyed the questions about team nicknames but was overwhelmed by the harder questions dealing with state abbreviations and with distances of the teams from his home town. The programmer therefore added the subroutine to keep Paul from being overwhelmed. While Paul continued to use the first two loops in the program (the teams and their nicknames), his family showed him maps on which to locate the teams and taught him that every state had a postal abbreviation. Even though Paul was never aware of this periodic change in the value of L in line 2400, he gradually became able to use the program to learn without becoming frustrated.

Question 3: Whenever it asks a new question, the computer randomly selects one of the several possible types. How does it accomplish this random variation?

```
10   REM   FOOTBALL BY ED VOCKELL
20   REM   COPYRIGHT 1982
30   REM   ALL RIGHTS RESERVED
40   HOME
45   REM   **** THE FOLLOWING LINES PRESENT A TITLE PAGE.
50   PRINT : PRINT : PRINT : PRINT  TAB(15);"FOOTBALL"
60   PRINT : PRINT  TAB(18);"BY"
70   PRINT :. PRINT  TAB(14);"ED VOCKELL": PRINT : PRINT
     TAB(9);"(ALL RIGHTS RSERVED)"
80   PRINT : PRINT : PRINT
90   PRINT : PRINT "ARE YOU READY TO START (PRESS RETURN)";
92   REM   **** THE FOLLOWING LINES INITIALIZE THE RANDOM NUMBER
     GENERATOR.
94   LET Y =  PEEK(78) + 256 *  PEEK(79)
96   LET X =  RND(-Y)
100   INPUT R$: HOME
110   PRINT "WHAT IS YOUR NAME?"
120   INPUT N$
130   HOME
140   REM   **** L SETS THE LIMIT ON THE RANGE OF QUESTIONS.
150   REM   **** 1 GIVES ONLY A VERY SIMPLE TYPE OF QUESTION.
160   REM   **** 8 GIVES A RANGE FROM VERY SIMPLE TO VERY
     DIFFICULT QUESTIONS.
170   LET L = 8
175   REM   **** THE FOLLOWING SUBROUTINE CHANGES THE VALUE OF L
     IF THE COMPUTER 'RECOGNIZES' THE PLAYER.
180   GOSUB 2400
210   REM   **** UNRECOGNIZED PLAYERS GET THE DEFAULT LIMIT OF 8
     FROM LINE 140.
215   REM   **** THE FOLLOWING LINE SETS THE NUMBER OF TEAMS.
220   LET N = 28
230   DIM C$(N + 1),F$(N + 1)
240   DIM D(N),T$(N),S$(N + 1),D$(N)
250   DIM U$(51),V$(51)
255   REM   **** READ LOOP
260   FOR I = 1 TO N
270   READ C$(I),F$(I),D(I),T$(I),S$(I),D$(I)
280   NEXT I
290   FOR I = 1 TO 50
300   READ U$(I),V$(I)
310   NEXT I
320   PRINT "QUESTION NUMBER ";R + W + 1;":": PRINT
325   REM   **** THE FOLLOWING LINE SELECTS A TEAM ABOUT WHICH TO
     ASK A QUESTION.
330   LET X =  INT(RND(1) * N) + 1
335   REM   **** THE FOLLOWING LINE SELECTS A TYPE OF QUESTION TO
     ASK.
340   LET A =  INT(RND(1) * L) + 1
345   REM   **** THE FOLLOWING LINE BRANCHES TO ONE OF THE EIGHT
     POSSIBLE QUESTION FORMATS.
350   ON A GOTO 1000,1100,1400,1300,1200,1500,1600,1700
1000   PRINT "WHAT TEAM COMES FROM"
1005   PRINT : PRINT  TAB(5);C$(X): PRINT
1010   IF K > 0 THEN 1025
1015   PRINT : PRINT "TYPE THE NAME OF THE TEAM"
1020   PRINT "OR TYPE L TO SEE THE LIST."
1025   PRINT : INPUT A$: HOME
1030   IF A$ = "L" THEN 2000
1035   GOTO 2200
1040   IF A$ = F$(X) THEN 2900
1045   IF X = 17 AND A$ = "GIANTS" THEN 2900
1050   IF X = 18 AND A$ = "JETS" THEN 2900
1055   GOTO 2700
1100   PRINT "WHAT PLACE HAS A TEAM NAMED THE"
1105   PRINT : PRINT  TAB(5);F$(X): PRINT
1110   IF K > 0 THEN 1125
1115   PRINT : PRINT "TYPE THE NAME OF THE PLACE"
1120   PRINT "OR TYPE L TO SEE THE LIST."
1125   PRINT : INPUT A$: HOME
1130   IF A$ = "L" THEN 2100
1135   GOSUB 2300
```

Figure 10.1. The listing of FOOTBALL (written for the Apple).

```
1140   IF A$ = C$(X) THEN 2900
1145   GOTO 2700
1200   LET Y =   INT(RND(1) * N) + 1
1205   IF X = Y THEN 1200
1210   IF C$(X) = C$(Y) THEN 1200
1215   PRINT : PRINT "WHICH TEAM COMES FROM A PLACE"
1220   PRINT : PRINT "THAT COMES EARLIER IN THE ALPHABET:"
1225   PRINT : PRINT  TAB(3);"THE ";F$(X);" OR THE ";F$(Y);"?"
1230   PRINT : INPUT A$: HOME
1235   IF A$ = "L" THEN 2100
1240   IF X > Y THEN 1260
1245   IF A$ = F$(X) THEN 2900
1250   IF A$ = C$(X) THEN 2900
1255   GOTO 2700
1260   IF A$ = F$(Y) THEN 2900
1265   IF A$ = C$(Y) THEN 2900
1270   GOTO 2700
1300   LET Y =   INT(RND(1) * N) + 1
1305   IF X = Y THEN 1300
1310   IF D(X) = D(Y) THEN 1300
1315   PRINT "WHICH TEAM IS FURTHER FROM HAMMOND?"
1320   PRINT : PRINT "THE ";F$(X);" OR THE ";F$(Y)
1325   PRINT : INPUT A$: HOME
1330   IF D(X) > D(Y) THEN F$ = F$(X)
1335   IF D(Y) > D(X) THEN F$ = F$(Y)
1340   IF A$ = F$ THEN 2900
1345   GOTO 2700
1400   PRINT "WHAT TEAM IS NAMED AFTER A ";
1405   PRINT : PRINT D$(X);"?"
1410   IF K > O THEN 1425
1415   PRINT : PRINT "TYPE THE NAME OF THE PLACE."
1420   PRINT "OR TYPE L TO SEE THE LIST."
1425   PRINT : INPUT A$: HOME
1430   IF A$ = "L" THEN 2100
1435   GOTO 2300
1440   IF A$ = C$(X) THEN 2900
1445   IF A$ = F$(X) THEN 2900
1450   IF X = 27 AND A$ = "RAIDERS" THEN 2900
1455   IF X = 20 AND A$ = "BUCCANEERS" THEN 2900
1460   GOTO 2700
1500   PRINT : PRINT "IN WHAT STATE DO WE FIND"
1505   IF X = 28 THEN X = 27
1510   PRINT : PRINT "THE ";F$(X);"?"
1515   PRINT : INPUT A$: HOME
1520   IF A$ = S$(X) THEN 2900
1525   GOTO 2700
1600   PRINT "WHAT IS THE ABBREVIATION OF THE STATE"
1605   IF X = 28 THEN X = 27
1610   IF K = O THEN  PRINT
1615   PRINT "WHERE THERE IS A TEAM CALLED"
1620   IF K = O THEN  PRINT
1625   PRINT "THE ";F$(X);"?"
1630   IF K > O THEN 1645
1635   PRINT : PRINT "TYPE THE ABBREVIATION OR TYPE L"
1640   PRINT "TO SEE A LIST OF STATE ABBREVIATIONS."
1645   PRINT : INPUT A$: HOME
1650   IF A$ = "L" THEN 2500
1655   IF A$ = T$(X) THEN 2900
1660   GOTO 2700
1700   PRINT : PRINT "TELL ME THE NAME OF A TEAM FROM": PRINT
1705   IF X <  > 28 THEN  PRINT "THE STATE OF ";
1710   PRINT  TAB(5);S$(X);"."
1715   IF K > O THEN 1730
1720   PRINT : PRINT "TYPE THE NAME OF A TEAM"
1725   PRINT "OR TYPE L TO SEE THE LIST."
1730   PRINT : INPUT A$: HOME
1735   IF A$ = "L" THEN 2000
1740   GOTO 2300
1745   IF A$ = C$(X) THEN 2900
1750   IF A$ = F$(X) THEN 2900
1755   IF S$(X) = S$ THEN 1765
```

Figure 10.1. The listing of FOOTBALL (written for the Apple). (Continued.)

```
1760    GOTO 2700
1765    PRINT "THE ";A$;" ARE ONE TEAM FROM"
1770    PRINT S$". NAME ANOTHER TEAM FROM"
1775    PRINT S$;".": GOTO 1730
1999    REM ****  LIST ROUTINE FOR NICKNAMES
2000    FOR I = 1 TO  INT(N / 2 + .5)
2010    LET K = 1
2020    PRINT F$(I); TAB(20);F$(I +  INT(N / 2 + .5))
2030    NEXT I
2040    PRINT
2050    ON A GOTO 1000,1,1,1,1,1,1,1700
2099    REM  **** LIST ROUTINE FOR PLACES
2100    FOR I = 1 TO  INT(N / 2 + .5)
2110    LET K = 1
2120    PRINT C$(I); TAB(20);C$(I +  INT(N / 2 + .5))
2130    NEXT I
2150    PRINT : ON A GOTO 1,1100,1400,1,1215,1,1,1
2199    REM  **** SPELLING CHECK FOR NICKNAMES
2200    FOR I = 1 TO N
2210    IF A$ = F$(I) THEN 2270
2220    NEXT I
2230    PRINT : PRINT A$" IS NOT THE CORRECT SPELLING "
2240    PRINT "OF ANY TEAM."
2250    PRINT : PRINT "TRY AGAIN OR TYPE L TO SEE THE LIST."
2260    PRINT : ON A GOTO 1000,1100,1400,1315,1215,1500,1600,1700
2270    LET S$ = S$(I)
2280    ON A GOTO 1040,1140,1440,1340,1245,1520,1655,1745
2299    REM  **** SPELLING CHECK FOR PLACES
2300    FOR I = 1 TO N
2305    IF A$ = C$(I) THEN 2345
2310    NEXT I
2315    IF A = 8 THEN 2200
2320    IF A = 3 THEN 2200
2325    PRINT : PRINT A$" IS NOT THE CORRECT SPELLING "
2330    PRINT "OF ANY PLACE WITH A TEAM."
2335    PRINT : PRINT "TRY AGAIN OR TYPE L TO SEE THE LIST."
2340    PRINT : ON A GOTO 1000,1100,1400,1315,1215,1500,1600,1700
2345    LET S$ = S$(I)
2350    ON A GOTO 1040,1140,1440,1340,1245,1520,1655,1745
2399    REM  **** NAME RECOGNITION ROUTINE
2400    IF N$ = "PAUL" THEN L = 8
2410    IF N$ = "ED" THEN L = 2
2420    IF N$ = "MARC" THEN L = 6
2430    RETURN
2499    REM **** STATE ABBREVIATION LIST
2500    PRINT "STATE ABBREVIATIONS:"
2510    PRINT : FOR I = 1 TO 50 STEP 3
2520    PRINT V$(I);" ";U$(I); TAB(13);V$(I + 1);" ";U$(I + 1);
        TAB(26);V$(I + 2);" ";U$(I + 2)
2530    NEXT I
2540 K = 1
2550    PRINT : GOTO 1600
2599    REM  **** ANOTHER QUESTION ROUTINE
2600    PRINT : PRINT "DO YOU WANT ANOTHER QUESTION (Y/N)";
2610    LET K = 0
2620    INPUT R$
2630    HOME
2640    IF R$ = "Y" THEN 320
2650    IF R$ = "N" THEN 3100
2660    PRINT "ANSWER Y FOR YES OR N FOR NO, PLEASE."
2670    GOTO 2600
2699    REM  **** WRONG ANSWER ROUTINE
2700    PRINT "WRONG.
2705    LET W = W + 1
2709    REM  **** R1 COUNTS CONSECUTIVE RIGHT ANSWERS
2710    LET R1 = 0
2714    REM  **** SPECIFIC ERROR MESSAGES BASED ON TYPE OF
        QUESTION (A)
2715    PRINT : ON A GOTO 2720,2720,2755,2730,2725,2775,2790,2805
2720    PRINT "THE ";F$(X);" ARE FROM ";C$(X);".": GOTO 2600
2725    IF X > Y THEN  PRINT C$(Y);" COMES BEFORE ";C$(X);".":
        GOTO 2600
```

Figure 10.1. The listing of FOOTBALL (written for the Apple). (Continued.)

```
2727   PRINT C$(X);" COMES BEFORE ";C$(Y);".": GOTO 2600
2730   PRINT C$(X);" IS ";D(X);" MILES AWAY."
2735   PRINT C$(Y);" IS ";D(Y);" MILES AWAY."
2740   PRINT : PRINT "THAT MAKES THE ";F$
2745   PRINT  ABS(D(X) - D(Y));" MILES FURTHER AWAY."
2750   GOTO 2600
2755   PRINT "THE TEAM WHICH GETS ITS NAME FROM
2760   PRINT : PRINT "A ";D$(X);" IS "
2765   PRINT : PRINT "THE ";F$(X);" FROM ";C$(X);"."
2770   GOTO 2600
2775   PRINT "THE ";F$(X);" ARE FROM "
2780   PRINT S$(X);"."
2785   GOTO 2600
2790   PRINT "THE ";F$(X);" COME FROM "
2795   PRINT S$(X);", WHICH IS ABBREVIATED ";T$(X);"."
2800   GOTO 2600
2805   PRINT "THE ";F$(X);" ARE FROM ";S$(X);"."
2810   GOTO 2600
2899   REM  **** RIGHT ANSWER ROUTINE
2900   PRINT "THAT'S RIGHT, ";N$;"!"
2909   REM  **** R1 COUNTS CONSECUTIVE RIGHT ANSWERS
2910   LET R1 = R1 + 1
2920   LET R = R + 1
2930   IF R1 < 2 THEN 2600
2940   PRINT : PRINT "THAT MAKES ";R1;" RIGHT ANSWERS"
2950   PRINT "IN A ROW, ";N$;"."
2960   IF R1 = 5 THEN   PRINT : PRINT "NOT BAD, ";N$;"."
2970   IF R1 = 10 THEN  PRINT : PRINT "WAY TO GO, ";N$;"."
2980   IF R1 = 15 THEN  PRINT : PRINT "YOU KNOW A LOT, ";N$;"."
2990   IF R1 = 20 THEN  PRINT : PRINT "FANTASTIC JOB, ";N$;"."
3000   IF R1 = 25 THEN  PRINT : PRINT "SUPER JOB, ";N$;"."
3010   IF R1 = 30 THEN  PRINT : PRINT "GREAT JOB, ";N$;".":
       PRINT "I NEED A BREAK NOW.": GOTO 3100
3020   GOTO 2600
3099   REM  **** END ROUTINE
3100   PRINT : PRINT "YOU GOT ";R;" RIGHT OUT OF ";R + W;"."
3110   PRINT : PRINT "THAT'S " INT((((R /(R + W)) + .005) *
       100);" PERCENT."
3120   END
4999   REM  **** FOOTBALL TEAM INFORMATION
5000   DATA  ATLANTA,FALCONS,674,GA,GEORGIA,BIRD LIKE A HAWK
5010   DATA  BALTIMORE,COLTS,668,MD,MARYLAND,YOUNG HORSE
5020   DATA  BUFFALO,BILLS,522,NY,NEW YORK,PERSON NAMED WILLIAM
5030   DATA  CHICAGO,BEARS,30,IL,ILLINOIS,LARGE FURRY ANIMAL
5040   DATA  CINCINNATI,BENGALS,280,OH,OHIO,TYPE OF TIGER
5050   DATA  CLEVELAND,BROWNS,335,OH,OHIO,A COLOR
5060   DATA  DALLAS,COWBOYS,917,TX,TEXAS,PERSON WHO WORKS ON A
       RANCH OUT WEST
5070   DATA  DENVER,BRONCOS,997,CO,COLORADO,WILD HORSE
5080   DATA  DETROIT,LIONS,266,MI,MICHIGAN,A LARGE CAT THAT'S
       NOT A TIGER
5090   DATA  GREEN BAY,PACKERS,197,WI,WISCONSIN,PERSON WHO PUTS
       MEAT IN PACKAGES
5100   DATA  HOUSTON,OILERS,1067,TX,TEXAS,PERSON WHO LOOKS FOR
       OIL
5110   DATA  KANSAS CITY,CHIEFS,499,MO,MISSOURI,BOSS OF INDIANS
5120   DATA  LOS ANGELES,RAMS,2054,CA,CALIFORNIA,STRONG SHEEP OR
       GOAT
5125   DATA  MIAMI,DOLPHINS,1329,FL,FLORIDA,FRIENDLY KIND OF
       FISH
5130   DATA  MINNESOTA,VIKINGS,405,MN,MINNESOTA,SAILOR FROM
       EUROPE
5135   DATA  NEW ORLEANS,SAINTS,912,LA,LOUISIANA,PERSON WHO IS
       IN HEAVEN
5140   DATA  NEW ENGLAND,PATRIOTS,963,MA,MASSACHUSETTS,PERSON
       WHO LOVES HIS COUNTRY
5150   DATA  NEW YORK,GIANTS,802,NY,NEW YORK,VERY LARGE PERSON
5160   DATA  NEW YORK,JETS,802,NY,NEW YORK,VERY FAST PLANE
5170   DATA  OAKLAND,RAIDERS,2132,CA,CALIFORNIA,PIRATE
5180   DATA  PHILADELPHIA,EAGLES,738,PA,PENNSYLVANIA,LARGE BIRD
       THAT STANDS FOR AMERICA
```

Figure 10.1. The listing of FOOTBALL (written for the Apple). (Continued.)

```
5190   DATA   PITTSBURGH,STEELERS,452,PA,PENNSYLVANIA,PERSON WHO
       MAKES METAL
5200   DATA   ST. LOUIS,CARDINALS,289,MO,MISSOURI,RED BIRD
5210   DATA   SAN DIEGO,CHARGERS,2064,CA,CALIFORNIA,PERSON WHO
       ATTACKS SOMEONE
5220   DATA   SAN FRANCISCO,49ERS,2142,CA,CALIFORNIA,PERSON WHO
       LOOKED FOR GOLD
5230   DATA   SEATTLE,SEAHAWKS,2013,WA,WASHINGTON,BIRD THAT LIVES
       NEAR THE SEA
5240   DATA   TAMPA BAY,BUCCANEERS,1150,FL,FLORIDA,PIRATE
5250   DATA   WASHINGTON,REDSKINS,671,DC,THE DISTRICT OF
       COLUMBIA,INDIAN
5999   REM   **** STATES AND ABBREVIATIONS
6000   DATA
       ALABAMA,AL,ALASKA,AK,ARIZONA,AZ,ARKANSAS,AR,CALIF,CA,COLORAD
       O,CO,CONN'CUT,CT,DELAWARE,DE,FLORIDA,FL,GEORGIA,GA,HAWAII,HI
       ,IDAHO,ID,ILLINOIS,IL
6010   DATA
       INDIANA,IN,IOWA,IA,KANSAS,KS,KENTUCKY,KY,LOU'ANA,LA,MAINE,ME
       ,MARYLAND,MD,MAS'ETTS,MA,MICHIGAN,MI,MIN'SOTA,MN,MIS'IPPI,MS
       ,MISSOURI,MO
6020   DATA   MONTANA,MT,NEBRASKA,NE,NEVADA,NV,NEW HAMP,NH,N
       JERSEY,NJ,N MEXICO,NM,NEW YORK,NY,N C'LINA,NC,N
       DAKOTA,ND,OHIO,OH
6030   DATA   OKLAHOMA,OK,OREGON,OR,P'VANIA,PA,R ISLAND,RI,S
       C'LINA,SC,S
       DAKOTA,SD,TEN'SEE,TN,TEXAS,TX,UTAH,UT,VERMONT,VT,VIRGINIA,VA
6040   DATA   WASH'TON,WA,W V'INIA,WV,W'CONSIN,WI,WYOMING,WY
```

Figure 10.1. The listing of FOOTBALL (written for the Apple). (Continued.)

Answer: In line 170, L stands for "limit." There are eight levels of questions in FOOT-BALL, and by altering L, the programmer can allow a player to select from all eight levels or limit the player to a smaller range. This selection of the type of question occurs in line 340, and a new number between 1 and the upper limit (L) is chosen each time the player is recycled to line 320 after answering a question.

Question 4: How does the computer store in its memory the facts about the football teams?

Answer: Lines 230 to 250 contain dimension statements, which set aside storage space in the computer for the arrays of data that the computer will read into its memory. In labeling these arrays, the programmer chose those that were meaningful to him. For example, C$ stands for "city" and F$ stands for "football team," but the choice was completely arbitrary. The programmer could just as easily have chosen P$ for "place" or T$ for "team."

Technical note: You may be surprised by the choice of N + 1 instead of N for the size of the arrays in line 230. This unusual choice was made because the programmer wanted to generate lists of teams and cities on the screen, and these lists would be in two colums (see lines 2020 and 1110). If one of these lists contained an uneven number of items (e.g., twenty-five teams), the computer would have to print a "blank" city or team in the bottom right-hand corner of the list. (A similar problem occurred in CAPS, Chapter 8). If this sounds complex and obscure to you, don't worry about it. Suffice it to say that the programmer had learned from experience that such a strategy would keep him from getting a "Subscript Out of Range" error message when he tried to print such lists. The same logic was used in line 250: even though there are only fifty states, the programmer reserved fifty-one spaces in the array. The list of states and abbreviations would be in three columns, and when the programmer tried to print three rows of seventeen states, he knew that he would need to allow for the blank space in the bottom right-hand corner of his list.

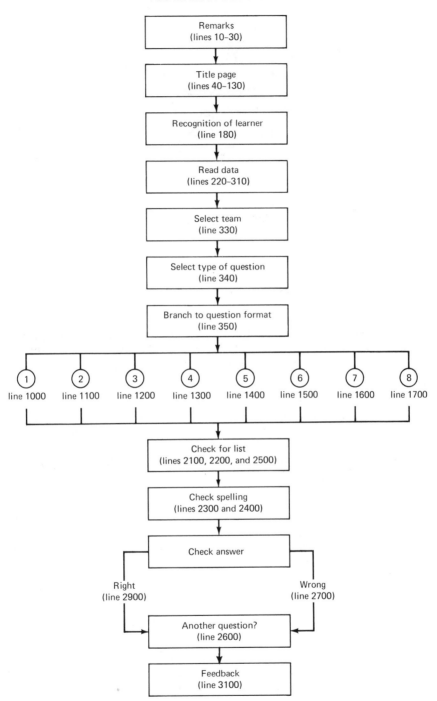

Figure 10.2. The logic of FOOTBALL.

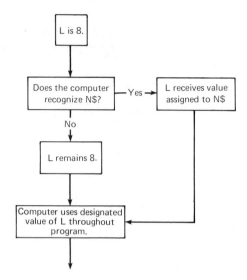

Figure 10.3. The logic of a recognition routine.

The computer memorizes the DATA through READ loops in lines 260 to 310. The first loop (lines 260 to 280) obtains the information about the teams, and the second loop (lines 290 to 310) obtains the states and abbreviations for use in the abbreviation list in line 2520.

Question 5: How does the computer actually present the questions on the screen?
Answer: The drill actually starts in line 320, which permits the player to keep track of how many questions he or she has attempted to answer. Line 330 randomly selects a team about which the computer will ask a question, and line 340 randomly selects a type of question. Line 350 routes the computer to one of the eight subroutines that ask the eight types of questions. The computer will return to this branching point before each new question.

Technical note: Notice the unusual sequence of eight line numbers in the ON GOTO statement in line 350. The programmer had originally written the eight subroutines in the order in which they occur (1000, 1100, 1200, 1300, 1400, 1500, 1600, and 1700). His plan was to use all eight of them in a normal run of the program. But, it immediately became clear to him that Paul was overwhelmed by the complexity of some of the questions and found it easier to name the team when a description was given (1400 subroutine) than to identify the alphabetical order of cities when only the nickname was given (1200 subroutine). Therefore, the programmer introduced the different questions gradually, over a period of two weeks, with the 1400 sequence pushed ahead of the 1200 sequence, thus explaining the unusual order of the line numbers in line 350.

Question 6: How does the computer know if an answer is correct?
Answer: To check the accuracy of the answer, the computer simply compares the player's input with the team nickname (or other array item) that is attached to the corresponding value of X (e.g., line 1040).

Question 7: How does the computer present the list of teams or nicknames?
Answer: The computer informs the player that it is possible to see a list of all the teams or nicknames by entering the letter "L." A player who chooses this option is routed to line 2000 or 2100, where the computer provides the list and then repeats the question.

Technical note: The purpose of line 1010 is to omit the message in lines 1015 to 1020 whenever the list is already on the screen. (If the message were repeated, it would clutter up the screen and waste valuable space. Besides, a player might wonder why he or she would want a list when that very list is already present.) Whenever the computer generates a list (in subroutine 2000 or 2100), the value of K changes to 1 and stays at 1 until line 2610 changes it back to zero before each new question. Therefore, the computer can tell by checking the value of K whether or not it would be appropriate to present the "list" message. (Note that even when this message is not presented, an L will still generate the list.)

Question 8: How does the computer check for accurate spelling?
Answer: When it is appropriate to do so, the computer goes to a subroutine in lines 2200 to 2300 to check the spelling of the player's response. The player is counted wrong only for entering a correct spelling of a wrong team. Otherwise, he or she is instructed to spell the entry differently or to examine the list of correct spellings. (This has some obvious disadvantages, but the programmer decided that this would be the most useful approach for the learner he had in mind. It would be easy to alter this option.)

Note that the spelling and list subroutines are entered by means of a GOTO statement rather than a GOSUB statement and therefore are terminated by another GOTO statement rather than by a RETURN statement. This strategy was necessary because the computer would not necessarily return to the line immediately following the statement that sent the computer to the subroutine (as would have happened with the GOSUB/RETURN combination). Therefore, each of the sequences ends with an ON GOTO statement, which sends the computer to an appropriate place in the program. (Note that this procedure was also used in CAPS, Chapter 8.)

Technical note: Lines 2050 and 2150 contain some "dummy lines"—line numbers which simply take up space but to which the computer will never actually be sent. This occurs because there are eight question formats (represented by the variable A), but only a few of them will ever require the presentation of a list. For those values of A which will never require the list, the programmer has merely inserted a "1" as the line number in the ON GOTO statements. Line 1 doesn't even exist, but the computer will never know this, since A will never have a value to send it to that line.

Question 9: New York has two teams (the Giants and the Jets). How does the computer cope with this ambiguity?
Answer: The programmer decided that he would accept either answer, and instructed the computer accordingly in lines 1045 and 1050. Note that the 1700 sequence (question 13) follows a different course of action to deal with a similar problem.

Question 10: When the computer asks what team comes from what city, why does it use the term "place" instead of "city?"
Answer: The programmer was forced to use the word "place" instead of "city" because Minnesota and New England have teams but are not cities. This may seem to be a trivial point. However, it is a very real problem that occurs in many instructional programs. If the computer will pull an item out of an array and insert it as a completion of an introductory statement, then this stem must logically fit all the possible endings.

Question 11: One of the question formats asks which team came first in alphabetical order. How does the computer know the answer to this question?
Answer: The 1200 sequence begins by randomly selecting a second team, by selecting Y, a second number between 1 and 28. If the second number happens to be the same as the first, then line 1205 will instruct the computer to try another number. The 1200 sequence will ask the player which city comes first in alphabetical order, and so it would

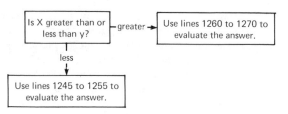

Figure 10.4. The logic of determing whether the player has chosen the team whose city comes first in alphabetical order.

make no sense to choose two teams from the same city. Therefore, line 1210 instructs the computer to try again if the names of the two cities are identical.

The programmer entered the DATA lines in alphabetical order so that when the computer reads the data in lines 260 to 280, the first city in alphabetical order will be assigned the number 1 in each of the arrays, the second city the number 2, and so on. Therefore, the computer will be able to identify City X or City Y as first in alphabetical order by simply determining whether X or Y is a lower number. This logic of evaluating the correct answer is diagrammed in Figure 10.4. The programmer decided to accept either the name of the city or the name of the team as a correct answer in lines 1245 to 1255 and 1260 to 1270.

Question 12: When the computer asks for the abbreviation of the team's state, it provides an optional list that looks like none of the other lists. Where does this list come from?
Answer: An L at line 1650 will send the computer to a subroutine that will supply a list of the abbreviations for all fifty states. The programmer wanted all fifty states to be displayed on a single screen, and this necessitated some modifications in the spelling of the state names. In addition, the programmer decided to deal with the problem of Washington D. C. by excluding it in line 1605. Other programmers might have resolved these problems differently.

Question 13: The computer asks the player to name a team from a given state. Many states have more than one team. How does the computer deal with this problem?
Answer: The programmer resolves this problem in line 1755 by directing the computer to a subroutine that states, "Your answer was correct, but give me another one." The logic of this routine is described in Figure 10.5. Notice that this is a different solution to the problem than the programmer used in the 1400 sequence (question 9), in which the computer simply accepted either answer. The programmer chose this course of action in the 1700 sequence because (1) there were many more duplications and (2) he planned to use the same pattern in baseball and in other sports, and he did not want to type in all the duplications that he was sure he would discover.

Question 14: What does the computer do if the player gives the wrong answer?
Answer: The wrong answer sequence at line 2700 adds 1 to the wrong-answer counter (W), resets the consecutive right-answer counter (R1) to zero, and tells the player what was wrong with the answer. The ON GOTO statement in line 2715 matches the corrective feedback with the appropriate question. The computer then proceeds to the 2600 sequence to see if the player wants another question.

Question 15: What does the computer do if the player gives the correct answer?
Answer: The right answer sequence at line 2900 tells the player that he or she was right, adds 1 to the right-answer counter (R), adds 1 to the consecutive right-answer counter (R1), and tells the player how many answers in a row he or she has answered

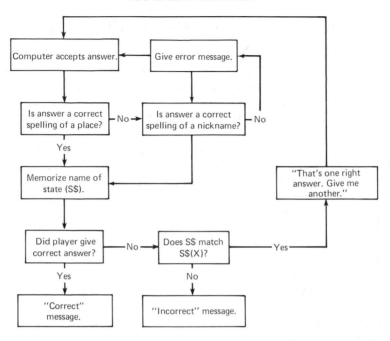

Figure 10.5. The logic of accepting answers for states that have several professional football teams.

correctly. The computer provides additional intermittent reinforcing feedback after each set of five consecutive correct answers (lines 2960 to 3010). If the player has answered correctly thirty questions in a row, the computer will declare the game to be over; otherwise the computer will go to the 2600 sequence to see if the player wants another question.

Question 16: How does the computer end the drill?
Answer: At the end of the drill, the 3100 sequence states the number of right and wrong answers during that run of the drill. The imposing formula in line 3110 simply states the player's performance as a rounded percentage of correct answers.

Question 17: What has the programmer done to promote the adaptability of the program to different numbers of teams and to different sports?
Answer: In line 220, N stands for "number of teams," which will always be 28 for the FOOTBALL game. Then why use N in such lines as 230, 260, and 330? Why not simply use 28 instead? There are two reasons. First, when the programmer was writing the program, he did not include all twenty-eight teams during the earliest stages of program writing. (Why should he enter data on twenty-eight teams when he was not even sure the program would work?) Rather, he started with a smaller number of teams and added the rest as he decided to keep the program. By using N throughout the program, he could keep it up to date by simply inserting the current number of teams in line 220. The N throughout the program automatically inserted this correct number whenever it was needed. Secondly, from the beginning the programmer was aware of the possibilities of adapting this program for use with professional baseball, college basketball, and other sports as Paul's interests changed. The programmer's plan was to duplicate the program and "edit" it by changing a few lines in it. Thus it would be much easier to alter a single N in line 220 than to find and alter the number 28 in several different lines.

Further Development of FOOTBALL

The preceding discussion suggested some changes that could be made in FOOT-BALL, and it is possible to expand FOOTBALL to ask additional questions. For example, the player's interest might be enhanced by having the computer ask him or her to identify the team on which several outstanding players play. Likewise, the computer could easily ask the player which team is located farther north, south, east, or west. It would also be possible to ask the player to identify the team that plays in the city in which a famous landmark is located or to estimate traveling time or traveling expenses between certain cities. In most cases such changes would require additional information in the DATA lines, the insertion of READ and DIM statements, and a few extra lines in the program. Such improvements are relatively easy to make once an initial set of data has been compiled and entered into the program.

If the programmer wanted to encourage the player to pay close attention to the words on the screen, it would be possible to add parallel sequences to 1200 and 1300 in order to ask the player to identify the team whose city comes latest in the alphabet or the team that is closest to the player's hometown.

It would take very little effort to convert this program to other sports. If the programmer has access to a good editing system or a word-processing language, the changes could require as little as fifteen minutes of work beyond entering new DATA lines, and it would be possible to have the child himself or herself (or other children) collect the information for these DATA lines.

Although FOOTBALL was written to fit the motivational and learning needs of one child, it should be clear that many other children in the same class or in other classes could benefit from it. Effective teachers have long known that children's outside interests can be incorporated into educational programs, and children who would consider this program a game would be able to use it to practice and "overlearn" useful skills.

Chapter 11
BEHMOD: The Universal Drill

THIS chapter will describe a program that is difficult to write but comparatively easy to adapt. At your present level of expertise, you may have trouble writing this program, but you should be able to understand major portions of it and integrate parts of it into programs of your own. In addition, you should be able to feed data into the format provided by this program to achieve your own goals. By doing so, your programs can apply educational methodologies that would be unavailable with less sophisticated programming techniques.

In its current format BEHMOD is a drill to help learners master thirty-one common terms associated with behavior modification. BEHMOD has the following characteristics:

1. It takes statements of any length up to 50 words (or 255 characters) and presents them on the screen with no wraparound problems; that is, the words are not arbitrarily split in the middle when the computer runs out of room while printing a line on the screen.
2. It furnishes immediate feedback regarding the correctness or incorrectness of each answer.
3. It keeps track of right and wrong answers and evaluates the learner's overall performance at the end of the program.
4. It supplies a list of the terms when the learner requests it. This list provides ten terms at a time in alphabetical order. After each portion of the list has been presented, the learner has the option of either entering the correct term or looking at more of the list.
5. It requires correct spelling. If a learner enters an incorrect spelling, the answer is rejected but not counted as an error. The learner receives the same question until he or she enters a correct spelling of one of the terms.
6. When a learner has answered a question on a term correctly one more time

than he or she has answered it incorrectly, that term will be removed from the item pool. This means that if the learner gets a term right on the first try, that term will not appear again in that run of the drill. But, if he or she gets the term wrong on the first try, it will appear two more times—and if the learner persists in getting it wrong, even more often.

7. When the learner gives an incorrect answer, the computer will provide as feedback both the correct term and the correct definition of the inaccurate term.

8. The program is written so that it is easy to add terms or to convert to terms related to a completely different topic.

Figures 11.1 to 11.4 show sample screens from BEHMOD. Students who are trying to study behavior modification terms find using this drill a useful way to become familiar with the terms. However, by merely changing the DATA lines, the program can easily be altered to serve as a drill on any topic in which it is important to connect a term with a definition or description of that term.

This chapter will first describe how BEHMOD accomplishes some of its functions. In addition, it will attempt to show how some of these strategies can be incorporated into other programs. This information will help you write better programs of your own, if you need to do so. In addition, it will help you know what you can expect and demand from programs you acquire from other sources.

```
QUESTION NUMBER 1:

HERE IS A DEFINITION OF A TERM.

TYPE THE CORRECT SPELLING OF THE TERM
OR TYPE L TO SEE THE LIST.

    THE STRATEGY OF REINFORCING ONE'S
    INTERIOR THOUGHTS RATHER THAN ONE'S
    EXTERNAL ACTIONS.

?COVERT REINFORCEMENT
```

```
RIGHT!

DO YOU WANT ANOTHER DEFINITION (Y/N)?

?Y
```

Figure 11.1. Typical screens from BEHMOD.

```
QUESTION NUMBER 1:

HERE IS A DEFINITION OF A TERM.

TYPE THE CORRECT SPELLING OF THE TERM
OR TYPE L TO SEE THE LIST.

     THE TITLE FOR THE PRIME MINISTER OF
     GERMANY.

?KAISER
```

```
WRONG.

CHANCELLOR IS DEFINED AS
     THE TITLE FOR THE PRIME MINISTER OF
     GERMANY.

KAISER IS DEFINED AS
     A TITLE GIVEN IN THE PAST TO THE
     EMPEROR OF GERMANY.

DO YOU WANT ANOTHER DEFINITION (Y/N)?
```

Figure 11.2. An example of BEHMOD adapted to a unit on Western European History.

Finally, this chapter will show you how to insert data into the program format to accomplish your own goals.

Our assumption is that most readers can profit greatly from this chapter without understanding BEHMOD in detail. The topics are clearly identified so that individual readers can examine those parts which are of greatest interest to them.

```
QUESTION NUMBER 1:

HERE IS A DEFINITION OF A TERM.

TYPE THE CORRECT SPELLING OF THE TERM
OR TYPE L TO SEE THE LIST.

     TWO EQUATIONS IN A SYSTEM WHICH ARE
     EQUIVALENT.

?DEPENDENT EQUATIONS
```

Figure 11.3. An example of BEHMOD adapted to a unit of analytic geometry.

```
QUESTION NUMBER 1:

HERE IS A DEFINITION OF A TERM.

TYPE THE CORRECT SPELLING
OF THE TERM
OR TYPE L TO SEE THE LIST.

ANY ONE OF A GROUP OF CONDITIONS
AFFECTING CONTROL OF THE MOTOR
SYSTEM DUE TO LESIONS IN VARIOUS
PARTS OF THE BRAIN.

?CEREBRAL PALSY
```

Figure 11.4. An example of BEHMOD adapted to a unit on special education.

The BEHMOD Program

Figure 11.5 provides a listing of BEHMOD, which is written for an Apple computer, and Figure 11.6 diagrams the overall strategy. Although BEHMOD appears to be a very complex program, the basic task of BEHMOD (stating a definition and asking for the corresponding term) is actually extremely simple. The complexities arise from attempts to make the program user friendly—by making the words appear on the screen without breaking them up at the wrong points, by allowing the learner to view the list of terms and enter the correct answer in the middle of the list, by withdrawing items from the item pool after the learner appears to have digested them, by providing corrective feedback, and so on. In other words, BEHMOD is complex because providing this degree of user friendliness is a complex task. BEHMOD is typical of good instructional programs. Easy and convenient use by the learner requires patient and often difficult work by the programmer.

How BEHMOD Does What It Does

This section will raise questions about what happens in BEHMOD. Each question identifies a specific topic. Some questions may be so easy that they appear to have obvious answers. Others may appear so complex that you will feel overwhelmed. You may wish to avoid both complicated and obvious questions and instead zero in on those questions which you feel are both understandable and profitable.

Question 1: How does the computer "memorize" the terms and definitions?
   Answer: The DIM statements at lines 70 and 80 reserve space for the arrays which will be used throughout the program. Then, in lines 90 to 110 the computer memorizes the terms and definitions. Note that the programmer has made T$(I) stand for "term" and D$(I) for "definition" or "description."

Question 2: Once the computer has memorized the terms and statements, how does it select a definition to put on the screen?
   Answer: At line 170 the computer selects a random number between 1 and the limit

```
10   REM   WRITTEN BY ED VOCKELL
12   REM   SEPTEMBER, 1982
14   REM   ALL RIGHTS RESERVED
15   REM   *** THE FOLLOWING LINES PRESENT A TITLE SCREEN
16   HOME
18   PRINT : PRINT : PRINT
20   PRINT   TAB(7);"BEHAVIOR MODIFICATION TERMS"
22   PRINT : PRINT   TAB(19);"BY"
24   PRINT : PRINT   TAB(12);"EDWARD VOCKELL"
26   PRINT : PRINT   TAB(10);"(ALL RIGHTS RESERVED)"
27   PRINT : PRINT
28   PRINT : PRINT "ARE YOU READY TO START (PRESS RETURN)";
30   INPUT Z$
31   REM   *** THE FOLLOWING LINES INITIALIZE THE RANDOM NUMBER
     GENERATOR
32   LET Y =  PEEK(78) + 256 *  PEEK(79)
34   LET X =  RND(-Y)
40   HOME
45   REM   *** PAUSE ROUTINE (TO KEEP SCREEN FROM GOING BLANK)
50   GOSUB 1240
55   REM   *** THE FOLLOWING LINE SETS THE NUMBER OF TERMS AND
     DEFINITIONS
60   LET N = 31
70   DIM T$(N + 10),D$(N),U(N)
80   DIM Y$(50)
90   FOR I = 1 TO N
95   REM   *** READ LOOP
100  READ T$(I),D$(I)
110  NEXT I
120  FOR I = 1 TO N
130  LET U(I) = 1
140  NEXT I
150  HOME
160  PRINT "QUESTION NUMBER ";R + W + 1;":": PRINT
165  REM   *** THE FOLLOWING LINE SELECTS A TERM AT RANDOM
170  LET X =  INT(RND(1) * N) + 1
180  LET T = 3
185  LET S = T
189  REM   *** THE FOLLOWING LINE CHECKS TO SEE IF THE TERM IS
     STILL IN THE ITEM POOL
190  IF U(X) < 1 THEN 170
200  LET Y$ = D$(X)
205  REM   *** THE FOLLOWING SUBROUTINE BREAKS THE DEFINITION
     DOWN INTO ITS COMPONENT WORDS
210  GOSUB 400
220  PRINT "HERE IS A DEFINITION OF A TERM."
230  PRINT : PRINT "TYPE THE CORRECT SPELLING OF THE TERM"
240  PRINT "OR TYPE L TO SEE THE LIST."
250  PRINT
255  REM   *** THE FOLLOWING SUBROUTINE PUTS THE WORDS OF THE
     DEFINITION ONTO THE SCREEN WITH NO WRAPAROUND PROBLEMS
260  GOSUB 830
270  PRINT : INPUT A$: HOME
275  REM   *** THE 950 SUBROUTINE SUPPLIES THE LIST IF IT IS
     REQUESTED
280  IF A$ = "L" THEN 950
285  REM   *** THE FOLLOWING SUBROUTINE CHECKS TO SEE IF THE
     RESPONSE IS A CORRECT SPELLING OF ONE OF THE TERMS
290  GOSUB 1110
295  REM   *** IF THERE WAS A MISSPELLING THE FOLLOWING LINE
     REROUTES THE PROGRAM TO RESTATE THE QUESTION
300  IF E = 1 THEN E = 0: GOTO 250
310  IF A$ = T$(X) THEN  GOSUB 570: GOTO 330
320  GOSUB 680
330  PRINT : PRINT "DO YOU WANT ANOTHER DEFINITION (Y/N)?":
     PRINT
340  INPUT R$: HOME
350  IF R$ = "Y" THEN 160
360  IF R$ = "N" THEN 1210
370  PRINT "ANSWER Y FOR YES OR N FOR NO, PLEASE."
380  GOTO 330
```

Figure 11.5. The listing of BEHMOD (written for the Apple).

```
390   REM  **** THE FOLLOWING ROUTINE BREAKS THE DEFINITION DOWN
      INTO WORDS.
400   LET K = 1
410   FOR I = 1 TO 50
420   LET L = 0
430   FOR J = K TO  LEN(Y$)
440   LET K = J
450   IF  MID$(Y$,J,1) = " " THEN  GOSUB 530: GOTO 490
460   LET L = L + 1
470   NEXT J
480   GOTO 500
490   NEXT I
500   GOSUB 530
510   LET L2 = I
520   RETURN
530   LET Y$(I) =  MID$(Y$,J - L,L)
540 K = K + 1
550   RETURN
560   REM  **** RIGHT ANSWER ROUTINE
570   PRINT "RIGHT!"
580 R = R + 1
590   REM  **** THE FOLLOWING LINES CHECK TO SEE IF THERE ARE
      ANY MORE QUESTIONS TO ASK.
600   LET U(X) = U(X) - 1
610   FOR I = 1 TO N
620   IF U(I) > 0 THEN 660
630   NEXT I
640   PRINT : PRINT "YOU'VE ANSWERED ALL THE QUESTIONS."
650   GOTO 1210
660   RETURN
670   REM  **** WRONG ANSWER ROUTINE
680   PRINT "WRONG."
690 W = W + 1
695   REM  *** THE FOLLOWING LINE CAUSES THE TERM (WHICH THE
      LEARNER GOT WRONG) TO STAY IN THE ITEM POOL LONGER.
700   LET U(X) = U(X) + 1
710   PRINT : PRINT T$(X);" IS DEFINED AS"
720   LET T = 2
730   PRINT  TAB(2);
740   GOSUB 830
750   PRINT
760   REM  **** THE FOLLOWING LINES GIVE THE CORRECT DEFINITION
      FOR THE LEARNER'S INCORRECT TERM.
770   PRINT S$;" IS DEFINED AS"
780   LET T = 2
790   LET Y$ = S1$
800   PRINT  TAB(2);
810   GOSUB 400: GOSUB 830
820   RETURN
830   REM  **** PRINT ROUTINE
840   FOR I = 1 TO L2
850   LET S =  LEN(Y$(I)) + S
860   IF S > 38 THEN  PRINT : PRINT  TAB(T);: LET S = T +
    LEN(Y$(I))
865   PRINT  TAB(T);
870   PRINT Y$(I);
890   PRINT " ";
900   LET S = S + 1
910   NEXT I
920   PRINT
925   LET S = T
930   RETURN
940   REM  **** LIST ROUTINE
950   LET K2 = 1: LET A$ = ""
960   IF K2 > N THEN 220
970   FOR I = K2 TO K2 + 9
980   PRINT T$(I)
990   NEXT I
1000  LET K2 = K2 + 10
1010  PRINT
1020  PRINT "ENTER THE CORRECT SPELLING."
```

Figure 11.5. The listing of BEHMOD (written for the Apple). (Continued.)

```
1030   IF K2 < N THEN  PRINT "OR PUSH THE RETURN KEY": PRINT "TO
       SEE MORE OF THE LIST."
1040   PRINT : GOSUB 830
1050   PRINT
1060   INPUT A$
1070   HOME
1080   IF A$ = "" THEN 960
1090   GOTO 280
1100   REM  **** SPELLING CORRECTION ROUTINE
1110   FOR I = 1 TO N
1120   IF A$ = T$(I) THEN 1180
1130   NEXT I
1140   PRINT A$
1150   PRINT "IS NOT THE CORRECT SPELLING OF ANY TERM."
1160   PRINT : PRINT "TRY AGAIN OR TYPE L TO SEE THE LIST."
1170   LET E = 1: RETURN
1180   LET S$ = T$(I)
1190   LET S1$ = D$(I)
1200   RETURN
1210   PRINT : PRINT "YOU GOT ";R;" RIGHT OUT OF ";R + W;"."
1220   PRINT : PRINT "THAT'S " INT((R / (R + W) + .005) * 100);"
       PERCENT."
1230   END
1240   PRINT : PRINT : PRINT : PRINT : PRINT
1250   PRINT  TAB(10);"ONE MOMENT PLEASE
1260   RETURN
5000   DATA    ARTIFICIAL REINFORCEMENT,REINFORCEMENT IN WHICH
       THERE IS NO OBVIOUS OR NATURAL CONNECTION BETWEEN THE
       REINFORCER AND THE BEHAVIOR PERFORMED TO OBTAIN THE
       REINFORCER.
5010   DATA    COUNTERCONDITIONING,THE ELIMINATION OR ALTERATION
       OF A CONDITIONED REFLEX THROUGH CLASSICAL CONDITIONING
       PROCEDURES.
5020   DATA    CONTINUOUS REINFORCEMENT,THE STRATEGY OF
       REINFORCING EVERY CORRECT PERFORMANCE OF A DESIRED BEHAVIOR.
5030   DATA    COVERT REINFORCEMENT,THE STRATEGY OF REINFORCING
       ONE'S INTERIOR THOUGHTS RATHER THAN ONE'S EXTERNAL ACTIONS.
5040   DATA    DRL,ABBREVIATION TO DESCRIBE STRATEGY OF TEACHING
       A PERSON A BEHAVIOR AT A MUCH LOWER RATE RATHER
       THAN ELIMINATING IT COMPLETELY.
5050   DATA    DRO,ABBREVIATION TO DESCRIBE STRATEGY OF
       REINFORCING ABSOLUTELY ANY BEHAVIOR OTHER THAN THE ONE
       TARGETED FOR ELIMINATION.
5060   DATA    DISCRIMINATION,LEARNING TO PERFORM A RESPONSE IN
       DESIGNATED SITUATIONS BUT NOT IN OTHERS.
5070   DATA    EXTINCTION,THE ELIMINATION OF A BEHAVIOR BY
       SYSTEMATICALLY WITHHOLDING THE REINFORCERS WHICH PREVIOUSLY
       MAINTAINED THAT BEHAVIOR.
5080   DATA    FEEDBACK,INFORMATION REGARDING THE CORRECTNESS OR
       INCORRECTNESS OF ONE'S BEHAVIOR.
5090   DATA    GENERALIZATION,LEARNING TO PERFORM A BEHAVIOR IN
       AN INCREASINGLY WIDER VARIETY OF APPROPRIATE SITUATIONS.
5100   DATA    INTERMITTENT REINFORCEMENT,THE STRATEGY OF
       REINFORCING CORRECT BEHAVIORS ON AN IRREGULAR BASIS RATHER
       THAN REINFORCING EVERY CORRECT PERFORMANCE.
5110   DATA    NATURAL REINFORCEMENT,REINFORCEMENT IN WHICH THERE
       IS A NATURAL AND OBVIOUS CONNECTION BETWEEN A REINFORCER AND
       THE BEHAVIOR PERFORMED IN ORDER TO GAIN THAT REINFORCER.
5120   DATA    NEGATIVE PRACTICE,A FORM OF PUNISHMENT WHICH
       REQUIRES A PERSON TO PERFORM A PREVIOUSLY ENJOYABLKE
       BEHAVIOR TO THE POINT WHERE THAT BEHAVIOR BECOMES SEVERELY
       UNPEASANT.
5130   DATA    NEGATIVE REINFORCEMENT,A TECHNIAL TERM FOR TYPE II
       OR TYPE III REINFORCEMENT.
5140   DATA    OVERCORRECTION,THE FORM OF PUNISHMENT WHICH
       REQUIRES A PERSON TO ENGAGE IN A PATTERN OF BEHAVIOR WHICH
       LOGICALLY CORRECTS A MISBEHAVIOR TO SUCH A DEGREE THAT THIS
       CORRECTIVE ACTION BECOMES SEVERELY UNPLEASANT.
5150   DATA    POSITIVE REINFORCEMENT,A TECHNICAL TERM FOR TYPE I
       REINFORCEMENT.
5160   DATA    PUNISHMENT,THE CONTINGENT PRESENTATION OF AN
       AVERSIVE SITUATION.
```

Figure 11.5. The listing of BEHMOD (written for the Apple). (Continued.)

```
5170  DATA    REINFORCEMENT,THE CONTINGENT PRESENTATION OF A
      PLEASANT SITUATION.
5180  DATA    RESPONSE COST,THE REMOVAL OF TOKENS IN A TOKEN
      REINFORCEMENT PROGRAM.
5190  DATA    SATIATION,THE ELIMINATION OF A BEHAVIOR BY LETTING
      THE BEHAVIOR CONTINUE UNTIL IT LOSES ITS REINFORCING VALUE.
5200  DATA    SHAPING,THE STRATEGY OF REINFORCING SMALL STEPS IN
      THE DIRECTION OF THE ULTIMATELY DESIRED BEHAVIOR.
5210  DATA    SUPERSTITIOUS REINFORCEMENT,THE STRATEGY OF
      REINFORCING EVERY ATTEMPT AT A BEHAVIOR (WHETHER IT IS
      CORRECT OR NOT).
5220  DATA    SYSTEMATIC DESENSITIZATION,THE ELIMINATION OF A
      CONDITIONED FEAR THROUGH A PROCESS OF GRADUAL INTRODUCTION
      TO THE FEARED OBJECT OR SITUATION.
5230  DATA    TIME OUT,THE STRATEGY OF REMOVING A PERSON FROM AN
      ENJOYABLE ACTIVITY FOR A CERTAIN PERIOD OF TIME.
5240  DATA    TOKEN REINFORCEMENT,THE STRATEGY OF USING A SET OF
      TEMPORARY REINFORCERS WHICH ARE LATER TURNED IN FOR BACKUP
      REINFORCERS.
5250  DATA    TYPE I PUNISHMENT,THE CONTINGENT PRESENTATION OF AN
      AVERSIVE STIMULUS.
5260  DATA    TYPE II PUNISHMENT,THE CONTINGENT REMOVAL OF A
      PLEASANT STIMULUS.
5270  DATA    TYPE III PUNISHMENT,THE PRESENTATION OF A NEW
      PLEASANT STIMULUS FOLLOWED BY THE REMOVAL (OR THREATENED
      REMOVAL) OF THIS STIMULUS.
5280  DATA    TYPE I REINFORCEMENT,THE CONTINGENT PRESENTATION
      OF A PLEASANT STIMULUS.
5290  DATA    TYPE II REINFORCEMENT,THE CONTINGENT REMOVAL OF AN
      UNPLEASANT SITUATION.
5300  DATA    TYPE III REINFORCEMENT,THE CONTINGENT AVOIDANCE OF
      A FUTURE UNPLEASANT SITUATION.
```

Figure 11.5. The listing of BEHMOD (written for the Apple). (Continued.)

established in line 60. In the present case, the computer selects a number at random between 1 and 31.

Question 3: How does the computer know which term is the right answer for the definition it will print on the screen?

Answer: Assuming that the DATA lines have been entered in the appropriate order, the random number (X) chosen in line 170 can be used to match a definition with a term; that is, Definition D$(X) will always be the correct definition of Term T$(X).

Question 4: How does the message "One Moment Please" get on the screen while the computer is reading the data?

Answer: Line 50 sends the computer to a subroutine at line 1240. The computer follows this sequence:

Make the screen go blank (line 40).
Put "One Moment Please" on the screen (line 1250).
Read the data (lines 90 to 110).
Make the screen go blank again (line 150).
Continue with the program (line 160).

This message keeps the screen from remaining blank while the computer reads the data. Because the computer reads so rapidly, for a set of thirty-one terms and definitions this message may be unnecessary. But if the program were much longer, a learner might be confused if the screen simply went blank or if nothing at all happened for several seconds. It is always a good idea to have the computer respond immediately to the user's input, by indicating that the computer is preparing itself to accept another input or to respond.

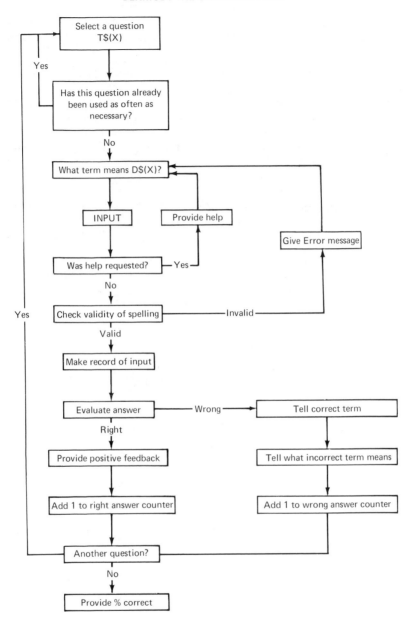

Figure 11.6. The overall logic of BEHMOD.

Question 5: How does the computer know what question number to print at the top of the screen?

Answer: In line 160 the computer prints R + W + 1. The number of right plus wrong answers is a good definition of how many questions the learner has answered; and so R + W + 1 is a good definition of the current question number. Many learners do not care how many questions they have answered, but others like to monitor their own progress. Learners can either pay attention to or ignore this information, and so there is no harm in providing it. (The information may also be of interest to teachers who are loosely monitoring learners while they work at the computers.)

Question 6: The computer withdraws each item from the item pool as soon as it has been answered correctly one more time than it has been answered incorrectly. How does it accomplish this?

Answer: At lines 120 to 140 the computer sets the value of each item in the "U" Array to 1. U stands for "use" and indicates how often each term will be used in the drill. At the beginning of the drill, the plan is to use each term only once *unless* the learner gets the term wrong. If a learner gets a term wrong, then the corresponding value of U(X) will increase, whereas a correct response will reduce the corresponding value of U(X). When U(X) drops below 1, the term corresponding to U(X) will drop out of the item pool. The logic of the Use Array is shown in Figure 11.7.

At line 190, the computer checks to see if the term that it plans to use as the correct answer—T$(X)—still belongs in the pool of acceptable items. If the value of U(X) has fallen below 1, the computer is directed to return to line 170 and get a new random number.

The computer "thinks longer" on its later questions than it did on its earlier items, because as the run of the program progresses it becomes harder for the computer to find a new random number that has not already been used. On its first question, any value of

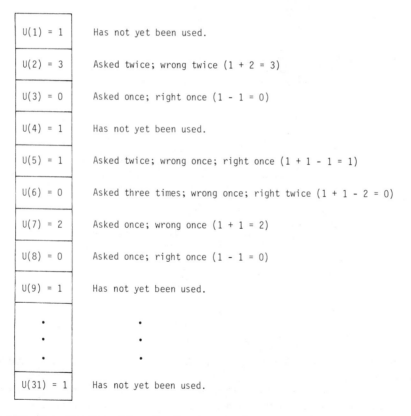

U(1) = 1	Has not yet been used.
U(2) = 3	Asked twice; wrong twice (1 + 2 = 3)
U(3) = 0	Asked once; right once (1 - 1 = 0)
U(4) = 1	Has not yet been used.
U(5) = 1	Asked twice; wrong once; right once (1 + 1 - 1 = 1)
U(6) = 0	Asked three times; wrong once; right twice (1 + 1 - 2 = 0)
U(7) = 2	Asked once; wrong once (1 + 1 = 2)
U(8) = 0	Asked once; right once (1 - 1 = 0)
U(9) = 1	Has not yet been used.
.	.
.	.
.	.
U(31) = 1	Has not yet been used.

Figure 11.7. An explanation of how the Use Array works. Items 3, 6, and 8 will not be used again during the current run of the drill. All the other items shown in the figure may be used at least one more time.

X will be acceptable, but by the thirtieth question the computer may have to reject a hundred random numbers at line 190 before it comes up with one that it is allowed to use.

Question 7: How does the computer print the definitions without any words being arbitrarily cut in two parts when the computer reaches the side of the screen?

Answer: This is the most complex part of the program. The computer accomplishes this "wraparound procedure" with two major subroutines. It is not necessary to understand these subroutines to understand and apply the program, and so only a brief description will be provided here.

First, the computer takes the definition it has selected—D$(X)—and converts it to Y$ in line 200. It does this (believe it or not) in order to make the subroutine beginning at line 1000 simpler. There is a second reason for converting D$(X) to Y$. This strategy for stringing definitions onto a screen with a nice wraparound is one of the modules outlined in Appendix C. Rather than reinventing the strategy, the programmer was able to "lift" it and "plug it into" his program. Because the existing module used the variable Y$, it is much easier to plug it in by using line 200 as an "adapter" than to alter every Y$ in the module.

Next, the subroutine at lines 400 to 530 takes the overall definition and breaks it down into its separate words. The logic is diagrammed in Figure 11.8.

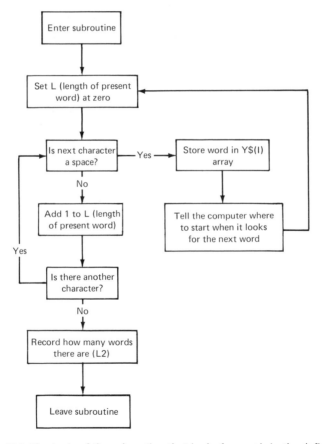

Figure 11.8. The logic of the subroutine that looks for words in the definition.

Once the computer has broken the string down into its component words, the next major subroutine writes the definition of the term on the screen. This happens in lines 220 to 270. The logic of this subroutine is diagrammed in Figure 11.9.

Before the computer prints any word on the screen, it first checks in line 860 how long the line would be if the next word in its storage were printed on that line. This program was written for an Apple computer with a screen able to hold forty letters, and the programmer wanted a little room to spare in the right margin. Therefore, he decided that if the new word caused the length of the line to exceed the limit of thirty-eight, the new word would not go on the present line but would go on the next line instead. So if the word fits on the line, it will be printed on the current screen line, and the size of

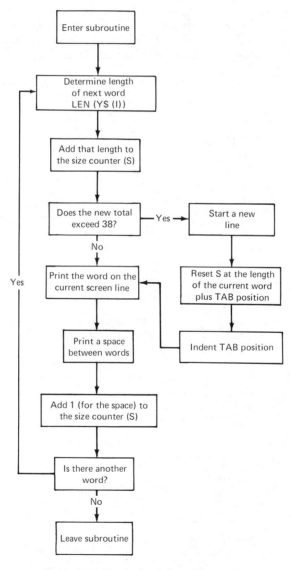

Figure 11.9. The logic of the print routine.

the S counter will increase accordingly. Otherwise it will print the word on the next line.

Finally, after it finishes this FOR/NEXT loop, line 930 sends the computer back to the main program, where the computer will wait at line 270 for the learner's response.

Question 8: How does the computer provide the list of terms?

Answer: If the learner responds with an "L" in line 270, then line 280 sends the computer to the 950 subroutine. The list is presented in a manner similar to that in CAPS and FOOTBALL in previous chapters.

Question 9: When the list goes on for several screens, the computer permits the learner to answer in the middle of a list rather than waiting for the entire list. How is this possible?

Answer: The computer sets A$ to a blank space in line 950. Later (at line 1060) the learner will respond after seeing part of the list. The computer will examine this input (line 1080) to see if the learner entered a response or merely wants to see more of the list. Because line 950 set A$ as a blank space, the computer will interpret anything other than a simple stroke of the return key (a blank) as an attempt at an answer, and line 1090 will therefore send the computer back to the main program to evaluate that answer. If the answer is blank (the return key alone), the computer will return to line 960 to continue with the list of terms. This combination of lines permits the learner to respond as soon as he or she recognizes the correct term in the list, rather than waiting until several additional and unnecessary lines of the list have been displayed. The logic of this procedure is explained in Figure 11.10.

Question 10: The computer accepts only correct spellings of the terms as appropriate answers. How does it accomplish this?

Answer: In line 1100 the computer starts through a loop that will examine all thirty-one terms unless it is interrupted. The only way such an interruption can occur is if the learner's answer (A$) matches one of the terms in line 1120. If there is such a match, the computer will go to line 1180 and eventually will continue with the program at line 300. If there is no match, the computer will set the value of E to 1 to indicate that there has been an error, will state that the learner's answer was not one of the words on the list (lines 1140 to 1160), and will go back to line 250 to restate the question. Note that "correct spelling" is operationally defined as "entering a word that matches one of the terms on the list." This is an inaccurate definition of spelling perfection. But the programmer decided that this imperfect approach was better than permitting learners to be diagnosed as wrong simply because they had made a typing error.

Question 11: How does the computer provide feedback for correct answers?

Answer: In line 310 the computer compares the learner's answer with the correct answer, and if they match, the computer will go to the correct subroutine at line 570. Line 570 provides feedback to the learner; line 580 adds 1 to the right answer counter (R); and line 600 reduces the corresponding U(X) by 1. Then lines 610 to 630 check to see if any of the U(I) values (Figure 11.7) are still above zero. (In other words, the computer checks to see if there are any questions left to ask.) If the computer finds a U(I) that is greater than zero, the computer will return to the main program and ask if the learner would like another question. On the other hand, if all the U(I) values have reached zero, the computer will state that there are no more questions and will go into the exit routine at line 1210.

Question 12: What does the computer do if the learner gives the wrong answer?

Answer: By the time the computer reaches line 320, it has verified (1) that the learner has not requested a list, (2) that the learner's response is a correct spelling, and (3) that

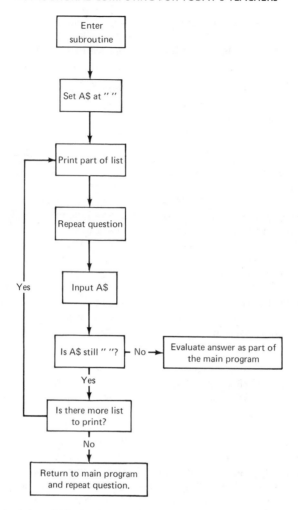

Figure 11.10. The logic by which the computer is able to accept a response in the middle of the list routine.

the response does not match the correct answer. The only remaining possibility, therefore, is that the answer was wrong; and so without further ado, the computer will go to the wrong answer subroutine at line 680. At line 680 the computer notifies the learner that the answer is wrong. Then line 690 adds 1 to the wrong answer counter (W). Next, line 700 adds one to U(X), which means that the term will remain in the item pool a little longer than had previously been scheduled. Next, the computer gives the correct answer in lines 710 through 740.

Question 13: If the learner gives a correct spelling of a wrong answer, the computer is actually able to "recognize" this wrong answer and provide the correct definition of it. How does the computer accomplish this recognition and feedback?
Answer: Lines 1180 and 1190 enable the computer to store the learner's response and the corresponding definition for that term. If the answer is correct, the computer will never do anything with this information. But if the learner's response is incorrect, this stored information will be used to provide feedback regarding the specific inaccuracy.

The logic by which the computer incorporates this "recognition" into the spelling correction routine is shown in Figure 11.11.

In line 770, the computer prints the (incorrect) term that it had recognized. In line 790, it inserts the definition of this incorrect term into the Y$ string. In line 810, the computer breaks down this new Y$ string into its component words and displays them on the screen. Notice the quality of the feedback that the computer has provided. The learner has entered one term, mistakenly thinking that this was a correct term. It is safe to assume that the learner will be motivated at this time to see the difference between his or her term and the correct term. Lines 770 through 810 offer exactly the information the learner needs in order to make this comparison. Finally, the computer returns to the main program to see if the learner wants another question.

Question 14: How often can the learner request another question?

Answer: As often as the learner answers yes when the computer asks if he or she would like another question. The computer will continue to ask this question as long as at least one of the U(I) values is above 0.

Question 15: The percentage of correct answers is always correctly rounded. How does this happen?

Answer: Line 1220 rounds off the proportion of correct responses and converts this to a percentage. For example, if a learner got two out of three answers correct, the computer would add 0.005 to 0.666666667, would multiply the result by 100, and then would drop everything after the decimal point. The result would be 67, and the computer would insert this before the word *percent.*

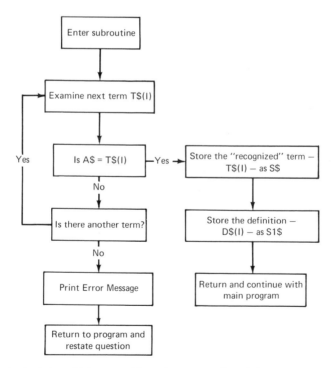

Figure 11.11. The logic by which recognition of a term and its definition are incorporated into the spelling correction routine.

Adapting the Program to Your Own Needs

This program is extremely flexible. In almost any area of learning, there are terms with which learners must become familiar in order to make intelligent use of the subject matter. In most cases, terms and definitions from such fields can be fed into the BEHMOD format to provide a very useful drill. Instructors can make this adaptation by following the guidelines presented in this section. It is not necessary to understand the complexities of the program or to do anything very complicated.

Figure 11.12 shows an example of an adaptation of this program to a home economics unit dealing with fabrics. Figure 11.13 shows part of a program applying BEHMOD to a review of terminology in a middle school science class. To make these adaptations, the programmers merely made minor changes within the framework of the BEHMOD program shown in Figure 11.5.

To adapt the program to a new set of terms and definitions, two main steps are necessary.

First, the programmer must add the new terms and definitions in the proper

```
QUESTION 1:

HERE IS A DEFINITION OF A TERM.
TYPE THE CORRECT SPELLING OF THE TERM
OR TYPE L TO SEE THE LIST OF TERMS.

NEEDLEWORK CONSISTING OF THE
INTERLOCKING OF LOOPED STITCHES
FORMED WITH A SINGLE THREAD AND
A HOOKED NEEDLE.

?
```

Figure 11.12. An adaptation of BEHMOD to teach a unit on fabrics in a home economics class.

```
QUESTION NUMBER 4:

HERE IS A DEFINITION OF A TERM.

TYPE THE CORRECT SPELLING
OF THE TERM
OR TYPE L TO SEE THE LIST.

  THE COLORED PART OF THE EYE.

?
```

Figure 11.13. An adaptation of BEHMOD to teach a unit on plant life in a junior high school science class.

```
QUESTION 1:

HERE IS A BRIEF SEQUENCE OF BEHAVIOR.
TYPE THE NAME OF THE TERM WHICH
BEST DESCRIBES THIS SEQUENCE,
OR TYPE L TO SEE THE LIST OF TERMS.

JOHN HAS BEEN READING COMIC BOOKS
INSTEAD OF DOING HIS HOMEWORK.  HIS
MOTHER JUST LETS HIM DO THIS FOR AN
HOUR.  EVENTUALLY, JOHN GETS TIRED OF
READING COMIC BOOKS AND STARTS TO DO
HIS HOMEWORK.  WHAT STRATEGY DID HIS
MOTHER USE TO GET JOHN TO STOP READING
COMIC BOOKS?

? EXTINCTION
```

Figure 11.14. An adaptation of BEHMOD to deal with the application of terms, rather than the mere recognition of these terms.

format. This information is added in the DATA lines at the end of the program. Each DATA line contains a term followed by a comma and then the definition of the term. There are no commas in any of the definitions, because the computer would interpret a comma as an indication that the definition was completed and would regard what came after the comma as if it were the next term. (If it were necessary to use a comma in the definition, the programmer would simply put the entire definition inside quotation marks. The computer would then not respond to the comma as a data separator.) This pattern of entering data terms and definitions on DATA lines must be followed if the program is expected to use these words correctly, as the program is presently written. Had the program been written differently, then it might be necessary to use a different format to enter the data.

Second, the programmer must change the value of N in line 60. N indicates the

```
WRONG.  THE ANSWER WAS SATIATION, NOT EXTINCTION.

SATIATION REFERS TO LETTING A BEHAVIOR
CONTINUE UNTIL THAT BEHAVIOR LOSES ITS
REINFORCING VALUE.

EXTINCTION REFERS TO WITHHOLDING THE
REINFORCERS WHICH PREVIOUSLY MAINTAINED
A BEHAVIOR.

TYPE R TO REPEAT THE ANECDOTE AGAIN.
TYPE Y TO GET ANOTHER QUESTION.
TYPE N TO QUIT.

?
```

Figure 11.15. The feedback provided for the error in Figure 11.14.

number of terms and definitions in the drill. Using a variable allows the programmer to change the number of terms and definitions, simply by adding more DATA lines in the proper order and changing the value of N. Without line 60, increasing the number of terms would require changes in lines 70, 90, 120, 170, and elsewhere. If the programmer had to find each of these places to change a number, there would be a good chance that he or she would miss some of them.

Note that it is not necessary to adhere rigidly to the exact phraseology found in the original program. For example, a programmer could write "incidents" instead of definitions within the same format. To the extent that the programmer would wish to alter the original format, greater modifications in BEHMOD may become necessary. Figures 11.14 and 11.15 show the outcome of an adaptation of BEHMOD. Note that the drill now focuses on the application of the concepts from the original drill, rather than on mere recall or understanding of the terms.

Concluding Comment

BEHMOD is an example of a complex but flexible program. It contains a large number of user-friendly and pedagogically effective strategies. It is useful to examine these strategies in order to understand how instructional programs carry out many of the functions they accomplish. This understanding will help you know what you can expect from other instructional programs. In addition, it is possible to take a program like BEHMOD and adapt it to a wide variety of instructional uses.

Chapter 12
Getting Started in Instructional Computing

YOU don't have to be around teachers very long these days to hear conversations like this:

Teacher A: Our school board wants to buy some microcomputers for our school.

Teacher B: No kidding. We've been talking about getting a few ourselves. Hey, did you know that Mountain View Middle School bought a whole laboratory full of micros at the end of last year?

Teacher A: That sounds great. What are they doing with them?

Teacher B: A teacher I know there said that the computers had been unpacked and set up but that no formal program had been developed. But I think a couple of the math teachers have been playing around with them.

Teacher A: I wonder how long it will take them to set up a program to use them?

Teacher B: It's hard to tell. Shouldn't they have decided things like that before they bought them?

Or if you hang around with school principals, you have probably heard conversations like this:

Principal A: Our board bought my elementary school five Ajax microcomputers.

Principal B: Have your teachers been trained to use them yet?

Principal A: No, but we hope to get started at that in the near future.

Principal B: Do you know what kind of applications you want to use them for?

Principal A: Probably drill and practice. I have a stack of catalogues with drills and programmed instruction on computers. But I haven't really had time to look at them very closely.

Principal B: Why did your district pick this time to buy the computers?

Principal A: Oh, some parents and teachers thought it would be a good idea. I'm not too sure myself. Do you want to hear what I think is the real reason?

Principal B: Sure, I think I can handle it.

Principal A: The business agent got a good deal on them. Four for the price of five.

Conversations like these are common and reflect an ambivalence. Teachers and administrators are perceptive enough to recognize that the current technology must be important for the educational process, but at the same time they are uncertain exactly what they should do about putting computers into their classrooms. The confusion is compounded by the overwhelming variety of hardware and software on the market and the constant barrage of new developments.

This chapter will attempt to bring some order into this chaos by asking and answering a number of important questions.

Questions and Answers

Question 1: What steps should I take to get instructional computing started in my classroom or school?

Answer: There are three important steps:

> Step A: First, find out what sorts of things the microcomputer can help you do in your particular field. Determine whether the available software will help you do a better job at something you already do now or will add important elements (such as expanded problem-solving opportunities) to your instructional capabilities.

> Step B: Talk to other teachers who have used microcomputers, and visit a classroom where the type of computing you are interested in is used. Ask questions and observe students. See how flexible the software is and ask yourself whether you could use this effectively in your classroom.

> Step C: Make a list of applications and assign them priorities. Show the list to the person in your school or school system who will buy the equipment and programs. Point out your particular needs in terms of hardware, software, costs, and the environment in which you wish to make your applications.

Question 2: What do you mean when you say that the software should be flexible?

Answer: Flexibility refers to the ease with which a computer or software package can be adapted for use in a variety of settings. With minor adaptations, flexible materials can be used with more than a single set of objectives and in different instructional settings (for example, individual, small groups, or large groups). Software documentation that suggests alternative uses is an indicator that the publisher is concerned about flexibility.

Question 3: After I've submitted my list, do I just sit back and wait for the equipment to arrive?

Answer: No! Work with the committee or individual that is writing the bid specifications so that the micros that meet your real needs are actually purchased. Be assertive and be nearby when the decisions regarding the type, number, placement, software, and allocation of time on the computers are made. If you know what you want to accomplish and how you want to do it, you will probably be chosen to participate in the early stages of computer introduction.

Question 4: What if the school board will not buy computers for my classroom?

Answer: If you are the sponsor of a science or similar club, encourage the students in your school to raise money to buy a computer. The enthusiastic use by students of computers elsewhere during lunch periods and after school provides a very powerful inducement to school authorities to investigate the issue. If you are an elementary school teacher, get the support of the PTA or a similar organization. Have someone demonstrate the computer to the members of the organization and show them that microcomputers are not mere toys. Many such organizations are able to buy a computer or software packages. If people are convinced that their school needs microcomputers, the computers will usually find a way into the school.

Question 5: Should my school develop a "twenty-year plan" for instructional computing?

Answer: Probably not. Things are happening too fast in this area. Attend conferences, consult instructional computing specialists, read professional journals, and talk to dealers. Decide what you want to do in the next year. At the same time, make tentative plans for the second year. Update the second year's plans as you obtain feedback from the first year's experience.

Question 6: Which microcomputer is the best?

Answer: There is no one answer to this question. Microcomputers vary in their attributes, such as cost, useable memory, ease of use, visual display characteristics, type of graphics, keyboard arrangement, available languages and courseware, quality of word processing and editing, level of documentation, expandability, and quality of maintenance service. Design your own system based on a careful assessment of your needs and the likelihood that a given combination of hardware and software can help you meet these needs. When more than one computer system fills the bill, then base your decision on cost, vendor support, and reputation. Remember that the cheapest system is not necessarily the most cost effective. A detailed model for the selection of a microcomputer system appears in Figure 12.1.

Question 7: With costs dropping and materials improving, wouldn't it be better to wait a while to make any purchases?

Answer: That's a valid point. But if you push it too far, you will never get started in instructional computing. If you wait, you will probably get more real value per dollar, but you may skip a generation of students while you procrastinate. No matter how long you wait, within the foreseeable future it will always be true that if you wait a little longer you will get more sophisticated machines for the money you spend. A better solution is to buy equipment with an eye on expandability so that you can change your system to meet your needs and to take advantage of new opportunities. When you hear that new developments are likely to make current hardware and software obsolete, it does not mean that you will have to throw away the old equipment; it merely means that the materials have improved. But your old equipment will still serve the purpose it was designed to serve.

Question 8: Should my school buy many inexpensive computers or a few more expensive computers?

Answer: Sorry, no firm answer. It depends on how you want to get started and what applications receive high priority in your plan. For example, if your goal is to help junior high students get involved in BASIC programming and if you already have a large number of TV monitors and cassette recorders, then it might be good to buy ten $500 microcomputers. On the other hand, if you are an elementary school teacher starting from scratch, with the goal of using LOGO to help young learners develop logical thinking in elementary science and mathematics, then you would probably have to spend $10,000 to set up a laboratory of five $2,000 computers (at current costs).

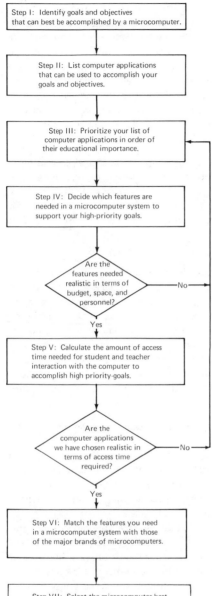

Figure 12.1. A microcomputer system selection model. In the model, *applications* refer to the drill and practice, tutorials, problem solving, programming, simulation, testing, computer literacy, word processing, data analysis, and computer-managed instruction. *Features* refer to such things as amount of usable memory in RAM, lowercase characters, sound, color and graphics capability, availability of multiple languages, an easy-to-use editor, disk drive(s), printers, and speech devices.

Question 9: What if I want my computers to serve both purposes?

Answer: If you want to buy computers to serve both of the preceding purposes, you will have to make a difficult decision: (1) to buy five expensive computers and five inexpensive computers, with the result that there would be minor variations that would confuse students and that the five inexpensive computers would probably never be able to support LOGO; (2) to scrape up an extra $10,000 and buy ten of the more expensive computers, with the result that all ten could be used for either purpose but that the money would have to be diverted from some other project; or (3) to buy only the five more expensive computers and require the BASIC students to "double up," with the result that each student will have less access to a computer. There are, of course, other possibilities. The point is that these decisions can be made only by the persons who can examine the specific situation. The number of computers you purchase will limit the breadth and speed of your implementation.

Question 10: Will I need one computer per student?

Answer: For some applications, yes. But in many cases several students can share a computer. Even in a programming course, for example, half the students can be at their desks planning or debugging their programs while the others are seated at the terminals. In many other applications, such as using computers to simulate laboratory experiments in a science class, it appears to be quite effective to have students work in groups of three to five rather than individually. In such cases, it is not impossible to have thirty-five students share a single computer. No known application requires that each student be seated at a single terminal all day. With appropriate scheduling, the computers can be spread throughout the classroom or throughout the school.

Question 11: People tell me that most of the courseware for elementary and secondary schools is junk! If that is the case, why not wait until better courseware is developed?

Answer: There is a large amount of inferior courseware on the market, but there is also a growing supply of excellent software, and major publishers are committing substantial resources to its development. Don't cheat the current students out of some useful educational opportunities, but start now with software in which you have confidence because you have carefully selected it and integrated it into your curriculum. Incidentally, the quality of software varies greatly for different types of computers. Some of the least expensive computers have few educational software programs, which are seldom of high quality. Keep this in mind when you buy a microcomputer.

Question 12: What is the most important thing to look for in educational software and courseware?

Answer: Look for software that meets your present and future instructional goals and objectives. Know what you want to do with it. Outstanding computer courseware is useless to you unless it is directed toward your needs. A plan for evaluating courseware for local school use appears in Figure 12.2.

Question 13: All right. Suppose that I have determined that a set of courseware will meet some of my needs. How do I know that it is good courseware?

Answer: Good courseware has accurate content that is appropriate for the intended grade level. It should be well constructed and interesting to the students and free of sexual, racial, or other biases. It should be well documented—accompanied by a thorough teacher's guide written in plain English. Specific courseware characteristics are outlined in the Courseware Evaluation Form in Figure 12.3.

Another key characteristic is the appropriateness of the computer as a vehicle for meeting the objectives of the software package. Some computer programs merely provide electronic workbooks. Better programs require the computer to do something that

Step I: Using courseware reviews and vendor descriptions, order for preview several programs that you feel might be appropriate for your instructional goals and microcomputing equipment. At the same time, request from the vendor the names of schools in your area that are using the programs you plan to review. If the program really interests you, don't hesitate to visit the school.

Step II: When the courseware arrives, load it on your computer. RUN through it briefly to establish in your mind the structure of the program.

Step III: Now run the courseware as one of your best students would, making few mistakes and "testing the limits of the program." Lack of program flexibility might be diserned at this point! Better yet, get one of your students to try it out for you. Note the behavior of the student as he or she tries it out.

Step IV: Run the program again, making intentional mistakes and errors. If an erroneous response results in the task being presented to you again, make repeated incorrect responses of the same type and of different types. Make typing errors, errors in input form (letters instead of numbers and vice-versa), and errors in following directions. Technical programming problems will be revealed when you do this.

Step V: Use a courseware evaluation form to help you describe the positive and negative attributes of the courseware under review. One suggested form is contained in Figure 12.3. Others, some more comprehensive, are available from a variety of sources (see Appendix F). Your responses to the questions should be based on your own experiences and observations with the courseware. When you finish, you should compare your responses with published reviews and vendor's claims.

Step VI: Make a decision, remembering the following:

1. There is no such thing as the "perfect" courseware package. If you respond positively to most of your criteria, then consider purchase seriously. The most important criterion, of course, is whether the courseware meets your instructional goals and can be easily integrated into the instructional flow.

2. Make sure that you have all the peripherals needed (printer, light pen, disk drives, sufficient memory) to run the courseware to its full potential. If you don't, include their cost in the total cost of the package.

3. Try to work out with the vendor an equitable lease or purchase agreement. You need one copy of the program for each CPU (microprocessor). Most publishers will reduce the fee or cost for multiple copies authorized or produced by them. Don't make unauthorized duplicates of programs in an attempt to reduce costs.

4. Make sure you have carefully considered student-access time, class schedules, physical space, and organization needed to take advantage of the courseware. If major problems are seen in this area, it may not be realistic to purchase the courseware at this time.

Figure 12.2. A courseware evaluation plan.

Courseware Evaluation Form

COURSEWARE CHARACTERISTICS	EVALUATION	
	Yes	No

I. TEACHING

    A. Does the courseware meet my instructional objectives?

    B. Are the objectives of the courseware package clearly stated or easily discernable?

    C. Is the courseware content accurate and appropriate for the intended users?

    D. Are the instructional strategies appropriate for the objectives of the courseware?

    E. Is the reading level appropriate for the intended users?

    F. Are the prerequisite skills needed by students to complete successfully the courseware objectives clearly identified?

    G. Is the content free of ethnic, racial, sexual, or political bias?

II. LEARNING

    A. Is the student put in the role of an active learner?

    B. Does the courseware motivate the student to learn?

    C. Is the courseware flexible; does it accommodate to a range of ability levels, a range of difficulty with respect to a given student or the class of skills or concepts involved?

    D. Are lesson goals and objectives made clear to students?

    E. Is feedback timely and effective?

    F. Can students control the pace and sequence of instruction?

    G. Can the amount of time needed to complete courseware goals be realistically allocated to the individual or group of student users?

III. TECHNICAL PRESENTATION

    A. Are courseware instructions clear to the student?

    B. Does the courseware ensure that a student user knows when and in what form input is needed?

    C. Do graphics, sound, and color, if used, enhance the package's instructional intent?

    D. Is the display of each "page" or frame uncluttered and easy to read?

    E. Does the program allow students to review previous frames or pages?

    F. Is the order of presentation logical and well organized?

    G. Does the courseware run reliably?

IV. TEACHER CONCERNS

    A. Is record keeping possible (either within the program or on work sheets)?

    B. Does the teacher have to monitor student use closely?

    C. Can the program be easily modified by the teacher to meet instructional goals?

    D. Is courseware documentation clear and comprehensive?

    E. Are support materials (teacher guide, operating instructions, organizational plans) clear and comprehensive?

Figure 12.3. A courseware evaluation form for teachers.

cannot easily be done through other classroom modalities. Good software also lets the students control the pace of instruction and gives them constructive feedback.

In many cases, you will be able to use the software exactly as it is written. But in other cases, you will need to modify the program to meet your own educational needs. If this is so, then a "good" program will also permit easy modification, and you should incorporate the cost in time of making such modifications into your selection of courseware.

Question 14: What sort of information should I expect from the vendor to prove that the courseware is effective?

Answer: You should be permitted to examine the package on approval. We recommend not dealing with a vendor who will not permit this. You should also request and review field test data to evaluate the package's effectiveness. In addition, you may wish to visit a location that uses the proposed package. At a minimum, you should consult software and courseware evaluations in reputable professional publications.

Question 15: Are there some situations in which I should avoid using the computer?

Answer: Certainly! It's easy to program a computer to simulate the movement of a pendulum for elementary school students, but why bother? The students can easily get more benefit by swinging their own, easily constructed pendulum. There are several computer applications that actually make instruction more costly and less effective. Avoid them.

Question 16: Is it important to evaluate the effectiveness of a computer application?

Answer: You bet your Horace Mann it is! The computer is an expensive piece of equipment, and it is a waste of money to use it without knowing whether it is producing the desired results. Without evaluation, how would you be able to improve next year's instruction? Make plans ahead of time to assess the students' attitudes, achievement, and problem-solving skills at the beginning and the end of the implementation.

Question 17: Should I be able to examine the listing of a program before I buy it?

Answer: If you have met the objectives of this book, you will certainly benefit from looking at the listing. However, in many cases, the program is delivered to you in a format that prevents you from being able to see the listing. Should this inability to examine the program be enough to keep you from purchasing it? In many cases, the answer is yes, especially if there is another vendor who will let you see the listing. In other cases, you may want the software badly enough to waive your right to see the listing.

Question 18: Why is it that some programs are delivered in a format that prevents me from examining the listing?

Answer: A programmer or vendor who writes or sells instructional programs has a valid interest in keeping users from obtaining the programs without paying for them. On the other hand, the buyer or user has an equally valid interest in being able to modify a program to make it more useful for a specific instructional application. One of the major problems in software dissemination is to balance the needs and interests of these two groups.

One of the most common ways for programmers and vendors to protect their interests is to disseminate the programs in such a way that the user is unable to do anything but run the program. This is accomplished by putting special instructions into the program that cause it automatically to start running when the system is "booted" and automatically to "reboot" any time the program is interrupted (as by pushing a break or reset key). A user who cannot even interrupt a program will find it impossible to make a copy of that program through the normal process of loading it and saving it. In addition, the vendor is able to build into the software the strategies for disabling the copy routines that normally enable a user to reproduce a disk or cassette. Such strategies effectively prevent the duplication of programs by persons who have no right to them. At the same time, however, these strategies make it impossible for the purchaser either to see or modify a program in order to make it more useful for a particular instructional application.

We find this concealment of the contents of commercially available instructional programs to be unfortunate and inappropriate. By reading a book such as this, educators can understand the principles of BASIC programming and evaluate the merits of a program by examining its listing. And so in order to take full advantage of the computer's ability to individualize instruction, it is often necessary to modify commercially available programs. Persons who have read this textbook, for example, can add or delete data, alter feedback, insert record-keeping and timing strategies, allow the computer to recognize the names of students in order to individualize instruction, and perform several other operations to improve existing programs.

In addition, because disks and cassettes can be easily damaged if they are mishandled, it is proper that a purchaser be able to make a back-up copy to replace a disk that is accidentally destroyed. For these reasons, it seems to be unwise to buy programs that prohibit one from evaluating and modifying the programs. Programmers and vendors should be encouraged to find ways to protect their own interests without violating those of the purchasers and users.

In some cases, however, a person who buys a computer program will not have the need (or ability) to make alterations in that program. Some users may have no intention whatsoever of interrupting the program to see its listing. This is especially likely in "advanced" applications, such as word-processing and graphics packages purchased by non-experts. In such cases, it makes greater sense to buy a program that one cannot examine or modify.

Question 19: Are there any major pitfalls to watch for in software selection?
Answer: In your evaluation of software, beware of gimmicks. We use the term *gimmicks* to refer to strategies (often graphic strategies) that give the impression that the computer is accomplishing a great deal, when in fact it is doing very little.

For example, we have recently reviewed a program in which a multicolored, fire-breathing dragon appeared on the screen to "devour" a learner who missed a designated number of vocabulary words, whereas the successful learner reached a pot of gold as a reward. When we showed this program to our graduate students, they were initially impressed by the quality of the program: the dragon looked neat, the game sounded like fun, and the words were worth learning. But the students who field tested the program all concluded that it was not as good as it had first appeared. They cited three shortcomings: (1) learners found it more interesting to lose the game (that is, to get the words wrong) than to win, because they found the dragon to be more interesting than the pot of gold; (2) every time the learners reran the program, they received exactly the same set of words; and (3) it was impossible to interrupt and modify the program. In addition, the program worked for only a single set of fifteen words, which were always presented in the same order. But anyone who has met the objectives of this textbook could easily modify that program to provide a random assortment and a much wider variety of words.

Question 20: But what if the gimmicks work? Then shouldn't we take advantage of them?
Answer: In the preceding example we are not arguing that using the multicolored, fire-breathing dragon is bad. Rather, we are saying that this particular application was very weak. It gave an impression of quality, whereas very little actually happened, and therefore we classified it as a gimmick. At the same time, it is important to note that children *did* find the dragon to be motivating. If a dragon could be incorporated into a program

in such a way as to eliminate the weaknesses, then we would regard it as a motivational device rather than a gimmick.

Likewise, we recently reviewed a series of programs that taught students to recognize important musical terms. Correct answers were accompanied by computerized musical feedback. This feedback was interesting, but obviously unrelated to the program's objectives. The vendors were selling this programs for approximately $200. Our judgment was that any music teacher who knew the subject matter and had mastered the objectives of this textbook could produce a better program (without the gimmick) within a couple of hours of programming time, by using BEHMOD as a model.

Our criticism of gimmicks is not intended to obviate the need for legitimate graphic displays. Undoubtedly, many weak programs can be made more interesting by introducing graphic displays. Rather, our advice is to beware of gimmicks that serve no useful educational purpose or that actually detract from a program while simply inflating the price that vendor is able to charge for that program.

Question 21: Can you give me some examples of more effective use of motivational graphics?

Answer: Good idea. For several years we let our students run a program that simulates a trip by pioneers across the Oregon Trail. The unadorned version of the program simply presented information on the screen and provided feedback to the students as they made their preparations and carried out their simulated trip from Kansas City to Oregon. Recently we found a newer version of this same program which presented a map of Oregon that displayed a picture of a covered wagon traveling toward Oregon as the students made decisions regarding appropriate courses of action. In addition, when hostile parties attacked the wagon train, they were graphically represented as coming across the screen, and the student was required to "shoot" at them by pressing keys on the keyboard. This clearly attracted the students' attention. The moving targets on the screen could have degenerated into a gimmick, but we found that they did not; rather, they served as a gamelike motivational strategy to make the students want to learn to do better at the program.

In addition, we recently examined a program that taught gifted elementary school children some of the fundamentals of genetics by showing them certain characteristics of mated birds, which were graphically represented on the screen, and having them predict the color of subsequent generations of birds. The birds were well done (much as the dragon in the other program), and the students found that they were fun to look at. We judged this to be a motivational use of graphics rather than a gimmick, because the strategy obviously enhanced instruction. The children found it much easier to learn by looking at concretely pictured birds than by studying the abstract symbols often used to represent genetic characteristics.

Finally, programs are beginning to appear that introduce educational elements into some of the arcade games. For example, a student might be required to perform some mathematical computation in order to overcome an alien spacecraft. In one sense, this use of arcade games is obviously a gimmick, but it contains a useful motivational strategy, as the arcade strategies require students to perform educational tasks that they probably would not otherwise. The best approach, therefore, is not to ignore the computer's graphic and gamelike capabilities but, rather, to combine them with educational goals.

Question 22: Should I expect to write most of my own programs, or should I be able to buy what I need?

Answer: Our feeling is that you should know how to write programs but that most of your programs should be written by someone else. If you know how to write programs and are able to do so on your system, you can effectively adapt programs to your individual needs and more intelligently choose the software to use to meet your educational goals.

Question 23: If I plan to write or modify programs, will this influence my choice of computers?

Answer: Yes. In addition to differing in the dialect of BASIC that they support, the various models and brands of computing systems will also differ in their error messages and editing capabilities, that is, the ease with which it is possible to identify language errors as they occur and modify lines in a program. The degree of help offered by different systems varies considerably.

For example, assume that you have misspelled the word *print* in the following line

```
10 PRIT ''WHAT IS YOUR NAME'';
```

On three different systems you might get the following three different messages:

```
SYNTAX ERROR
SYNTAX ERROR IN LINE 10
SYNTAX ERROR IN LINE 10; PRIT UNRECOGNIZED
```

A highly skilled programmer can, of course, find and correct the error with any of these three error messages. But a less experienced programmer will need more help from the computer to discover it. In addition to differing in degree of specificity, various operating systems also differ in the time at which they give feedback. For example, most operating systems do not notify a programmer of a language error until the program tries to run that line of the program. On some systems, however, the computer identifies many language errors as soon as the programmer enters such an error into the computer. In selecting a computer system, it is important to identify these differences in the operating system and to weigh the cost of the computer system against its benefits.

Question 24: What if I buy a computer with a weak editing system and later decide that I want to do some programming or modifying on my own? Am I stuck with my original investment?

Answer: Probably not—unless you bought a computer with really weak support. Relative deficiencies in the operating or editing systems of a computer can often be overcome by buying additional software. For example, it is possible to purchase the LDOS operating system from Apparat to replace the normal TRSDOS operating system on the TRS-80. The LDOS system gives more precise error messages and makes it easier to edit than does the TRSDOS system. (The LDOS also provides other advantages over the TRSDOS.) Likewise, the Apple disk-operating system does not permit the programmer automatically to renumber lines in a program, but the software package called the Apple Tool Kit does provide this option as one of its features. Editing capability can also be greatly expanded by applying word-processing software (such as Electric Pencil on the TRS-80 or Screenwriter II on the Apple) to the editing process.

Such upgrading of your computer's abilities can greatly increase its effectiveness. But you should keep in mind such additional costs when determining the comparative values of different brands and models of computers. If a given computer costs $500 less than another but will require an expenditure of an additional $700 to make it equally usable, then the first computer is not actually less expensive than the second.

Question 25: What do you mean by a "weak editing system"?

Answer: Once an error has been identified, it is necessary to correct that error. Various computers differ considerably in the ease with which they enable the programmer or user to correct errors or modify lines in a program. For example, the second of the lines below contains an error:

```
100 LET X=INT((R/(R+W)+.005)*100)
100 LET X=INT(R/(R+W)+.005)*100)
```

There is a missing parenthesis after the word INT. One way to correct this error is to retype the whole line, and on some systems this is the only editing capacity available to the programmer. More sophisticated systems, however, permit the programmer simply to insert the parenthesis in the correct place. Beside being annoying, the more primitive editing system has the additional disadvantage that the programmer is likely to make a new error while retyping a complicated line to correct the original error.

Question 26: To what extent can computer programs written for one brand or model of computer be transferred to another?

Answer: In one respect, BASIC programs are not very transferable at all, but in another respect they are extremely transferable. Programs are not easily transferable in that it is usually impossible to take a tape or disk directly from one computer and simply insert it into another system. This is because the format in which programs are stored for use on the one computer may differ considerably from the way in which programs must be formatted for use on the other computer. It is this format, rather than any idiosyncrasy of the program itself, that makes it initially impossible to transfer programs from one computer to another.

But in a different respect, BASIC computer programs are very versatile. By this we mean that if you were to sit down at the terminals and type the same lines of a computer program into two different computers, it is likely that the program would run on both systems. This is because the BASIC language has fairly universal characteristics, and therefore the commands needed to run a program on one computer are likely to be the same as those needed to run the same program on a computer of a different brand.

Question 27: Are you saying that BASIC is identical on all computers?

Answer: Different computers are likely to support different "dialects" of BASIC, which means that there will be slight differences in the commands necessary to carry out specific programming strategies. These differences are usually so slight that a person who has learned to program on one machine will be able to transfer to another machine with little or no difficulty. The term *dialect* suggests a useful metaphor: the different versions of BASIC differ from one another much as British English differs from American English, rather than as English differs from Japanese or Russian. The differences are greatest with regard to graphic commands, whereas the dialects are similar with regard to the ordinary nongraphic commands discussed in this book.

Table 12.1 summarizes some of the important dialect differences among the versions of BASIC supported by the TRS-80 and the Apple computers. As this table indicates, a person transferring a program from a TRS-80 to an Apple would have to change CLS to HOME each time that the command occurred in the program. The failure to make this change would result in an error message every time the term CLS appeared. Likewise, the term ELSE would have to be eliminated from the Apple version of the program. This would be accomplished by changing a single line TRS-80 command into sets of two Apple commands, as shown in Figure 12.4. A person who intends to adapt programs to

Table 12.1. Some Examples of Dialect Differences
Between the TRS-80 and Apple Versions of BASIC

TRS-80	*Apple*
CLS	HOME
IF . . . GOSUB	IF . . . THEN GOSUB
IF . . . PRINT	IF . . . THEN PRINT
LET X = RND (5)	LET X = INT (RND (1) * 5 + 1)
ELSE	(See Figure 12.1)

TRS-80 version:

```
100 IF X=2 THEN 200 ELSE 300
```

Apple version:

```
100 IF X=2 THEN 200
110 GOTO 300
```

Figure 12.4. Conversion of a TRS-80 ELSE command to the Apple equivalent.

several models of computers would be well advised to write (or buy) programs that contain as few dialectic discrepancies as possible. A person who may later wish to adapt the program to an Apple could avoid using the ELSE command when writing a TRS-80 program. Such a program would be more easily transferable to the Apple computer. The program would still run (perhaps somewhat less efficiently, but this would not even be perceptible to the ordinary user) on the TRS-80. A programmer who wishes to transfer materials to different models or systems should look for such areas of compatibility when developing programs. In most instances, other computers (such as Pet, Texas Instruments, and Atari) will present similar differences in dialect.

In most cases, therefore, programs written for one computer can be transferred to another computer. To a large extent, the incompatibility results from differences in format, which can be overcome by simply typing a command from one computer directly into the other computer. Astute readers will realize that if this process can be carried out by a human being at the computer terminal, it should also be possible to have the computer do it. Such computerized reformatting is, in fact, possible, and programs to make such transfers are available. One of the difficulties, however, is that there is a wide range of computers and that this "translation service" requires a unique translator program for each combination of machines. Therefore, although it is possible to overcome the differences in format, such differences are likely to present a serious obstacle to the easy transfer of programs in the forseeable future.

Question 28: How should these differences in dialect influence my choice of computers?
Answer: Educational users need an ample supply of instructional programs to meet their needs. These programs may be purchased, or they may be developed by the user. Therefore, when selecting a computer, you will wish to ascertain that either commercially available programs are readily available or that the BASIC language supported by the computer lends itself to effective programming at your level of expertise.

The versatility of transferring programs from one machine to another should be kept in mind when purchasing both hardware and software for instructional use. For example, one brand of computer might be inexpensive but might support a relatively "weak" dialect of BASIC. This means that some of the functions that accompany the "stronger" dialects would be impossible to perform on that model. (For example, the MID$ or the ELSE command might be omitted.) In addition to making your programming efforts more difficult, such weaknesses in the dialect make it necessary to reprogram major portions of any program containing such commands. This problem may arise in the very program that you would like to transfer to your system.

Appendix A
Glossary

THIS glossary briefly defines many of the terms commonly used in educational and instructional computing. When possible, citations are given to chapters in the text that discuss or give examples of the terms. In addition to many of the terms used in this book, this glossary contains terms that were not used here but that readers are likely to encounter in their reading or in their use of computers. Words in a definition that are *underlined* are themselves defined in this glossary.

Access Time. The time lapse between the moment a request is made (e.g., a command is entered at the keyboard) and the moment at which the computer begins to deliver its response.

Acoustic Coupler. A modem device that connects a terminal or microcomputer (which would be acting as a smart terminal) by an ordinary telephone line to another computer. The other computer is usually a central minicomputer or mainframe computer.

Address. The location in the computer's memory in which one byte of memory is stored. Every piece of information processed by the computer has at least a temporary address. It is not necessary to know the addresses in order to use the computer to run programs.

Algorithm. A step-by-step procedure or set of directions for performing a task or solving a problem: a logical decision rule. Good computer programs usually use algorithms. A flowchart is a schematic representation (diagram) of an algorithm.

Alphanumeric Characters. Any of the digits, letters, or symbols on a computer's keyboard. The term is often used to distinguish the subclass of symbols referred to as numeric symbols, which are restricted to those that can be treated mathematically (see discussion in Chapter 6).

APL. Stands for A Programming Language, a high-level mathematically oriented language that uses symbols for complex mathematical or string operations. APL uses the computer much more efficiently than BASIC does, but it is not as user friendly.

Apple. A widely used microcomputer developed by the Apple Corporation.

Applesoft. The version of BASIC that is used by many Apple computers.

Application Program. A computer program written by a programmer for some specific purpose. CAI programs, electronic video games, and test-scoring programs all are examples of application programs.

Arithmetic Logic Unit (ALU). The electronic circuits in the Central Processing Unit (CPU) that control the computer's mathematical and logical operations.

Arithmetic Operations. In most computers, these include addition, subtraction, multiplication, division, exponentiation, and combinations of these. In addition, most computers include a number of mathematical functions (such as sine, cosine, and square root) which make it simpler to perform common mathematical calculations (see also Hierarchy of Operations). Arithmetic operations are normally distinguished from string manipulations.

Array. A storage area in the computer that contains variables with certain common characteristics. In BASIC, arrays are symbolized as subscripted variables—for example, A$(5)—and are often established with DIM statements (see discussion in Chapter 7).

Artificial Intelligence (AI). AI uses the computer to simulate processes that occur in the human mind. Its purpose is to develop better computers and to come to a better understanding of the human mind. AI has been used in chess playing, medical diagnosis, and war games. LOGO is an attempt to apply some aspects of AI to educational settings.

ASCII Code. The *A*merican *S*tandard *C*ode for *I*nformation *I*nterchange, a method that uses seven bits of computer memory space to store symbols (such as letters or numbers) in the computer's memory. The ASCII code is often distinguished from more compressed codes that may be unique to various computers. At times it may be useful to store information in the ASCII code (or at least to know in which code the information is stored) in order to perform certain operations on a program or on the data in the program.

Assembly Language. A low-level language of the computer which is highly symbolic. Although they use the computer's time more efficiently than high-level languages do, assembly languages are much too tedious for the typical programmer to use, and therefore higher level languages such as APL, BASIC, FORTRAN, LOGO, and Pascal were designed for such use. Before execution, the assembly language is translated into an even more abstract and enigmatic set of symbols called machine language (consisting entirely of ones and zeros) which the computer actually executes. These translations are performed by the computer and take place in very small amounts of time.

ATARI. A widely available microcomputer developed by the Atari Corporation.

Authoring Language. A language, such as PILOT, which is exceptionally user friendly, and so users (such as teachers) who wish to develop software or courseware may do so without learning a complete computer language (such as BASIC). This increased user friendliness is usually accompanied by a loss of flexibility which would be present in the complete computer language.

Auxiliary Storage Device. A device such as a magnetic tape or disk on which programs or data can be stored away from the actual main computer. Auxiliary storage devices permit the programmer to save programs for later use. It is the availability of auxiliary storage devices that enables users to acquire programs from other programmers. The appropriate use of auxiliary storage devices greatly expands the computer's capacity.

Back-up File. A copy of a current file (for example, of a current program) that can be used if the active copy is accidentally destroyed. Both programmers and program users should have back-up copies of all important files.

BASIC. Stands for "Beginners All-purpose Symbolic Instruction Code," a relatively easily learned programming language that handles both string and numeric functions. It is extremely popular and therefore runs on almost all computers to which educators are likely to have access.

Batch Processing. An approach to data processing that requires one computer job (program) at a time to be submitted in a job queue. Programs either are run in the order submitted or are assigned a priority according to some decision rule. When cards were the primary medium of input, most jobs were submitted through batch processing. Many applications (such as statistical analysis, report cards, and payrolls) are still suited to batch processing. However, most educational settings require an interaction between a learner and the computer, and so these applications are much better suited to interactive processing.

Binary Numbers. Numbers in the base-2 system of counting. In this system, only the digits zero and 1 are used to represent all the numbers, letters, and symbols programmed into the computer. The computer uses binary numbers because 1 can represent the presence of an electric current in a given circuit, and zero the absence of current; thus electronic impulses can achieve "meaning." A computer strings together these bits (*binary digits*) in machine code to perform all mathematical and logical operations and to represent string characters. The computer's machine language consists of binary digits.

Bit. The smallest unit of information that the computer can "know." One bit is one binary digit, either zero or 1. A bit can be thought of as an on-off switch: "on" representing "yes" or "true" and "off" representing "no" or "false." Computer programs at their most basic level are nothing but a series of these on-off switches strung together in certain patterns. A programmer does not need to understand this process to program in high-level languages.

Boot. The act of starting or restarting the computer's disk-operating system. On most systems, the system is booted by pushing a special button or issuing a special command.

Branching Program. A type of programmed instruction in which the learner is "branched" to another point in the program based on his or her response to a preceding question. Branching instruction is more tailored to the individual needs of learners than is linear programming, but it is also more time-consuming to write (see discussion in Chapter 2).

Buffer. A storage area in the computer in which information is temporarily stored. For example, input data may be stored temporarily in a buffer before they are actually used by the computer, or output data may be temporarily stored in a buffer before they are actually transmitted to a printing device.

Bug. A mistake or problem in the operation of a program. A hardware bug is a problem in the operation or design of the computer itself or in its peripheral devices. A software bug is a mistake or problem in the logic of the computer program (see discussion in Chapter 9).

Bus or Buss. A connective device in the computer that transfers information from one part of the computer to another.

Byte. A combination of 8 *bits* that makes up the smallest unit for a particular memory storage location in a computer. The number of bytes that a computer is capable of storing often indicates its "memory size." Thus a computer with 48,000 bytes of storage can be said to have three times as much memory space as one with 16,000 bytes has.

CAI. See Computer-Assisted Instruction.

CAL. See Computer-Assisted Learning.

Calculator. A device for performing mathematical computation and analysis. A computer can act as a calculator, and in fact it is sometimes difficult to distinguish between a programmable calculator and a computer. The computer differs from the calculator in its ability to perform logical and string functions as well as mathematical operations.

Card Reader. A device that reads the data stored on punched computer cards and transmits these data to the main computer storage. Data thus transmitted are eventually treated like those entered through any other means, for example, through the keyboard.

Cards, Punched Computer. See Computer Cards.

Cathode Ray Tube (CRT) Terminal. A computer terminal that has a televisionlike screen for displaying data and a typewriterlike keyboard for data entry and response.

CBE. See Computer-Based Education.

Central Processing Unit (CPU). That portion of the computer that takes instructions from the computer memory, determines the type and order of operations that should be carried out, and then directs their execution and output. The CPU is made up of the ALU (Arithmetic Logic Unit) and the CU (Control Unit).

Chip. A small piece of silicon capable of maintaining and systematizing electronic impulses. A silicon chip contains transistors, etchings, and other electronic components integrated into a memory or logic circuit. The chip's microscopic technology makes it possible to put into a quarter-inch piece of silicon the computing capability that required room-sized computers in the late 1960s. These chips can be used to form the CPU and other elements of the computer and are mass produced at extremely low cost.

CMI. See Computer-Managed Instruction.

COBOL. Stands for the *Common Business Oriented Language*, one of the most widely used languages in business applications. It is extremely useful for preparing payrolls, making schedules, and printing report cards. It is much less effective for such applications as interactive instructional programming or word processing.

COM. See Computer Output Microfilm.

Command Mode. When in this mode, the computer responds by executing the BASIC or other language commands when they are entered without line numbers. When commands are entered with line numbers, they are stored and then executed in the programming mode.

Commodore 64. A widely available microcomputer developed by the Commodore Corporation.

Compiler. A program that takes the source statements written in a computer language and converts them into a machine language for a particular computer. In certain applications, it may be useful to store permanently the compiled program for later use on the computer. In many cases, the program is interpreted each time it is run. This interpreting causes the program to run more slowly, as the computer must both interpret and *execute* the program's instructions. But because most instructional programs are relatively short, this initial time is usually not important. In addition, the compiled program reduces flexibility, because different compilers are used on different computers and because in order to make changes in the program it is necessary to return to the program's original (uncompiled) version. In other cases (for example, when the program is long or has numerous loops, when there are other reasons to want it to operate more rapidly, or when the user is not likely to want to make changes in the program) the use of a compiled program is quite feasible. The logic of the compiled program is exactly the same as the logic of an uncompiled program; however, it is one more step removed from the level of the user.

Computer. A device that can accept input and follow directions to perform mathematical or logical operations on that input without additional intervention by a human being. In electronic computers these operations are performed by the computer's electronic circuitry.

Computer-Assisted Instruction (CAI). At the present time there is widespread disagreement on the definition of CAI. For example, some people define CAI as consisting only of those educational applications that involve drill and practice and use other terms for the more creative applications of the computer in education. These people distinguish among CAI, CAL, CMI, and the use of simulations in instruction. In this book, we use the term CAI to refer to any application of the computer to "assist" the instructional or learning processes. Thus, any instructional use of the computer is an example of Computer-Assisted Instruction, and other terms are used to designate ways in which the computer can assist instruction.

Computer-Assisted Learning (CAL). This is a more recent term than CAI and focuses on the learner rather than on the process or device that helps the learner acquire information or skills. Because the real purpose of education is to promote learning, rather than to promote instruction, it makes sense to use a label that refers to this more important aspect. The term *instruction* refers to what the instructor must do to facilitate learning, whereas the term *learning* focuses on what the learner does while learning. When the computer is used effectively in education, therefore, the terms CAI and CAL often refer to the same educational process.

Computer-Based Education (CBE). This term is essentially a synonym for Computer-Managed Instruction (CMI).

Computer Card. A heavy piece of paper with holes punched into it to code symbols that represent bits of information that the computer can store and interpret according to instructions. Information stored on computer cards is interpreted by a card reader each time that it is necessary to make this information available to the computer's memory. Information stored on computer cards is treated like information entered from any other source (for example, magnetic tape or keyboard entry) but is entered by a card reader rather than through one of the other sources. Punched cards are much more useful for batch processing than for interactive computing, and when interactive programs are initially written on punched cards, they are often stored on a disk or tape to make them more accessible for interactive use.

Computer Language. A set of words, symbols, and rules for using these words and symbols in order to instruct the computer to carry out mathematical or logical operations. A computer language can range from the very high-level languages that are easy to understand to low-level languages that are enigmatic combinations of obscure symbols.

Computer-Managed Instruction (CMI). The use of the computer to coordinate (manage) educational activities. A CMI application might include educational drills and simulations integrated into a package or almost no usage of a computer beyond the computerized storage of information regarding a student's performance on noncomputerized activities. With CMI, the teacher (student, administrator, or parent) is able to prescribe, score, analyze, store, retrieve, and integrate information in ways that can facilitate other educational processes.

Computer Program. A set of instructions that directs the computer to perform mathematical or logical operations in a specified order so as to achieve a desired outcome.

Computer Programmers. The people who design, write, and debug the sets of instructions to be carried out by the computer for a particular purpose.

Computer System. The entire assemblage or configuration of computer hardware that operates together to carry out the work of the computer. The computer system includes such hardware as the central processing unit, the console, input devices, output devices, and auxiliary storage devices.

Computer Users. The people who use an existing program for a certain purpose. Computer programmers and computer users can be the same persons but do not need to be. In education, computer users are usually teachers, administrators, counselors, students, and various support personnel.

Computerized Testing. The computer can be used in testing at various levels. At one level, the computer can be used to score and analyze the results of a test, by using mark-sense cards or keypunching the answers from the test sheet into the computer. At a different level, the student can take a test at a computer terminal, at which the test is actually generated by the computer; the results are immediately scored, analyzed, and reported by the computer; and subsequent steps of instruction or remediation are provided by the computer.

Console Terminal. A device by which the computer operator communicates with the computer's central processing unit. On microcomputers, the cathode ray tube screen that accompanies the computer is the console unit. In larger systems (mainframes and minicomputers) the console is the one cathode ray tube screen that is reserved for use by the person responsible for operating the entire system at a given time.

CONT Statement. A BASIC command that indicates that the computer should resume a program that has been interrupted (see discussion in Chapter 9).

Control Key. A key on a computer keyboard that is pressed simultaneously with at least one other key and that gives this other key a different meaning than it would have if that key were pressed alone. Although the commands issued through the normal keys usually require that the return (or enter) key be pressed before the command is executed, in many cases the control commands are executed as soon as the keys are pressed.

Control Program. A program that is part of the computer's operating system and that provides automatic control of the computer's resources.

Control Unit. A part of the central processing unit that directs and coordinates the entire computer system.

Controls, System. See System Controls.

Core Storage. See Storage, Magnetic Core.

Counter. A variable in a program that counts the occurrence of some event. For example, a counter can count the number of right answers, the number of wrong answers, or the number of times the computer has performed a portion of a loop. Programmers often refer to this process as "incrementing a variable."

CPU. See Central Processing Unit.

CRT Terminal. See Cathode Ray Tube Terminal.

Daisy Wheel Printer. An impact-printing device that consists of rotating spokes containing embossed characters that are transferred to paper. It is called a Daisy Wheel Printer because it is round and looks like a daisy. Daisy Wheel Printers normally print more "typewriterlike" letters than do other means, such as the matrix printers, but they print more slowly.

Data. The codified collection of facts, information, or instructions that is suitable for communication, interpretation, and processing by the computer as input or output.

Data Bank. A collection of data stored on an auxiliary storage device.

Data Base. A collection of data for some purpose organized in a predefined structure. The information is entered into a data base in a highly structured format, which promotes accessibility and flexibility. Examples of computerized data bases include files of information on college programs throughout the country, census data, and extensive collections of journal citations. The term *data search* refers to retrieving information from a data base.

Data Entry. The process of putting data into a format for entering into the computer or the actual process of entering data into a computer system.

Data File. A storage area in which data are stored on an auxiliary storage device until they are read into the computer's main memory according to the instructions in a computer program.

Data Processing. The automated collection, analysis, tabulation, or other treatment of data by the computer.

Data Retrieval. The process of transferring data from an auxiliary storage unit to the computer's main memory.

DATA Statement. In BASIC, the command that provides a set of values to be entered through READ statements (see discussion in Chapter 7).

Data Storage. The process of transferring data from the computer's main memory to an auxiliary storage unit.

Debugging. The process of eliminating language and logical errors from a computer program (see discussion in Chapter 9).

Decision Rule. The statement of the logical prerequisites necessary before the computer will take action. In BASIC, decision rules are incorporated into IF/THEN Statements or their equivalents.

Delete Command. A command on some systems that requires the computer to eliminate a line from a program or that deletes a program from memory on an auxiliary storage device. All systems have strategies for performing these functions, but many use a command other than DELETE.

DIM Statement. In BASIC, the command that dimensions an array; that is, it sets aside storage space for arrays of data (see discussion in Chapter 7).

Direct Access Storage Device. An auxiliary storage device on which data can be stored and from which they can be retrieved in either a sequential or random order.

Disk Drive. A device on which a disk is mounted in order to permit the transfer of information from that disk into the computer.

Disk, Floppy. See Floppy Disk.

Disk-Operating System (DOS). A software system that manages the transfer of information and files between the disk in the disk drive and the CPU of the computer.

Disk Pack. A set of several disks mounted onto a single hub so that each of the surfaces of the disks can be easily accessed by the arms of the disk drive in order to store or retrieve data. Disk packs are used on large mainframes and minicomputers rather than on microcomputers.

Documentation. A detailed record of facts and information necessary to operate a program or to understand its logic. Documentation can be found either in a program (for example, in PRINT or REM statements) or in the printed or recorded materials that accompany a program package.

DOS. See Disk-Operating System.

Drill. The instructional strategy of requiring a learner to perform a task repeatedly in order to master the concept or principle underlying that task (see discussion in Chapter 3).

EBCDIC. Stands for the *Extended Binary Coded Decimal Interchange Code*, a widely used coding system for representing data in computer storage on auxiliary storage devices.

Editing. This term has related but separate meanings in computing. First, it can refer to the entry of any type of instruction into a program. In this sense (for example, in the initial writing of a program or in word-processing applications) the term is synonymous with writing. Second, the term can refer to an efficient process of correcting errors. For example, when a programmer finds an error in logic in a program and alters the program to correct this logical error, this is referred to as editing. Many computers have a special editing mode that enables the programmer to alter major portions of a program while retyping only a few of the symbols in them (see discussion in Chapter 9).

Editing Mode. The term given to the computer's frame of reference when it is oriented to receive instructions to alter existing lines in a program.

Electrographic Printer. A nonimpact printer that produces symbols through the use of specially coated paper. Such printers use electric or light impulses to change the chemical nature of this paper.

Electronic Mail. A system of transferring messages to people who share a common computer system, through the computer system itself rather than through an external message delivery service.

END Statement. A BASIC command that indicates the end of a computer program (see discussion in Chapter 6).

Error Trap. A strategy for identifying user errors and enabling the computer to continue without interruption after such errors.

Execution. The process during which the computer actually carries out the instructions written in the computer program.

Feedback. Information evaluating the correctness or appropriateness of a response (see discussion in Chapter 3).

File. A collection of instructions or data assembled under a common label (file name). Computer programs are examples of files, as are data files.

File Manipulation. Strategies for storing, retrieving, deleting, and altering files stored on an auxiliary storage device.

File Name. The label given to a file in the computer's main memory or on an auxiliary storage device.

File Organization. The strategies used to organize files so that they are acceptable for use by the computer.

File Security. The process of protecting files so as to avoid their accidental destruction or contamination or to prevent their use by unauthorized persons.

File Updating. The incorporation of additions, deletions, or changes into the existing files.

First-Generation Computers. Computers developed before 1959, which relied primarily on vacuum tubes.

Flexibility. The ability to use a program that has been developed in one situation (for example, on one computer) with little or no modifications in another situation.

Floppy Disk. A plastic disk (usually five to eight inches in diameter) that is coated with oxide and enclosed in a protective covering. This magnetic disk can be used to store and communicate data to and from the computer. The "floppiness" of the disk refers to the material from which it is made, but the disk does not actually flop at any time during its proper use.

Flowchart. A diagram that graphically represents the detailed steps (or decision rules) in the solution of a problem. A flowchart is a representation of an algorithm.

Flowchart Symbols. The standard symbols used to indicate the various logical steps in a flowchart.

FOR/NEXT Loop. A sequence of BASIC commands that instructs the computer to execute a specified set of commands a designated number of times (see discussion in Chapter 7).

FORTRAN. An abbreviation for "FORmula TRANslation," a high-level language used primarily by scientists, engineers, and mathematicians. It handles mathematical computations more efficiently than do languages such as COBOL or BASIC.

Frame. A single screenful of information in programmed instruction.

Friendliness. See User Friendliness.

Full-Duplex Line. A data communication line that allows data to be sent simultaneously both to and from a computer. It is distinguished from a half-duplex line.

GOSUB Statement. The BASIC command that requires the computer to deviate from its normal sequence, but to return to that sequence when it encounters a RETURN command (see discussion in Chapter 7).

GOTO Statement. The BASIC command that requires the computer to deviate from its normal rule of going to the next instruction and to go to another line instead (see discussion in Chapter 6).

Graphic Display Terminal. A CRT terminal that can display graphs and diagrams or pictures as well as words and numbers.

Graphics. Strategies for drawing diagrams or other images on an output device.

Half-Duplex Line. A communication line that permits data to be sent both to and from the computer but not in both directions simultaneously.

Hard Disk. A magnetic disk that is more solid and less portable than a floppy disk.

Hardcopy Output. Output from a computer program that is provided on paper at a printer (as opposed to the more temporary output that appears on a cathode ray tube screen).

Hexadecimal Number System. A number system used by many computers that uses the base sixteen. This means that such a system uses sixteen separate symbols (instead of ten) to represent values. A two-digit hexadecimal number represents a byte.

Hierarchy of Operations. A set of rules that governs the order in which mathematical or logical operations will be performed in a computer program (for example, adjacent multiplication is performed before adjacent addition).

High-Level Programming Language. A programming language that is relatively easy to understand but whose characteristics are far removed from the internal characteristics of the computer itself. For example, BASIC is a higher-level language than is assembly language, and assembly language is a higher-level language than is machine language.

High-Resolution Graphics. The graphic representation of output in which a diagram or picture is drawn with relatively clearly delineated (smooth) lines. This is done by breaking down the screen into more "dots" or drawing areas than is the case with low-resolution graphics.

Hollerith Code. The system of punched holes used to record data on computer cards.

IF/THEN Statement. The BASIC command that causes the computer to depart from its normal sequence of going to the next instruction if a certain condition or set of conditions is true. IF/THEN statements provide the basis for incorporating decision rules into computer programs.

Impact Printer. A printing device that produces images by striking a ribbon against a paper with some kind of hammerlike instrument. Matrix and daisy wheel printers are impact printers, whereas electrographic printers that use specially treated papers are not.

Input. Data that are entered into the computer for use or analysis. In BASIC, data can enter the program through READ or INPUT statements, from the keyboard, from cards, from disks, or from data files. Although input must necessarily have an original source outside the program itself, the computer can also generate its own input with LET statements based on previous external input.

Input Error. An error that occurs when data are converted to a machine-readable format or when the data are entered into the computer for processing.

Input/Output Error. An error that occurs when data are being transmitted to or from the computer, usually between the computer and an auxiliary storage device. For example, if a file is mislabeled or nonexistent, the computer will indicate an input/output error if it is instructed to read or write information to or from such a file.

INPUT Statement. The command that enables the computer during the run of a program to receive data from someone using the computer terminal (see discussion in Chapter 6).

Input Unites. Devices designed to permit the entry of data into the computer (for example, card readers, keyboards, and disk drives).

Inquiry. A request from the operator of a computer console or terminal for information from the computing system.

INT Statement. A BASIC command that instructs the computer to convert a decimal number to the next lowest integer. With positive numbers, this command has the effect of truncating a decimal number by dropping everything to the right of the decimal point (see discussion in Chapter 7).

Intelligent (or Smart) Terminal. A computer terminal that can process data independent of the larger computer to which it is attached. Such intelligent terminals often receive data from some other source (for example, by telephone lines) and then use their electronic capability to alter these data before transmitting them to a larger computer. Such a strategy effectively increases the larger computer's capacity by relegating to the terminal predictable or routine tasks that would otherwise consume part of the larger computer's capacity.

Interactive Processing. The use of the computer to execute commands and respond to inquiries as soon as possible after they are received. Interactive computing is distinguished from batch processing, in which several programs are entered and addressed one at a time in a certain order. In education, report cards are done by batch processing, but nearly all instructional applications use interactive processing.

Interpreter. A software or hardware machine language program that converts high-level language into a machine language that the computer can understand. This process of interpretation is performed line by line and is the main reason that high-level programs run more slowly than do machine language programs.

JCL. See Job Control Language.

Job Control Language (JCL). A system of commands that links the computer's operating system and the application programs that will be run on that system. The JCL regulates jobs being processed, programs to be executed, and the job-to-job transition within the computer. Therefore, the sequence and timing of application programs can be controlled. Note that it is possible to use the computer system effectively without understanding the intricacies of the JCL for that system.

Job Queue. The "waiting list" of programs waiting to be run on a system in which more than one job may be submitted at a time.

Keyboard Entry. The process of entering input into the computer by typing the input at a console or terminal or taking it from computer cards or magnetic disks.

Keypunching. The process in which a machine punches holes in computer cards to provide meaningful input when the cards are submitted to a card reader.

KILL Command. A command in some systems that deletes a file from storage on an auxiliary storage device (see discussion in Appendix E).

Language Error. A mistake in the way a command is expressed in a programming language. Language errors are corrected by rewriting the command, whereas logical errors are corrected by altering the logic of a series of commands (see discussion in Chapter 9).

LET Statement. The BASIC command that instructs the computer to assign numeric data to numeric variables either directly or indirectly through the execution of mathematical operations. This statement is also used to assign strings or characters to string variables (see discussion in Chapter 6).

Light Pen. A pencil-shaped device that allows data to be entered or altered by pressing the device against a CRT screen.

Linear Program. A type of programmed instruction in which all learners go through the material in exactly the same sequence.

LOAD Command. A command that instructs the computer to take a program from an auxiliary storage device and put it into the computer's main memory for current use (see discussion in Appendix E).

Logical Error. A programming error in the underlying logic of a program rather than an inaccuracy in how a line was written. A program with logical errors may run, but run incorrectly.

Logical Operations. The management of variables and loops in a computer program through logically appropriate instructions, such as IF/THEN, GOSOB, and FOR/NEXT statements.

LOGO. A very high-level computer language that is easily learned and can be used to simulate many real-life situations (see discussion in Chapter 5).

Loop. The repetition of a series of commands in a computer program (see discussion in Chapter 7).

Low-Level Programming Language. A programming language that is based on the characteristics of a particular machine. Low-level languages are highly symbolic and difficult to understand. BASIC, on the other hand, is a high-level programming language.

Low-Resolution Graphics. A graphic representation of output in which a diagram or picture is drawn with lines that look like a series of small boxes rather than clearly delineated lines. The distortion is more noticeable because the lines are diagonal or curved, as the screen is broken down into fewer drawing areas than with high-resolution graphics.

Machine Language. A series of symbols (numbers, letters, and other special configurations) that can be interpreted by the computer's electronic circuitry. These symbols cause the computer's various operations to be executed.

Magnetic Disk. A form of auxiliary storage in which data are stored on oxide-coated disks (for example, hard disks or floppy disks) which rotate inside the disk drives.

Magnetic Tape. A form of auxiliary data storage in which information is magnetically stored on tapes similar to those used in tape recorders. These magnetic tapes may be connected to the computer by devices ranging from a simple cassette recorder to a sophisticated high-speed tape mechanism.

Main Memory. Memory to which the CPU has direct access. Resident programs and variable information are found in the main memory.

Mainframe Computer. A large computer (usually costing hundreds of thousands or even millions of dollars) that is capable of processing billions of characters of data very quickly. Mainframes are usually used in education for administration or time-sharing purposes.

Maintenance. The processes of repairing the hardware when it malfunctions, purchasing consumable items (paper, ribbons, etc.), and upgrading both software and hardware when inadequacies or errors are found. In calculating the cost of a computer system or a computer application, it is important to consider its maintenance expenses.

Manual. The book of instructions that accompanies a computer or electronic device used in conjunction with the computer. It is important to examine the manuals to understand the correct use of the computer system's components. In many cases, it is necessary to consult the relevant manual to answer a question. For example, information on how to use data files will be found in the disk-operating system manual rather than in the computer manual itself. This is because data files are used only with disks, and therefore the information would not need to be in the general computer manual.

Mark-sense Cards. Computer cards on which respondents mark their answers in pencil. The marks are then interpreted electronically as one form of data entry.

Mass Storage Device. A large auxiliary storage device.

Mathematical Operations. See Arithmetic Operations.

Matrix Printer. An impact printer that forms characters by producing a series of small dots arranged in a matrix.

Memory. See Storage.

Memory, Programmable Read Only. See PROM.

Memory, Random Access. See RAM.

Memory, Read Only. See ROM.

Memory Size. The number of bytes of information that a computer or auxiliary storage device is capable of storing. The unit K is often used to represent memory size. One K consists of 1024 bytes. When comparing memory sizes, it is important to compare usable memory, that is, the memory that can be used for a particular purpose. See also Storage.

MERGE Command. A command on some computers or software packages that enables the computer to load two programs one after another without clearing the main memory. If the two programs have line numbers in common, the lines in the more recently added program will override those in the older program.

Merging Files. The process of combining two or more data or program files into a single file.

Microcomputer. A relatively inexpensive and small computer, often referred to as a personal computer. The microcomputer system usually consists of a CRT, and CPU with a keyboard, and an auxiliary storage device. Microcomputers are so named because they use microprocessors.

Microprocessor. A very small silicon chip that contains the electronic components of an entire central processor.

Microsecond. One-millionth of a second.

MID$. A BASIC command used in string manipulation. The "grammar" of the MID$ command varies on different computers.

Millisecond. One thousandth of a second.

Minicomputer. A computer whose size ranges between that of a microcomputer and that of a mainframe computer. When minicomputers are used for instructional applications, they are usually used on a time-sharing basis.

Modem. A device that receives a digital signal and transforms it into an analog signal, or vice-versa. Modems are used when the computer sends or receives information to or from some other source, such as over a telephone line. When computers use telephone lines, it is necessary to have a modem at both ends of the telephone connection.

Monitor. A cathode ray tube instrument designed to operate with a computer. The monitor has no antenna or tuner and will not "play" the normal television channels. It will take a video or audio signal directly from the computer, thereby enabling a programmer or other user (such as a learner) to observe or "monitor" input to and output from the computer. An RF modulator is necessary in order to use a normal TV set as a computer monitor.

Multiplexer. An electronic device that distributes the computer communication from a single line into several subsidiary channels for use by several separate computers. Multiplexers are widely used to put several microcomputers into a network.

Nanosecond. One-billionth of a second.

Negative Feedback. Information from the computer to the learner indicating that a response is incorrect.

Network. A system composed of several computers, terminals, and auxiliary storage devices.

Nonimpact Printer. A printer that prints letters and symbols using a process other than a hammer hitting a piece of paper. Many nonimpact printers use a specially coated paper that responds to some stimulus (such as heat) in order to make an image on the paper.

Numeric Variable. In BASIC, a variable that can be subjected to mathematical operations; in other words, a number as opposed to a string variable (see discussion in Chapter 6).

Object Program. A set of machine language instructions that results from compiling source statements written in a higher level language.

OCR (Optical Character Recognition). A strategy for reading data by scanning a location on an item (for example, a specially formatted form) entered into a reading device. The computer determines the meaning of the data by interpreting the shape that it encounters there.

Octal Number System. A number system that uses eight numeric symbols to represent values.

ON/GOSUB Statement. A BASIC command that combines several IF/THEN and GOSUB statements (see discussion in Chapter 7).

ON/GOTO Statement. A BASIC command that combines several IF/THEN statements (see discussion in Chapter 7).

Operating System. A collection of programs that allows a computer system to supervise and execute the operations in that system.

Optical Character Recognition (OCR). See OCR.

Optical Scanning Device. A device that senses data on forms and feeds them into the computer for processing.

Output. Information that is produced as a result of the computer acting upon some input. The output is transmitted to the user via some mechanism such as a CRT screen or a printer.

Output Device. A device that displays information from the computer's operations. Common output devices include the CRT, a printer, and the disk drive.

Output Error. An error that occurs when data are being transmitted from the computer to some output device, such as a CRT or a printer.

Pascal. A high-level programming language designed to make it easy to enter instructional programs in a structured fashion.

PET. A widely available microcomputer developed by the Commodore Corporation.

Plotter. A printing device that can produce diagrams or drawings as hardcopy output from a computer.

Polling. A strategy used in time-sharing applications of the computer in which each terminal in a network is examined in sequence to determine whether there are data to be sent to the main computer.

Positive Feedback. Notification by the computer that the learner has given a correct response.

PRINT Statement. The BASIC command that displays data as output on a screen or on some other output device (see discussion in Chapter 6).

Printer. A device that produces hardcopy output under the computer's control.

Printer Speed. The rate at which a computer is able to put letters, words, or lines on a page. For printers that accompany microcomputers, the printer speed is often expressed in letters (characters) per second. For larger systems, a printer speed is often expressed in lines or pages per second.

Processor Unit. The part of the computer system that stores the data and contains the electronic circuitry necessary to process these data. The processing unit consists of the central processing unit and the main computer storage.

Program. See Computer Program.

Program Documentation. See Documentation.

Program Size. The number of bytes of storage that a computer needs to run a program.

Programmed Instruction. A strategy that packages learning material into independent, sequential steps (frames). Learners go through these steps at their own pace and receive feedback after each. With an appropriately designed programmed learning package, a learner should be able to obtain positive feedback approximately 90 percent of the time. Programmed instruction may be either linear or branching (see discussion in Chapter 2).

Programming. The process of writing instructions to be executed by the computer.

Programming Languages. The software (programs) supplied as part of the computer system that instructs the computer to perform its operations. See also high-level programming languages, low-level programming languages, and machine languages.

Programming Mode. The computer is in the programming mode when there is a resident program in the main memory and that program is being executed.

PROM (Programmable Read Only Memory). A modified variation of Read Only Memory

(ROM). PROM can be read but not altered when used as a part of the computer system. It can be altered (programmed) by the user before being assembled as part of the system. It is therefore more flexible than ROM but less flexible than RAM.

Punched Card Reader. See Card Reader.

Punched Cards. See Computer Cards.

RAM (Random Access Memory). A type of data storage in which data may be read into and out of the storage area. The RAM provides the temporary storage space in which programs can be loaded in from disks and executed for a specific application. RAM is distinguished from ROM, which is not subject to modification. The RAM adds flexibility to the computer and increases its capacity by enabling it to receive into its temporary memory large amounts of data from auxiliary storage devices.

Random Access. The strategy of retrieving data from a data file without first reading previous records in that same file. This strategy is contrasted with sequential access.

READ Statement. The BASIC command that places the data listed in DATA statements into variable fields (see discussion in Chapter 7).

Record. A collection of fields related to a particular unit of information.

REM Statement. A BASIC command that enables the programmer to insert lines of documentation into a program. These lines of documentation are useful to the programmer and others who will read the programs, but they will be ignored by the computer during the execution of the program (see discussion in Appendix B).

Remote Job Entry. Putting jobs or programs into a computer system from a location remote from the computer site.

Resident Program. A program that has been loaded into the computer's main memory.

RETURN Statement. A BASIC command that signals the end of a subroutine that was entered through a GOSUB statement. When the computer encounters the RETURN statement, it returns to the next command after the pertinent GOSUB statement (see discussion in Chapter 7).

Reverse Video. The technique of highlighting characters, words, or lines on a CRT screen by reversing the color of the standard display.

RND Statement. A BASIC command that instructs the computer to select a random number (see discussion in Chapter 7 and Appendix B).

ROM (Read Only Memory). A type of storage in which data can be read from the storage but no data can be placed into it. ROM storage is therefore not subject to temporary modification in a specific run of a program. The ROM is the permanent or "hardwired" part of the computer's main memory. Because the data are permanently placed into the ROM, the ROM provides data more rapidly than does the RAM however, it lacks the flexibility of being able to accept information from the auxiliary storage for particular applications. An actual run of a computer program depends on a carefully arranged interaction of the ROM and the RAM.

RUN Statement. A statement that instructs the computer to go to the first line of a BASIC program and begin executing commands starting at that point (see discussion in Appendix E).

SAVE Command. A command that instructs the computer to take a file from its main memory and store it on an auxiliary storage device (see discussion in Appendix E).

Scrolling. The ability to move lines either up or down on a CRT screen.

Searching. The process in which files are examined to locate a certain piece of information.

Second-Generation Computers. Computers that were introduced around 1959 and contained transistorized rather than vacuum tube components.

Secondary Storage. See Auxiliary Storage Device.

Sectors. A series of individual storage areas on a magnetic disk.

Sequential Access. The strategy of retrieving data from a file, one record after another, in a predetermined sequence (as opposed to random access).

Silicon Chip. See Microprocessor.

Simulation. An artificial, structured, realistic imitation of an actual event or principle. Computerized simulations, of course, use the computer to provide these realistic settings (see discussion in Chapter 4).

Software. Programs written and stored on disk or tape for use on computers. The term is usually contrasted with hardware, which consists of the physical machinery on which these programs will be run. In recent years, as many functions that had previously been performed by software have become "hardwired" into electonic circuitry, the distinction between the two terms has become less clear.

Software, System. See System Software.

Sorting. The process of arranging data records in an appropriate sequence, for example, ascending or descending order.

Special Purpose Computer. A computer that performs a specific task and cannot easily be reprogrammed to perform a different task (for example, arcade games could be described as Special Purpose Computers).

STOP Statement. A BASIC command that signals an interruption in a BASIC program (see discussion in Chapter 9).

Storage Capacity. The number of bytes comprising the computer's main memory.

Storage, Magnetic Core. A type of internal computer storage consisting of very small ring-shaped pieces of material that can be magnetized in one of two different directions.

Storage, Main Computer. The electronic components in the main computer that can store symbols (letters of the alphabet, numbers, and special characters). Data are often transferred from auxiliary storage to main computer storage, where they are acted upon by the central processing unit. The main computer storage is part of the computer's RAM.

String Manipulation. The application of the computer's logical capabilities to string (letters, words, and symbols), as opposed to mathematical computation.

String Variable. In BASIC, a variable that cannot be subjected to mathematical operations, as opposed to a numeric variable.

Strings. In BASIC programming, words, letters, or symbols, as opposed to numeric data (see discussion in Chapter 6).

Structured Design. A method of developing computer programs in which a large program is visualized as consisting of several small modules or subprograms, each of which performs a specific function and can be programmed separately. These modules are combined using a minimum number of GOTO statements.

Subroutine. A group of instructions in a program that is used on different occasions in that program and that can be summoned as needed.

Subscript. A number in parentheses that follows a variable and identifies a specific member of an array.

Supervisor. A program in the operating system that controls and schedules a computer system's resources.

Synchronous Transmission. The transmission of data based on a timing mechanism in which data are transmitted at fixed intervals.

System Analyst. A person who plans and coordinates a computer system's hardware and software in order to achieve desired applications.

TAB Statements. The BASIC command that designates the location on a line at which the computer is to begin printing output. This command acts like a tab function on a typewriter (see discussion in Chapter 6).

Tape, Magnetic. See Magnetic Tape.

Tape Density, Magnetic. The number of characters per inch that can be stored on magnetic tape. Frequently used densities include 800, 1,600, and 6,250 bytes per inch.

Terminal, CRT. See Cathode Ray Tube Terminal.

Terminal, Dumb. A terminal that can accept input data and transmit them to a computer without any other processing capability.

Terminal, Hardcopy. A computer terminal capable of producing printed output.

Terminal, Intelligent. See Intelligent Computer Terminal.

Test Data. Data created to test whether a program has been correctly written.

Third-Generation Computers. Computers (designed primarily after the late 1970s) that use microprocessors.

Time Sharing. The simultaneous use of a minicomputer or mainframe computer by several users. The operating system includes decision rules for sharing the computer among the several users as time becomes available.

Track, Magnetic Disk. The concentric recording positions on a magnetic disk.

TRS-80. A microcomputer system developed by Radio Shack, a trademark of the Tandy Corporation.

Tutorial. An instructional programming strategy in which the computer functions as a "tutor" by presenting structured information to the learner. Tutorial programs can be either linear or branching programs (see discussion in Chapter 2).

UNIVAC. The first electronic computer dedicated to data processing applications. Developed by the Sperry-Rand Corporation.

Updating. The process of changing files through additions, deletions, and corrections in order to debug a program or to update it.

User Friendliness. The ability of the computer to respond to and accommodate mistakes made by persons running a computer program (see discussion in Chapter 9).

Variable Names. Symbolic labels used to designate specific areas of storage. See also string variables and numeric variables (see discussion in Chapter 6).

Virtual Storage. A storage strategy in which portions of a program or of a data file are stored on auxiliary storage until needed during a program's run. By having large enough auxiliary storage, this strategy gives the illusion that the computer's storage capacity is much greater than it really is.

Voice Input Device. A device that accepts as input sound waves (such as from the ordinary human voice) and interprets them as data input for the computer.

Voice Synthesizer. A device that causes the computer to provide output that resembles human speech. The output may be hardware or software based or both.

Word Processing. A strategy for using the computer to store and manipulate written information, such as that normally included in reports, letters, and other manuscripts.

Appendix B
BASIC Commands

THIS appendix will present a brief summary of some of the most important BASIC commands and a more detailed description of many of them. Not all BASIC commands used on all computers are included in this appendix: those commands that are not often used by beginners and commands that are used on one system but not on another have been omitted. The goal of this chapter is to introduce those commands that will enable you to read and write programs of moderate complexity. All of these commands are exemplified in the annotated programs contained in the earlier chapters of this book, and you should examine these programs for applications of these commands. For further information, you should consult the manual that accompanies your computer.

Summary of BASIC Commands

ABS. Provides as output the "absolute value" of a variable or an equation; that is, it drops the minus sign, if there is one.

CLS. Clears the entire screen by erasing everything printed on it and moves the cursor to the top of the screen.

CONT. Enables the program to continue if it has been interrupted. The CONT command will not work if the program has been modified since the interruption or if an error message has occurred since the interruption.

DATA. Enables the programmer to enter values for variables as part of the program. The DATA values are entered as the program encounters appropriate READ statements.

DIM. Enables the programmer to "reserve space" for an appropriate number of variables to be entered into subscripted arrays. A DIM statement is necessary whenever the programmer plans to enter more than ten values into a subscripted array.

END. Causes the execution of the program to stop and returns control to the user at the "command level."

FOR/NEXT. Allows the programmer to repeat a "loop" a designated number of times.

GOSUB. Causes the computer to depart from its normal sequence of going immediately to the next line (or to the next command if there is more than one on each line). The computer goes to the line designated by the GOSUB command, and then it continues to follow the normal rule of going to the next line until it encounters a RETURN statement. At that time it will return to the command immediately following the GOSUB statement.

GOTO. Causes the computer to depart from its normal sequence of going immediately to the next line (or to the next command if there is more than one on each line). The computer goes to the line designated after the word GOTO.

IF/THEN. Causes the computer to execute the command following the word THEN if, and only if, the condition described after the word IF is true. Otherwise, if this condition is not true, the computer will follow its normal rule of proceeding to the next line in the program. When THEN is followed by a line number, the IF/THEN combination acts as a conditional GOTO statement.

INPUT. Causes the computer to pause, display a prompt on the screen, and wait for the user to respond. This response then becomes the value of the variable identified in the INPUT statement.

INT. Provides as output the "integer" of a number or an equation; that is, it "truncates" the number by eliminating everything following the decimal point.

LEN. Provides as output a number indicating the length of a "string" expression. In other words, the computer counts the number of letters or symbols in a word or expression and indicates how long it is.

LET. Allows the programmer to assign values to variables as part of the program. The variable designated in the LET statement simply assumes the value indicated after the equal sign.

MID$. Isolates a string of letters or symbols in a larger string and provides these as output. This output can be used in the same ways as any other string variable.

NEXT. Returns the computer to the beginning of a loop. When the computer encounters a NEXT statement, it returns to the FOR statement at the beginning of the loop, unless the designated number of repetitions has already been performed. If this limit has already been reached, the computer will proceed to the command immediately following the NEXT statement.

ON/GOSUB. A combination of IF and GOSUB, analogous to ON/GOTO.

ON/GOTO. Sends the computer to the line designated by a combination of the value following ON and the line number designated after GOTO. This command is really a sophisticated combination of the IF and GOTO statements.

PRINT. Instructs the computer to print on the screen (or other output device) whatever values or symbols follow the word PRINT.

READ. Instructs the computer to examine a DATA statement and assign to a variable the value or symbol designated on that DATA statement.

REM. Allows the programmer to insert "remarks" into the text of the program. The computer actually ignores anything written in a REM statement; the information is there solely for the programmer and others who read the program lines.

RESTORE. Moves the computer's "pointer" back to the first DATA statement encountered in the program. Normally, as the computer encounters successive READ statements, it draws the data for such statements from successive DATA commands in the program. The RESTORE command tells the computer to start over with the first DATA statement in the program.

RETURN. Signifies the end of a GOSUB sequence and sends the computer back to the command immediately following the last GOSUB statement encountered.

RND. Provides as output a random number according to parameters defined by the programmer.

STOP. Interrupts the computer program and returns control of the computer to the user at the "command level." The user can examine lines and values before continuing with a CONT command.

TAB. Instructs the computer to begin printing the designated output at a specified column on the screen. This functions much like the tab key on a typewriter.

THEN. Tells the computer what action to take if the condition following an IF statement is true.

VAL. Converts a number that has been stored as a "string" variable to a numeric variable of the same value.

Detailed Description of BASIC Commands

CLS (TRS-80 Computers Only)

The CLS command tells the computer to "clear the screen" by eliminating everything currently printed on it and moving the cursor to the top left corner of the screen. The CLS command, therefore, offers a "clean slate" on which to start writing new output.

Format
Type CLS on an appropriately numbered line.

Example

```
10 CLS
```

Common Errors

1. Forgetting to include a CLS statement and therefore getting a cluttered screen.
2. Inserting a CLS in such a way that PRINT statements are erased a fraction of a second after they are printed on the screen, thus making such printed output invisible. This problem is eliminated by using the CLS command only after an INPUT statement or after the computer has been required to pause.

Examples in Programs
All the demonstration programs presented in this book contain either this command or its Apple equivalent (HOME), as discussed later in this appendix.

DATA

The DATA command supplies the values for a READ command.

Format
Type DATA and then the value. It is important to note the following:

1. The computer will read the data in the order listed, starting with the first piece of data and proceeding to the last. Therefore, it is essential that the data be in the exactly correct order.

2. It is permissible to list more than one piece of data on a line. Separate the data on a single line with commas.
3. If a READ statement calls for strings, the DATA statement must provide strings. If the READ statement calls for numeric variables, the DATA statement must provide numbers.

Examples

```
10 DATA 1,2,3,4,5
20 DATA MERCURY
30 DATA 120, HARRY
40 DATA ''TOM, DICK, AND HARRY'',''BILL''
```

Related Terms:

```
READ
RESTORE
variables
```

Common Errors:

1. See READ errors.
2. Omitting the word DATA.
3. Omitting the comma between data values.
4. Omitting one piece of data from a long list.
5. Inserting an additional comma after the word DATA, resulting in an error message.
6. Inserting an additional comma at the end of the DATA line, causing the computer to read an "extra" piece of data (actually a blank string), because it thinks that there is more on the line than is written there.
7. Inserting commas in a string of data, causing the computer to read the single piece of data as if it were several separate entries. This results in both an inaccurate reading of a specific piece of data and a misreading of all subsequent DATA lines. This problem is avoided by placing the data entry inside quotation marks (see line 40 in the examples).

Examples in Programs
See CAPS, FOOTBALL, and BEHMOD. This command is briefly discussed in Chapter 7.

DIM

The DIM statement enables the programmer to reserve sufficient space in the computer's memory to store the values that will be entered into subscripted arrays. For example, the command DIM X(20) provides storage space for twenty variables, designated X(1), X(2) . . . X(20). The command DIM Y(2,20) provides storage space for a matrix of forty variables, designated Y(1,1), Y(1,2) . . . Y(2,20).

Note that many computers provide, "by default," storage space for up to ten values in a subscripted array. This means that even if you do not have a DIM statement, you can still have an array with up to ten values in it. However, if there are more than ten values in the array, then the DIM statement will be mandatory.

Also note that it is possible to include several different arrays in a single DIM statement, as in lines 50 and 60 of the following examples.

Format
Type the word DIM, the name of the subscripted variable, and then (in parentheses) the number of values to be included in the array. If it is a two-dimensional array, indicate (in parentheses) the number of values to be included in each dimension of the array. If there is more than one array to be described, separate the arrays by commas.

Examples

```
10 DIM A(50)
20 DIM X$(25)
30 DIM B(5,50)
50 DIM A(50),B(50),C(100)
60 DIM X(25),A$(2,25),Y(10),Z(10,10)
```

Related Terms

```
arrays
READ Loops
```

Common Errors

1. Failing to write a DIM statement for a subscripted array that will contain more than ten values in a single dimension.
2. Setting the limit too low in a DIM statement. For example, you might have tried to put twenty-five values into an array when your DIM statement was designed to receive only twenty. This error often occurs when you modify a program by increasing the number of DATA statements to be read into an array but forget to alter the DIM statement responsible for this array.
3. Setting the limit too high in a DIM statement. This does not result in an error message but merely wastes space in the computer's memory. In many cases you can afford to waste such space, and so setting an unnecessarily high limit is not actually a mistake.

Examples in Programs
See CAPS, FOOTBALL, and BEHMOD. This command is discussed in Chapter 7.

FOR/NEXT

This command tells the computer to repeat another command or a series of commands a certain number of times.

Format
Type FOR, the names of a variable to serve as a counter (to record progress toward the upper limit—the number of times the command will be repeated), an equal

sign, a value which will serve as the starting point for the counter, the word TO, and finally a value to signify the upper limit—usually the number of times the command will be repeated. Next (usually on separate lines) enter the command or series of commands that you want the computer to repeat. After the last command in this series, type the word NEXT, followed by the name of the counter.

Examples

```
10 FOR I = 1 TO 5
20 PRINT ''HELLO''
30 NEXT I
```

This series will print the word "Hello" on five separate lines.

```
10 FOR K = 1 TO 10
20 LET X = X + 1
30 PRINT X
40 NEXT K
```

This series will print the numbers 1 to 10 on separate lines.

Related Terms

```
loops
nested loops
READ loops
```

Trying It Out for Yourself

Enter the following program into your computer:

```
10 CLS (or HOME)
20 FOR X = 1 TO 500
30 NEXT X
40 PRINT ''THIS MESSAGE WILL FLASH ON AND OFF.''
50 FOR X = 1 TO 500
60 NEXT X
70 GOTO 10
```

Stop now! Predict what you think this program will do. Then run it to see if you were right.

The FOR/NEXT loops in lines 20 through 30 and 50 through 60 do nothing other than spend time going through the loop. This has the effect of allowing the message to flash on and off the screen as the computer alternates between clearing the screen in line 10 and printing the message in line 40. The computer clears the screen and then counts to 500, prints the message and then counts to 500, clears the screen and counts to 500, *ad infinitum.*

```
THIS MESSAGE WILL FLASH ON AND OFF.



```

It will continue going through this loop until someone mercifully presses the break or reset key.

FOR/NEXT loops occur in most of the demonstration programs in this book. Chapter 7 discusses FOR/NEXT loops, and Figure 7.26 describes how a FOR/NEXT loop is used to draw the map in the PIZZA program. Almost any program that includes DATA lines uses one or more FOR/NEXT loops to read the data into arrays. The use of such arrays is discussed in Chapter 7. Examples of such READ loops are found in CAPS, BEHMOD, and FOOTBALL. Likewise, these same programs contain examples of FOR/NEXT loops for checking spelling and presenting lists of possible answers (e.g., lines 660 to 690 and 720 to 760 in CAPS).

GOSUB

The GOTO command tells the computer to break its normal sequence by going to a designated line rather than to the subsequent command. The GOSUB command has a similar function. GOSUB tells the computer to go out of the ordinary sequence to perform a command or set of commands but then to return to the command immediately following the GOSUB command when it is finished with that subroutine.

Note that once the computer goes to the line following the word GOSUB, it will continue to follow the ordinary rule of going to each subsequent command in the subroutine until it encounters a RETURN command. At that time it will return to the command immediately following the GOSUB that sent it to the subroutine.

Format

Type GOSUB, followed by the line to which you want the computer to go. Then insert the RETURN command at the end of the sequence of commands (the subroutine) to which you wish to send the computer.

Note that a GOSUB may come after an IF/THEN statement, as in the example on line 20 following.

Examples

```
10 GOSUB 500
20 IF X = 5 THEN GOSUB 500
```

Related Terms

```
GOTO
RETURN
ON/GOSUB
subroutines
```

Common Errors

1. Using a GOSUB without a RETURN.
2. Using GOSUB when you mean GOTO.
3. Putting the wrong line number after GOSUB.

Examples in Programs

See TRAP, PIZZA, CAPS, FOOTBALL, and BEHMOD. This command is discussed in Chapter 7.

GOTO

The normal rule is that when the computer completes one instruction it will go to the next. The GOTO statement tells the computer to break this rule. When the computer encounters a GOTO statement, it simply goes to where the instruction tells it to go rather than going to the next instruction in the natural order of the program. Then the computer continues to follow the normal rule of finishing one instruction and going to the next.

Format

Type GOTO and a line number. The line number must be an actual line number to which you want the computer to go. (GOTO may be written as either one or two words.)

Examples

```
10 GOTO 300
20 GOTO 500
30 GO TO 50
```

Related Terms

```
GOSUB
ON/GOTO
IF/THEN
```

Common Errors

1. Telling the computer to GOTO a wrong line.
2. Telling the computer to go to a nonexistent line.

Trying It Out for Yourself

Enter the following program into your computer:

```
10 CLS (or HOME)
20 LET C = 0
30 PRINT ''THIS PROGRAM WILL PRINT AS''
40 PRINT ''MANY LINES OF STARS AS YOU WANT''
50 PRINT ''ON THE SCREEN.''
60 PRINT ''HOW MANY LINES OF STARS DO YOU WANT'';
70 INPUT N
80 CLS (or HOME)
90 LET C = C + 1
100 PRINT ''*****************************''
110 IF C = N THEN 130
120 GOTO 90
130 END
```

Stop now! Predict what you think this program will do. Then run it to see if you were right.

This routine uses a counter (C) to place the desired number of lines of stars on the screen. The computer will continue to transfer control from line 120 to line 90 as long as C does not equal N in line 110. When C does equal N, the program will stop.

```
THIS PROGRAM WILL PRINT AS
MANY LINES OF STARS AS YOU WANT ON THE SCREEN.
HOW MANY LINES OF STARS DO YOU WANT?
?5
```

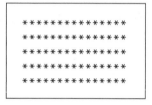

Note that the computer clears the screen in line 80 so that the lines of stars will start to appear at the top of the screen.

GOTO statements are found in all the demonstration programs in this book. A common use of the GOTO statement is to use it as a detour command to route the computer around the lines to be avoided. For example, if line 75 were omitted from HELLO, the computer would say, "I'm sorry to hear that. I am glad to hear that." Likewise, without GOTO statements, such programs as CAPS, FOOTBALL, and BEHMOD would tell learners that they were simultaneously right and wrong for the same answer! The GOTO statement is described in Chapter 6.

HOME (Apple Computers Only)

The HOME command tells the computer to go "home" by eliminating everything currently printed on it and moving the cursor to the top left corner of the screen. The HOME command, therefore, produces a clean slate on which to start writing new output.

Format
Type HOME on an appropriately numbered line.

Example

```
10 HOME
```

Common Errors
   1. Forgetting to include a HOME statement and therefore getting a cluttered screen.

2. Inserting a HOME statement in such a way that PRINT statements are erased a fraction of a second after they are printed on the screen, thus making them invisible. This problem is eliminated by using the HOME command only after an INPUT statement or after the computer has been required to pause.

IF/THEN

Most instructions make the computer take some action whenever they are encountered in the program. The IF/THEN command, on the other hand, will result in action only if the condition stated after IF is true. Otherwise (if this condition is not true), the computer will follow the normal rule of immediately going to the next instruction in the program.

There are two reasons for using the IF/THEN statement:

1. Interrupting the normal sequence of going to the next instruction in the program. If the condition following IF is true, the computer will go to the line following the word THEN. Otherwise, it will follow the normal rule of going to the next instruction.

Format

Type IF, the condition, THEN, and finally the line number to which you want the program to go if the condition is true.

Examples

```
10 IF X = 20 THEN 300
20 IF A$ = ''YES'' THEN 500
30 IF X$ = ''GEORGE'' THEN 1500
40 IF X>20 THEN 10
50 IF X + Y=5 THEN 500
60 IF X/Y<100 THEN 200
```

2. Having the computer execute an instruction only under certain circumstances. In this case, the computer will execute an instruction (such as a PRINT command or an arithmetic operation) only if the condition following IF is true. Otherwise, the computer will skip the instruction following IF and go immediately to the next instruction in the normal sequence.

Format

Type IF, the condition, the word THEN, and finally the instruction that you want the computer to carry out if the condition is true.

Examples

```
10 IF X = >20 THEN PRINT ''HELLO''
20 IF X<20 THEN PRINT ''GOODBYE''
30 IF X + Y=20 THEN A$=''TOO BAD''
40 IF X$<>''YES'' THEN STOP
```

Note

The condition is always stated in terms of equal to or not equal to, meaning that the following terms may be used:

- = means "is equal to"
- < means "is less than"
- > means "is greater than"
- <> means "is not equal to"

Common Errors

1. Omitting or using the wrong sign in a statement of condition or arithmetic operation.
2. Failing to direct the computer to do something when the IF condition is not true.
3. Directing the computer to go to a wrong line.

Trying It Out for Yourself

Enter the following program into your computer:

```
10 CLS (or HOME)
20 PRINT ''THIS PROGRAM TELLS YOU IF TWO''
30 PRINT ''NUMBERS ARE EQUAL. IF THEY ARE''
40 PRINT ''NOT, IT TELLS YOU WHICH IS LARGER.''
50 PRINT
60 PRINT ''PUT IN TWO NUMBERS (50,60 FOR EXAMPLE).''
70 INPUT B,C
80 IF B<>C THEN 110
90 PRINT ''YOUR NUMBERS ARE EQUAL.''
100 GOTO 130
110 IF B>C THEN PRINT B;'' IS GREATER THAN '';C;''.''
120 IF C>B THEN PRINT C;'' IS GREATER THAN '';B;''.''
130 END
```

Stop now! Predict what you think this program will do. Then run it to see if you were right.

Statement 80 asks if a condition is true. If the condition is true (that is, if B and C are unequal), then the computer will go to line 110. But if the condition in line 80 is not true, then the computer will continue to line 90. If the computer is sent from line 80 to line 110, then it will be necessary to evaluate another condition. If B is greater than C, the computer will print the message in line 110. If C is greater than B, the computer will print the message in line 120.

```
THIS PROGRAM WILL TELL YOU
IF TWO NUMBERS ARE EQUAL.
IF THEY ARE NOT, IT TELLS YOU
WHICH IS LARGER.

PUT IN TWO NUMBERS (50,60, FOR
EXAMPLE).
10,20
20 IS GREATER THAN 10.
```

If you examine the logic of the program, you will notice that if the computer arrives at line 110, it will necessarily print one, and only one, of the messages in lines 110 through 120. All of the demonstration programs in this book contain examples of IF/THEN statements. Chapter 6 discusses this command in the program HELLO.

INPUT

The INPUT command tells the computer to pause until the person at the terminal responds. Then the computer makes that response the value of the variable accompanying the INPUT statement.

Format

Type the word INPUT and then the name of the variable. Note that the name of the variable must be followed by a dollar sign if the response from the person at the terminal is a string. But if the response is to be treated as a number, then the variable name must not be followed by a dollar sign.

Examples

```
10 INPUT X
20 INPUT A$
```

Related Terms

```
LET
READ
variables
```

Common Errors

1. Giving a numeric variable a string value, or vice-versa.

Trying It Out for Yourself

Enter the following program into your computer:

```
10 CLS (or HOME)
20 PRINT ''WHAT IS YOUR NAME'';
30 INPUT A$
40 PRINT
50 PRINT ''HOW OLD ARE YOU, '';A$;
60 INPUT A
70 IF A = >40 THEN 100
80 PRINT ''YOU ARE JUST A SPRING CHICKEN, '';A$;''!''
90 GOTO 110
100 PRINT ''YOU ARE REALLY LIVING NOW, '';A$;''!''
110 END
```

Stop now! Predict what you think this program will do. Then run it to see if you were right.

The INPUT statement at line 30 sets the value of A$ at "Bob." The INPUT statement at line 60 sets the value of A at 41. The value of A$ is used in lines 50, 80, and 100. Line 70 uses the value of A to decide whether to branch to line 80 or 100.

```
WHAT IS YOUR NAME? BOB
HOW OLD ARE YOU, BOB? 41
YOU ARE REALLY LIVING NOW, BOB!
```

Note that the question mark provided by the INPUT statement is attached by a semicolon to the previous line. This eliminates the need for a second question mark and improves the program's format.

All the demonstration programs in this book contain examples of INPUT statements. A brief discussion of this statement accompanies the description of the program HELLO in Chapter 6.

INT

In many instances a programmer prefers to deal with whole numbers rather than with long strings of decimal places. The INT (integer) function accomplishes this by using the "greatest integer" function. For positive numbers, this means truncating the number—that is, eliminating everything to the right of the decimal point. (For negative numbers, the computer "rounds up"—for example, -12.1 becomes -13.)

Note that such truncating differs from the usual practice of rounding. It is possible to perform the more conventional rounding procedure by instructing the computer to add .5 to the number before truncating, as in line 50 in the following example. With a little imagination, we can even use the INT function to round off on the right side of the decimal point. For example, to round off a decimal reference to money, we could add .005 to an amount, multiply it by 100, truncate by using the INT function, and then divide by 100. This would round off to the nearest cent, as in line 70 following.

Format
Type INT and follow this with the value to be truncated in parentheses. This INT function can be inserted anywhere on a program line that a numeric variable is permitted.

Examples
```
10 LET X = INT(47.346)
20 LET X = INT(Y)
30 LET Y = INT(A/B)
50 LET Z = INT(A/B + .5)
70 LET S = INT(100*(T*4.47 + .005))/100
80 PRINT ''THAT'S '';INT(R/(R + W)*100);'' PERCENT CORRECT.''
```

Common Errors

1. Becoming confused by the mathematical intricacies in the equations. Just think the equation out calmly using a large sheet of paper.

2. Violating the logical ordering in which the computer performs mathematical operations. Use extra parentheses, if necessary, to make it clear. Or perform separate operations within separate computer statements and then combine them.

3. Imbalanced parentheses. The rule is that the number of end parentheses must equal the number of opening parentheses.

4. Leaving a space after INT and before the parentheses. The computer will recognize INT as a function only if it is followed immediately by a set of parentheses. Without the parentheses, the computer will try unsuccessfully to interpret the term INT as a variable, with a default value of 0.

Trying It Out for Yourself

Enter the following program into your computer:

```
10 CLS (or HOME)
20 PRINT ''THIS PROGRAM ROUNDS OFF NUMBERS''
30 PRINT ''FROM FOUR TO TWO DECIMAL PLACES.''
40 PRINT
50 PRINT ''WHAT IS YOUR NUMBER''
60 PRINT ''WITH FOUR DECIMAL PLACES'';
70 INPUT A
80 LET B = INT((A + .005)*100)/100
90 PRINT
100 PRINT ''HERE IS YOUR ROUNDED NUMBER: '';B
110 END
```

Stop now! Predict what you think this program will do. Then run it to see if you were right.

Your computer should have produced output like that shown below. Line 80 added .005 to 1.5023, making B equal to 1.5073. This result was then multiplied by 100, giving a temporary result of 150.73. The INT function next eliminated the .73, making B equal to 150. Finally, this number was divided by 100, giving the result of 1.50 which was printed in line 100.

```
THIS PROGRAM ROUNDS OFF
NUMBERS FROM FOUR TO TWO
DECIMAL PLACES.

WHAT IS YOUR NUMBER WITH
FOUR DECIMAL PLACES? 1.5023

HERE IS YOUR ROUNDED NUMBER: 1.50
```

Note

It is not necessary to put the INT function in a LET statement. The demonstration program could have been written with line 80 omitted and line 100 revised as follows:

```
100 PRINT ''HERE IS YOUR ROUNDED NUMBER:
''; INT((A+.005)*100)/100
```

One common usage of the INT function occurs when a programmer wants to tell players what percentage of their answers was correct. Examples of this usage can be found in line 3110 of FOOTBALL and line 1220 of BEHMOD. Further discussion of the INT function can be found in Chapter 7.

LET

One way to give a value to a variable is to use a LET statement.

Format

Type LET, the name of the variable, an equal sign, and finally the value you wish to assign to the variable. This value can take any of these forms:

1. It can be a number.
2. It can be another variable.
3. It can be an algebraic equation.
4. It can be a letter or a string of letters or symbols beginning with a letter.

Examples

```
10 LET X = 1
20 LET Y = 0
30 LET X = Y
40 LET X = X + 1
50 LET X = Y + 1
60 LET X = Y + Z/5
70 LET Y$ = ''LETTER''
80 LET A$ = A$ + B$
```

Note

The word LET is optional. Each of the preceding statements could be written without the word LET and retain their same meaning. For example:

```
10 X = 1
60 X = Y × Z/5
70 A$ = A$ + B$
```

Related Terms

```
INPUT
READ
mathematical operations
variables
```

Common Errors

1. Giving a numeric variable a string value, or vice-versa.

2. Accidentally using the same label for two different variables. This could result in your accidentally erasing a value you wished to retain. (The most recent value would be retained, and the earlier one would be discarded.)

Trying It Out for Yourself

Enter the following program into your computer:

```
10 CLS
20 LET X = 50
30 PRINT X
40 LET X = X + 5
50 PRINT X
60 END
```

Stop now! Predict what you think this program will do. Then run it to see if you were right.

Your computer should have printed the number 50 in the upper left-hand corner of the screen and 55 directly under it.

```
50
55
```

In line 20, the computer assigned the value of 50 to X. In line 30, it printed the value of X. Then in lines 40 and 50, the computer increased the value of X and printed the new value.

Now enter this program:

```
10 CLS
20 LET X$ = ''LETTERS''
30 LET Y$ = ''CAN BE ''
40 LET Z$ = ''ASSIGNED TOO.''
50 PRINT X$;Y$;Z$
60 END
```

Stop now! Predict what you think this program will do. Then run the program to see if you were right.

```
LETTERS CAN BE ASSIGNED TOO.
```

Your computer should have printed the message shown in the preceding diagram. The semicolon joins the sentence fragments on one line. Note that in order to have a period at the end of the sentence and spaces between the words, it was necessary to include these as part of the LET statements.

Other examples of LET statements can be found in any of the annotated programs in this book. LET statements in TRAP are discussed in Chapter 7.

MID$

The MID$ command is a "string manipulation" command enabling the computer to take apart a string and to use the selected part of the string as a separate variable.

Format

Type MID$, an opening parenthesis, the name of the string to be examined, a number to designate the position of the letter at which the computer is to start constructing the new string, a number to designate the length of the new string, and finally an end parenthesis. In many cases, both of the numbers in the parentheses are actually variables that represent numbers. The MID$ function can be inserted anywhere in a program that any other variable would constitute a valid statement.

Examples

```
100 IF MID$(X$,X,5) = ''HELLO'' THEN 500
200 LET X$ = MID$(A$,1,6)
300 LET Y$ = MID$(B$,X,L)
400 IF MID$(R$,1,1) = ''Y'' THEN 500
```

Related Terms

```
RIGHT$
LEFT$
```

Common Errors

1. Putting a wrong value into the parentheses. Avoid this error by counting and planning carefully.

Examples in Programs

```
BEHMOD (lines 450 and 530)
```

ON/GOSUB

The ON/GOSUB command is exactly the same as the ON/GOTO command, except that it uses the logic of the GOSUB statement rather than the logic of the GOTO statement. This means that after the computer goes to one of the designated lines following the word GOSUB, it will return to the command immediately following the ON/GOSUB command as soon as it encounters a RETURN statement.

Format

Use the ON/GOTO format. Type ON, a variable to indicate a number, the word GOSUB, and finally a list of lines from which the computer will select one based on the instructions after the word ON. The computer will go to the line in the list whose rank order is indicated by the number following ON.

Examples

```
100 ON X GOSUB 200,300,400
200 ON Y - 1 GOSUB 400,500,600,700,800
```

Related Terms

```
ON/GOTO
GOSUB
IF/THEN
```

Common Errors

1. Allowing the variable following ON to take a value higher than the list of choices can handle.
2. Allowing the variable following ON to take a value of 0.

ON/GOTO

The ON/GOTO command enables the computer to branch to any of several possible routes designated by the input in the statement. The ON/GOTO is really a combination of several separate IF/THEN statements compressed into a single command. In this statement, the computer is given a list of possible lines to which it could go, and it selects the line to which it will actually go based on the input after the word ON. The ON/GOTO statement often follows an INPUT statement, and in such cases the computer is usually sent to a line designated by the INPUT statement.

Format

Type the word ON, a variable to designate the choice the computer is to select, the word GOTO, and finally a list of lines the computer can select. From the list of possible choices, the computer will GOTO the one in the rank order that matches the number following the word ON. For example, in the statement ON X GOTO 100,200,300, the computer will go to line 100 if the value of X is 1, to 200 if the value of X is 2, and to 300 if the value of X is 3.

Examples

```
10 ON X GOTO 100,200,300
20 ON Y GOTO 310,320,330,340,350
30 ON Z - 1 GOTO 400,500,600,700,800,900
```

Related Terms

```
ON/GOSUB
GOTO
IF/THEN
```

Common Errors

1. Allowing the variable to take on a value higher than the list of choices can handle. For example, in line 10 of the examples, allowing X to take a value higher than three when there are only three lines to which the computer can go.
2. Giving a string response to the INPUT statement preceding the ON/GOTO statement. This results in the variable being assigned a 0 value, and so the computer does not know what to do with a statement reading ON 0 GOTO. . . .

Examples in Programs

CAPS (lines 280, 770, and 780), FOOTBALL (lines 350 and 2280).

PRINT

The command PRINT tells the computer to display some information on a computer screen.

The computer will PRINT three types of information ("output"):

1. A string of information.
2. A numerical value (which may be symbolized by a variable name or algebraic equation).
3. A blank space.

Format

Type the word PRINT and the item of information to be printed. For the types of information just described, the following guidelines apply:

1. *Strings*. The contents of the string must be enclosed in quotation marks or can be represented by a variable label accompanied by a $.

Examples

```
10 PRINT ''HELLO.''
20 PRINT ''MY NAME IS RALPH.''
30 PRINT A$
```

2. *Numeric Values*. The value may be a simple number, a variable label, or an equation producing a new value.

Examples

```
10 PRINT 16.34
20 PRINT X
30 PRINT X + 1
31 PRINT X/Y
```

3. *A Blank Space*. This requires the computer to fill a line (or the rest of a line if something else came first) with empty space. When PRINT is the only word on a line, this will cause the printer to "skip" a line.

Example

```
10 PRINT
```

Common Errors

1. Omitting quotation marks for string variables.

READ

The READ command tells the computer to give a variable a value listed in a DATA statement. The first time the computer comes to a READ statement during a run of a program, it will use the first value listed on the first DATA line in the program. The second READ statement will send the computer to the second DATA value, and so forth.

Format

Type READ and the name of the variable to which you wish to attach the value. Note that if you want this value to be a string, the variable must be accompanied by a dollar sign. But if you want to treat this value as a number, it must not be accompanied by a dollar sign.

Examples

```
10 READ X
20 READ A$
30 READ X(I)
40 READ A$(I,J)
50 READ X,Y,Z
```

Related Terms

```
DATA
variables
loops
arrays
RESTORE
```

Common Errors

1. Mismatch between the number of READ statements and the number of DATA statements.
2. READ statement calling for a number when the DATA line contains a string, or vice-versa.
3. Attempting to read the same data twice without a RESTORE command.
4. See data errors.

Examples in Programs

See CAPS, FOOTBALL, and BEHMOD. This command is discussed in Chapter 7.

REM

The command REM stands for "remark" and indicates that everything else in the statement after the word REM consists of a remark intended for the programmer and other interested readers. Therefore the computer does not even try to interpret the contents of the rest of this statement. As soon as it sees a REM, it will go immediately to the next command. Such "nonexecuted" REM statements are useful when you try to debug your program or wish to show your program to someone who is not familiar with it.

Format

Type REM and then the remark you wish to make. For the sake of neatness and clarity, you may prefer to include several consecutive REM lines rather than a single long REM statement.

Examples

```
100 REM THIS IS THE PRINT SUBROUTINE
200 REM ***THESE LINES CAN BE REMOVED WHEN
210 REM ***FEWER THAN THREE PLAY THE GAME.
```

Common Errors

1. Omitting the word REM.

Examples in Programs

See FOOTBALL (lines 10 to 30 and 140 to 160) and BEHMOD (lines 10 to 30 and 390).

RETURN

The RETURN command signifies the end of a subroutine that was entered through a GOSUB statement. When the computer encounters the RETURN command, it will proceed directly to the command immediately following the GOSUB statement that sent it into the subroutine. If there are several successive GOSUB statements, the RETURN command will send the computer back to the most recent GOSUB command.

Format

Enter the word RETURN on an appropriately numbered line.

Examples

```
100 RETURN
200 IF X>2 THEN RETURN
```

Related Terms

```
GOSUB
ON/GOSUB
subroutines
```

Common Errors

1. Failing to include the RETURN at the end of the subroutine entered through a GOSUB statement.
2. Using a RETURN instead of a GOTO or a IF/THEN at the end of a subroutine entered through a GOTO or an IF/THEN statement.
3. Accidentally allowing the computer to enter a subroutine by following its normal rule of going to the next line in sequence. When the computer does this and encounters a RETURN statement, it will not know what to do and so will give a "RETURN WITHOUT GOSUB" error message. The correct way to avoid this is to see that the computer enters the subroutine only when it is sent there by an appropriate GOSUB. This is usually accomplished by placing a GOTO or IF/THEN statement immediately before the first line of the subroutine.

Examples in Programs

All the programs with GOSUB statements also have RETURN statements, which includes most of the demonstration programs in this book.

RND

The RND function enables the computer to make a random selection of a number, which can be used in the same way that any other variable can be used in a program.

Format

On the TRS-80, simply type RND, and then put the upper limit in parentheses. The computer will then select a number between 1 and this upper limit. On other computers, the process is sometimes slightly more complex. For an explanation of this more complex process, see Chapter 7. This RND function can be inserted anywhere on a program line that a numeric variable is permitted.

Important Note

The computer does not actually invent random numbers. It selects numbers from a list stored in its memory. This list contains numbers which were originally generated in a truly random fashion. However, unless instructed otherwise, every time the computer first draws a number from this list, it will start at the same place. Consequently, if you turn your computer on and instruct it to select ten random numbers on two consecutive occasions, you will get the same series of ten "random" numbers in each set. This, in turn, means that if you randomly select items for a drill, you will get the same ten items on consecutive runs of the drill. This problem will occur only if prior to each run of the drill the computer is turned off and back on, but this often happens in actual use of the computer. This is hardly desirable.

To overcome this problem, it is necessary to initialize the random number generator. On the TRS-80, a single command accomplishes this. Simply put the word RANDOM alone on a line early in the program.

```
15 RANDOM
```

That's all it takes. On the Apple, the solution is slightly more complex. One solution is to insert lines like the following immediately after an INPUT statement and prior to your first RND statement:

```
15 LET Y = PEEK(78)+256*PEEK(79)
20 LET X = RND(-Y)
```

Other computers have different solutions to this problem. Consult your manual to determine what to do on your computer. CAPS provides an example of the TRS-80 solution. FOOTBALL and BEHMOD demonstrate the Apple solution. Other programs (AGE, TRAP, and PIZZA) do not control this problem.

Examples

```
10 LET X = RND(5)
20 LET Y = RND(N)
30 LET Z = RND(50) + 20
40 IF X>RND(25) THEN 300
50 IF RND(50)>25 THEN 500
60 ON RND(3) GOSUB 100,200,300
70 LET J = INT(10*RND(1)) + 1
```

Note

Different computers vary in their rules for selecting random numbers. Line 70, RND(1) is an example of the use of a *seed value* to select a random number between 0 and 1. The initial random number is then multiplied by 10 to get a number between 0 and 9. Adding 1 to this result produces a number between 1 and 10. This process is discussed in Chapter 7.

Trying It Out for Yourself

Enter the following program into your computer:

```
10 CLS (or HOME)
20 LET X = 0
30 LET A = RND(5)
   (or) 30 LET A = INT(5*RND(1)) + 1
40 PRINT A
50 LET X = X + 1
60 IF X = 5 THEN 80
70 GOTO 30
80 END
```

Stop now! Predict what you think this program will do. Then run it to see if you were right.

Your computer should have printed a sequence of numbers arranged vertically on the screen:

```
5
1
2
4
5
```

Of course, because the numbers are randomly selected, yours probably will not be the same as those shown here. Run the program several times. You should not get the same set of numbers each time you run the program. But if you do, this is an indication that your computer will require a separate command earlier in the program to "start up the randomizer." This separate command is usually RANDOM or RANDOMIZE. Check your manual.

Several of the annotated programs use the RND function. TRAP, for example, uses RND to select a number at random between 1 and 100. Likewise, PIZZA uses RND to select the coordinates to which the pizza is to be delivered, and CAPS, FOOTBALL, and BEHMOD all use RND to select the question and corresponding correct answers for these drills.

Examples in Programs
TRAP (line 350), PIZZA (line 580), CAPS (line 920), FOOTBALL (lines 330 and 340), and BEHMOD (line 170)

TAB

The TAB command enables the computer to start printing at a designated column on the screen. It works much like the tab key on a typewriter. If there is no TAB command, the output will appear on the screen wherever the cursor happens to be (usually at the beginning of a line or at the end of the previous output.)

Format
Enter the word TAB followed immediately (without a space in between) by a set of parentheses containing a number or a variable representing a numeric value. Then type a semicolon, followed by the output you wish to print at that TAB position.

Examples

```
100 PRINT TAB(5);''HELLO!''
200 PRINT TAB(X);A; TAB(X + 10);B
```

Related Terms

```
PRINT
screen display
```

Common Errors

1. Leaving a space after the word TAB and before the parenthesis. The computer will attempt to interpret the word TAB as a variable rather than as a function and will print the default value (zero) in an unexpected position.
2. Using a TAB position that represents a location that the cursor has already passed (e.g., TAB(15)), when the computer has already printed a string of twenty characters on that line.
3. Using an impossible TAB position (e.g., minus 1).
4. Imbalanced parentheses.

Examples in Programs
See HELLO (line 20), PIZZA (line 480), CAPS (lines 60 to 100 and 680), FOOTBALL (lines 50 to 70 and 1005), and BEHMOD (lines 860 and 865).

Appendix C
Modules

THE following pages contain "modules" that can be inserted into a variety of programs to improve their instructional effectiveness. In most cases, the modules have been demonstrated in the programs discussed in this book, and whenever appropriate, cross-references are made to them.

Module 1

Spelling Check

Objective

To verify that the answer entered by the learner is at least a correct spelling of one of several possible answers on a list. This minimizes the possibility that the learner's answer will be considered wrong merely because the correct answer is misspelled.

Strategy

Store a list of possible right answers in an array. (This will usually be the same array from which you will instruct the computer to select the correct answer.) When the learner enters an answer, compare this answer with each of the items in the array to see if there is a match. If there is a match, then consider the learner's response to be a correct spelling and continue with the program as soon as the match is found. If there is not a match, then print a message indicating that the response was not the correct spelling and ask the learner to respond again. The logic of this strategy is diagrammed in Figure 8.3.

Program lines

```
500 FOR I=1 to 50
510 IF A$=S$(I) THEN 600
520 NEXT I
530 PRINT A$;'' IS NOT A CORRECT SPELLING''
540 PRINT ''OF ONE OF THE ANSWERS. TRY AGAIN.''
550 GOTO 400
```

In this example, the computer has received an answer and is comparing that answer with a list of fifty possible answers. Line 400 asks the question again. Line 600 continues the program.

Examples

```
CAPS (Lines 720–780)
BEHMOD (Lines 1100–1200)
FOOTBALL (Lines 2200–2280 and 2300–2350)
```

Note

In some cases, you will not want to provide the spelling correction, as it may give inappropriate clues. See discussion in Chapter 8.

Module 2

Movement on the Screen

Objective

To make a word or object appear to move across the screen.

Strategy

Draw or print the item on the screen, leave it there barely long enough to be seen, and then erase it and draw it again a slight distance away. The principle is exactly the same as that involved in cartoon animation.

Module 3

Wraparound Routine

Objective

To have strings of words appear on the screen so that they will not divide in the middle when a string is too long to fit onto a single line.

Strategy

Establish the string of words in its entirety. You can do this with DATA statements, LET statements, or any other valid way to put together strings of words. Then have the computer break down the string into an array of words. (The computer can do this by looking for spaces between the words.) Then have the computer print the words on the screen one word at a time. Before it prints each word, have the computer first determine how many spaces on a given line will be used if that word is printed. If the length of the line with the new word falls below the desired limit (e.g., below forty or sixty characters), then have the printer print the word. If the new word causes the line to be excessively long, end the current line and start a new line with the new word. Continue this process until all the words in the array are printed. The logic behind this routine is described in Figures 11.3 and 11.4.

Program lines

```
2000 LET K = 1
2010 FOR I = 1 TO 50
2020 LET L = 0
2030 FOR J = K TO LEN(Y$)
2040 LET K = J
2050 IF MID$(Y$,J,1) = '' '' THEN GOSUB 2130: GOTO
     2090
2060 LET L = L + 1
2070 NEXT J
2080 GOTO 2100
2090 NEXT I
2100 GOSUB 2130
2110 LET L2 = I
2120 RETURN

2130 LET Y$(I) = MID$(Y$,J - L,L)
2140 K = K + 1
2150 RETURN

2160 REM **** PRINT ROUTINE
2170 FOR I = 1 to L2
2180 LET S = LEN(Y$(I)) + S
2190 IF S > 38 THEN PRINT : PRINT TAB( T);: LET S =
     T + LEN(Y$(I))
2200 PRINT TAB (T)
2210 PRINT Y$(I);
2220 PRINT '' '';
2230 LET S = S + 1
2240 NEXT I
2250 RETURN
```

Before this set of subroutines can be entered, Y$ must have a value assigned to it. This value will consist of a string of words, as in a definition of a term. It is necessary to dimension an array of fifty members for Y$(I). The preceding example assumes a limit of fifty words and a line length of forty characters, but both can be altered. The variable S records the current length of a line in terms of the number of characters. The variable L records how many of the characters in the Y$ string have been examined. The variable T indicates the tab position to which you want the string of words indented as you print them on the screen. If you want no indentation, set this value at 1.

Example

BEHMOD (Lines 390–520, 530–550, 830–890)

Note

The lines in the sample program have been written as subroutines, enabling you to call them at will and to use them several times (for different reasons) in the same program.

Module 4

Lists in Two Columns

Objective

To list the items of an array in two (or more) columns rather than in a single column. Such a strategy is helpful when the list is long and the items on it would go off the top of the screen before the learner had a chance to read them.

Strategy

Print one item from the list in column 1, use the TAB function to move across the screen on the same line, print the second item from the list at this new tab position, and then go on to the next line. Note that it is necessary to use a STEP 2 command in the FOR/NEXT loop to do this.

Note

The following example does not attempt to preserve an order, such as an alphabetical order, in the list, but Module 5 does preserve such an order. (Order can be preserved in a single page list by incorporating some of the strategies shown in Module 5.) The list of the states in CAPS (Chapter 8) provides an alphabetical order on a single screen.

Program Lines

```
500 FOR I = 1 TO 13 STEP 2
510 PRINT T$(I);TAB(20);T$(I + 1)
520 NEXT I
```

These lines will produce a list of twenty-six items in two columns. No item in the list should exceed nineteen characters in length.

Examples

```
CAPS (Lines 660–700) (50 items in 4 colums)
FOOTBALL (Lines 2000–2050 and 2100–2150 (26 items in two
columns), and 2500–2550 (50 items in 3 columns)
```

Note

After providing a list, it is usually best to repeat the question, as in the examples cited.

Module 5

Lists on Several Screens

Objective

To permit a long list to be printed on several consecutive screens, pausing at the end of each screenful of information.

Strategy

Have the computer print a designated number of items from the list. Then insert an INPUT statement to make the computer pause. When the learner enters a response at the keyboard, have the computer resume the list where it left off. This logic is diagrammed in Figure C.1.

Program Lines

```
500 LET K2 = 1
510 IF K2>N THEN 300
520 FOR I = K2 TO K2 + 9
530 PRINT T$(I)
540 NEXT I
550 LET K2 = K2 + 10
560 PRINT
570 PRINT ''READY TO CONTINUE (PRESS RETURN)'';
580 INPUT A$
590 GOTO 510
```

Line 300 restates the question and continues with the program. This routine lists up to N items with ten items in a single column on each screen. By combining this module with Module 4, it is possible to put several columns on each screen. This routine has placed a *list* on the screen. The same logic could be used for other information, such as "pages of instructions."

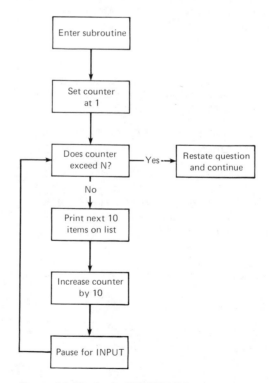

Figure C.1. The logic of MODULE 5.

Examples

>   CAPS (Lines 1150—1220)
>   BEHMOD (Lines 940—1090)

Note

This routine requires the learner to look at the whole list before responding. To permit the learner to respond as soon as the correct answer appears on the list, see Module 6.

Module 6

Permitting Responses During Lists

Objective

To give the learner the option of either seeing the rest of the list or immediately responding to a question. For example, if a learner has just seen the correct answer on the first screenful of list items, it may be unnecessary to look at the rest of the list.

Strategy

Set the variable that records the answer at "blank" at the beginning of the list loop. When the learner enters a response at the end of each screenful of the list, examine the response to see if the answer-recording variable is still blank. If it is blank, continue with the list. Otherwise, return to the main program. This logic is diagrammed in Figure 11.5.

Program Lines

```
500 LET K2 = 1
505 LET A$ = ''''
510 IF K2>N THEN 300
520 FOR I = K2 TO K2 + 9
530 PRINT T$(I)
540 NEXT I
550 LET K2 = K2 + 10
560 PRINT
570 PRINT ''ENTER THE CORRECT ANSWER''
575 PRINT ''OR PRESS RETURN KEY FOR MORE LIST.''
580 INPUT A$
585 HOME
590 IF A$ = '''' THEN 510
600 GOTO 400
```

A$ must be the label given to the student response elsewhere in the program. Line 300 restates the question and continues. Line 400 continues with the evaluation of the response entered at line 580.

Example

>   BEHMOD (Lines 940—1090)

Note

This routine parallels Module 5.

Module 7

Providing Feedback for Wrong Answers

Objective

To enable students to use incorrect responses as a basis for comparison and learning.

Strategy

(1) If either the question or the learner's response has been erased by clearing the screen, repeat enough of this information to enable the learner to compare the correct and incorrect answers. (2) State that the answer was wrong and give the correct answer. (3) If the learner's answer shows an incorrect understanding of something the computer can recognize, then offer a correct statement of this information. The logic of this routine is described in Figure 11.6.

Example

```
Question: What is the capital of New Mexico?
Learner's Response: Phoenix.
Computer's Response (on a new screen):
    Wrong. The capital of New Mexico is Santa Fe.
    Phoenix is the capital of Arizona.
```

Program Lines

```
500 PRINT ''WRONG.''
510 PRINT
520 PRINT T$(X);'' IS DEFINED AS ''
530 LET Y$ = D$(X)
540 GOSUB 2000
550 PRINT
560 PRINT A$;'' IS DEFINED AS ''
570 LET Y$ = S$
580 GOSUB 2000
```

This is a typical term/definition program. D$(X) represents the definition shown on the screen, and T$(X) represents the correct answer. GOSUB 2000 represents the wraparound routine described in Module 3 that prints the definitions.

Lines 560 through 580 rely on the previous recognition of S$ as the correct spelling of an incorrect alternative. This recognition can be built into this routine (e.g., between lines 560 and 570), and it can also occur elsewhere in the program, perhaps as part of the spelling correction routine. The following lines achieve this recognition:

```
1000 FOR I = 1 TO N
1010 IF A$ = T$(X) THEN 1050
1020 NEXT I
```

```
1030 (Optional spelling message)
1040 GOTO 1060
1050 LET S$ = D$(I)
1060 (Continue program)
```

Example
See BEHMOD, lines 680 through 820.

Note
A similar strategy can be applied in math: "The correct answer $2.75, not $4.50. You added instead of subtracting." See Figure 9.4.

Module 8

Exit Routine

Objective
To provide feedback to learners as they exit from the program.

Strategy
Indicate the number of correct and incorrect answers, and then state this as a percentage. If appropriate, offer additional evaluative feedback by comparing the learner's performance with some explicit or implicit standard.

Program Lines

```
900 PRINT ''YOU GOT '';R;'' RIGHT OUT OF '';R + W;''.''
910 PRINT
920 PRINT ''THAT MAKES '';INT((R/(R + W) + .005)*100);''
PERCENT.''
930 PRINT
940 IF R/(R + W)>.90 THEN PRINT ''THAT'S PRETTY GOOD!''
950 IF R/(R + W)<.60 THEN PRINT ''YOU COULD USE SOME MORE

PRACTICE.''
990 PRINT
999 END
```

This example assumes the existence of R and W as counters correctly incorporated into the program in order to keep track of right and wrong answers. The supplementary feedback at lines 940 and 950 is optional and arbitrary: there is nothing sacred about a percentage of 90 or 60. A PRINT statement immediately preceding the END statement often improves the appearance of the screen at the end of the program.

Examples

```
CAPS (Lines 1590-1610)
BEHMOD (Lines 1210-1230)
FOOTBALL (Lines 3100-3120)
```

Module 9

Right-Answer and Wrong-Answer Routines

Objective
To evaluate the learner's answer and provide feedback regarding its correctness or incorrectness.

Strategy
Compare the learner's response with the correct answer. If there is a match, go to the Right-Answer Routine. If the answers do not match, go to the Wrong-Answer Routine. Include in these routines (1) feedback, (2) continuous or intermittent reinforcement, (3) right-answer or wrong-answer counters, and (4) appropriate information regarding questions attempted or number of consecutive right answers. The logic behind such routines is described in Figure 8.5.

Program Lines

```
500 IF A$ = T$(X) THEN GOSUB 600:GOTO 550
510 GOSUB 700
550 PRINT ''DO YOU WANT ANOTHER QUESTION (Y/N)'';
560 INPUT R$
565 HOME
570 IF R$ = ''Y'' THEN 200
580 IF R$ = ''N'' THEN 900
590 PRINT ''ANSWER Y FOR YES OR N FOR NO.''
595 GOTO 550
600 PRINT ''RIGHT. GOOD ANSWER.''
610 LET R = R + 1
650 RETURN
700 PRINT ''WRONG. THE CORRECT ANSWER IS''
710 PRINT T$(X);'' (NOT '';A$;'').''
720 LET W = W + 1
750 RETURN
```

These program lines can be preceded by spelling corrections, list routines, and the like. Line 200 starts a new question. Line 900 enters the exit routine. Various other modules can be inserted between lines 610 and 650 and 720 and 750 in order to record consecutive answers, to control duplication of questions, to provide reinforcement, and so forth.

Examples

```
CAPS (Lines 350–380 and elsewhere in the program)
BEHMOD (Lines 310–320 and related subroutines)
FOOTBALL (Lines 1040–1050; also seven other places in the
program)
```

Note
When a learner gives a wrong answer, it is important to put enough information on the screen to permit him or her to profit from the error. In many cases, this

problem can be resolved by clearing the screen only after correct (but not incorrect) responses. In other cases, it is better to restate the information after clearing the screen. For additional help, see Module 7.

Note
If you use R and W to record the number of right and wrong answers, you can also use R + W + 1 to indicate the number of the upcoming question.

Module 10

Varying the Feedback
Objective
To avoid the constant repetition of the same feedback following a correct or incorrect response by the learner.

Strategy
Have the computer select a random number, and incorporate it into an ON GOTO statement to provide varied feedback.

Program Lines
These lines can be part of the Right-Answer Routine.

```
600 LET V = INT (5*RND(1) + 1)
610 ON V GOSUB 820,830,840,850,860
620 (Continue Right Answer Routine.)
820 PRINT ''RIGHT. GOOD ANSWER.'':RETURN
830 PRINT ''WAY TO GO, '';N$;''!'':RETURN
840 PRINT ''NOT BAD!'':RETURN
850 PRINT ''YOU GOT IT RIGHT!'':RETURN
860 PRINT ''SUPER!'':RETURN
```

Note
The preceding example focuses on single-line PRINT statements, but it is also possible to use the same strategy for much longer routines. For example, each of the preceding PRINT lines can be replaced with a lengthy graphic display that would provide reinforcing feedback.

Module 11

Eliminating Duplications
Objective
To prevent the computer from selecting the same item more than once during a single run of a drill.

Strategy
Label each item in some way when it is selected. When a new item is selected, check to see if it is labeled as previously selected. If it is so labeled, have the computer select a different item; otherwise continue with the program.

Program Lines

```
200 LET X = RND(30)
210 IF T$(X) = ''USED'' THEN 200
220 LET T$(X) = ''USED''
```

The preceding lines will keep the computer from selecting the same value of X more than once during a single run through the program. In addition to these lines, the program needs some way to keep the learner from requesting more than thirty questions. (A request for a thirty-first value for X would "hang up" the computer in a perpetual loop between lines 210 and 200, because the condition at line 220 would always be true.)

Module 12

Permitting Only Specified Duplications

Objective
To eliminate from a drill items that have been answered correctly, while retaining those which were answered incorrectly. (More specifically, this module retains an item in the drill until the learner answers an item correctly one more time than he or she has answered it incorrectly.)

Strategy
Set up an array to indicate how often each item can still be used during a run of the drill. Start each member of this array with a value of 1. As part of the Right-Answer Routine, subtract 1 from the appropriate member of this array. As part of the Wrong-Answer Routine, add 1 to the appropriate member of this array. Before permitting the computer to ask a new question, have it check to see if there are any questions left that still have a value of 1 or greater. When the computer selects an item, have it check to see if the array value is greater than 0. If the value is greater than 0, continue with the program; otherwise select a new item. The logic behind this strategy is described in Figure 11.2.

Program Lines
First, you need to initialize the array:

```
100 DIM U(30)
110 FOR I = 1 TO 30
120 LET U(I) = 1
130 NEXT I
```

In your Right-Answer Routine, include a line such as the following:

```
630 LET U(X) = U(X) - 1
```

In your Wrong-Answer Routine, include a line such as the following:

```
730 LET U(X) = U(X) + 1
```

Then, use the following lines to select your random number:

```
200 LET X = RND(30)
210 IF U(X)<1 THEN 200
```

In addition, insert the following lines into your Next-Question Routine:

```
550 FOR I = 1 TO 30
552 IF U(I)>1 THEN 560
554 NEXT I
556 GOTO 900 (Exit Routine)
560 PRINT ''DO YOU WANT ANOTHER QUESTION?'' (etc.)
```

These final lines enable the learner to continue as long as there is one item in the pool but to exit from the program when each item has been answered correctly one more time than it was answered incorrectly.

Example

```
BEHMOD (Lines 70, 120–140, 190, 590–660, 700)
```

Module 13

Putting Responses into a Random Order

Objective

To present the possible responses on the screen in such an order as to conceal any pattern that would help the learner discover the correct answer.

Strategy

Start with an array whose members are arranged in some predictable pattern (e.g., with the correct answer as the first member of the array). Then assign a random number to each of these members. Have the computer put the list of alternatives on the screen in the order indicated by these random numbers.

Program Lines

The following sequence takes a list of five items labeled X$(1) to X$(5) and prints them on the screen in random order. The logic is diagrammed in Figures C.2 and C.3. By changing the number 5 in lines 5000, 5030, and 5040 to some other value, the programmer can use this sequence to handle different numbers of items on the list. The logic of this strategy is described in Figures C.2 and C.3.

```
5000 FOR J = 1 to 5
5010 LET V(J) = 0
5020 NEXT J
5030 FOR I = 1 TO 5
5040 LET V = INT(5 * RND(1) + 1)
5050 FOR J = 1 TO I
5060 IF V = V(J) THEN 5040
5070 NEXT J
5080 LET V(I) = V
5090 PRINT X$(V);
5100 NEXT I
5110 PRINT
```

The computer has through some designated process
compiled in its memory the following array of
items:

        X$(1) A wrong answer
        X$(2) A wrong answer
        X$(3) A wrong answer
        X$(4) A wrong answer
        X$(5) The correct answer

The computer prints one of these at random.
        The computer chooses X$(3).
The computer prints another one at random.
        The computer chooses X$(1).
The computer prints a third item at random.
        The computer chooses X$(5).
The computer prints a fourth item at random.
        The computer chooses X$(4).
The computer prints the fifth item.
        The computer chooses X$(2).

Figure C.2. The strategy involved in Figure C.3. The computer starts with a list of five items. If
these items are simply printed on the screen in their initial order, the learner will soon discover
that the fifth item is always the correct answer. But by printing the items in a random order,
the computer conceals this pattern. In this example, the correct answer is printed third in the
list. On another run, the correct answer may be fourth, first, and so on.

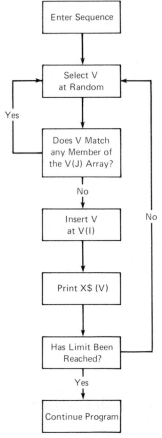

Figure C.3. The logic of a subroutine to put the items from a list into random order. V is the
number between one and the number of items in the list to be randomly arranged. The third
box in the diagram (line 5060) prevents any item from being printed twice. The second-last box
(line 5100) makes sure that all of the items will be printed.

Note

If the size of the list (for example, fifteen items) makes it difficult to fit onto the screen, additional strategies must be used.

Module 14

Keeping Track of Consecutive Answers

Objective

To keep track of the number of the learner's consecutive right or wrong answers.

Strategy

Insert a variable to count consecutive right answers in the Right-Answer Routine. Reset this counter to zero in the Wrong-Answer Routine. (A corresponding strategy can count consecutive wrong answers.) The line numbers in the following example are compatible with the Right- and Wrong-Answer Routines in Module 9.

Program Lines

To count consecutive right answers, insert the following line in the Right-Answer Routine:

```
630 LET R1 = R1 + 1
```

It is also necessary to insert the following line in the Wrong-Answer Routine:

```
730 LET R1 = 0
```

To count consecutive wrong answers, use the same strategy with W1.

Note

Based on the number of consecutive right or wrong answers, the computer can be programmed to (1) give intermittent reinforcement, (2) move to a higher or lower level of difficulty in the program, or (3) exit from the program. For example:

```
2000 IF R1>10 THEN PRINT ''YOU'RE DOING SUPER, '';N$;''!''
2010 PRINT ''THAT'S '';R1;'' RIGHT ANSWERS IN A ROW.''
```

Example

```
FOOTBALL (lines 2710, 2910, and 2960 to 3010)
```

Module 15

Nested READ Loops

Objective

To store data in a two-dimensional array. Such an array is shown in Figure 7.15.

Strategy

Use two FOR/NEXT loops, one inside the other. The first loop should control the first dimension of the array, and the second loop should control the second dimension.

Program Lines

This example stores a list of authors—A $(I)—and a list of three books by each author—B $(I,J). The authors will be stored in a one-dimensional array, and the books will go into a two-dimensional array.

```
100 FOR I = 1 TO 20
110 READ A$(I)
120 FOR J = 1 to 3
130 READ B$(I,J)
140 NEXT J
150 NEXT I
```

To select items from such an array, simply have the computer select two random numbers, one for each dimension:

```
200 LET X = RND(20)
210 LET Y = RND(3)
220 PRINT ''WHO WROTE '';B$(X,Y);
230 INPUT A$
240 IF A$ = A$(X) THEN correct answer routine
```

The correct answer, of course, is the name corresponding to A $(X). This process is shown in Figure C.4.

Module 16

Accepting a Number to Indicate a Word As an Answer

Objective

To list in order a set of possible responses, to precede each item on this list by a number, and to accept this number (instead of the entire response) as the answer.

A$(I)		B$(I,J)		
		1	2	3
1 Mark Twain	1	Huck Finn	Tom Sawyer	Conn Yankee
2 Jane Austen	2	Pride/Prej	Sense/Sense	Emma
3 Charles Dickens	3	Tale/Cities	Great Expec	Oliver T
"				
"				
"				
20 John Steinbeck	20	Red Pony	Pearl	Mice/Men

1. The computer reads both arrays of data (lines 100 to 150).
2. The computer selects X=3 at random in line 200.
3. The computer selects Y=2 at random in line 210.
4. The computer asks "Who wrote *Great Expectations?*" in line 220. It does so because *Great Expectations* is the value of B$(3,2).
5. The computer will recognize as the correct answer "Charles Dickens," as this is the value of A$(3).

Figure C.4. How the computer combines information from a two-dimensional array—B$(I,J)—with information from a one-dimensional array—A$(I)—to provide a drill on authors and their works.

This simulates the normal multiple-choice format on standardized tests (see Figure C.5).

Strategy
Use a FOR/NEXT loop to print the items in the list. Each item will be associated with a counter derived from the FOR/NEXT statement. Simply have the computer print the number along with each of the items. Then allow the student to enter the number instead of the entire response.

Program Lines
The following lines can be inserted into BEHMOD to permit the learner to respond by entering a number rather than spelling out a long response. The program with these modifications will accept either the number or the complete word as a correct response. Simpler modifications enable the program to accept only the number as a response.

First, change line 1110 to read as follows:

```
1110 PRINT I;''.  '';T$(I)
```

Then add this line:

```
525 IF VAL(A$) = X THEN GOSUB 900:GOTO 540
```

Module 17

Dealing with Dollar Signs

Objective
To permit students to prefix their answers with a dollar sign when such a sign is appropriate. Remember that the dollar sign is not accepted as numeric input, and

```
11.  INTERMITTENT REINFORCEMENT
12.  NATURAL REINFORCEMENT
13.  NEGATIVE PRACTICE
14.  NEGATIVE REINFORCEMENT
15.  OVERCORRECTION
16.  POSITIVE REINFORCEMENT
17.  PUNISHMENT
18.  REINFORCEMENT
19.  RESPONSE COST
20.  SATIATION


ENTER THE CORRECT SPELLING
OR PUSH THE RETURN KEY
TO SEE MORE OF THE LIST.

THE CONTINGENT PRESENTATION OF
AN AVERSIVE SITUATION.
```

Figure C.5. Sample screen from BEHMOD. With the proposed modification, the numbers in the left column have been added. The learner can enter either the correct answer (PUNISHMENT) or the number accompanying that answer (17).

therefore, programmers often write their programs with instructions to omit dollar signs. The result is that learners occasionally receive a message such as "Wrong. The correct answer was $2.32, not $2.32."

Strategy
In your INPUT statement, accept the input as a string variable rather than as a numeric variable. Then check to see if the input is introduced by a dollar sign. If it is, drop the dollar sign. Then use the VAL command to convert the string variable to a numeric variable. This strategy is diagrammed in Figure C.6.

Program Lines
```
500 INPUT A$
510 IF LEFT$(A$,1) = ''$'' THEN A$ = A$ - LEFT$(A$,1)
520 LET A = VAL(A$)
```

Module 18

Accommodating Rounding Errors

Objective
To overcome the rounding problem described next.

Strategy
Use a combination of $<$ $>$ equations to replace the $=$ equation.

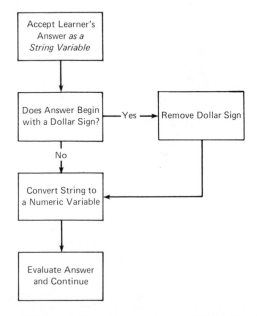

Figure C.6. The strategy for removing an initial dollar sign.

Problem

When the computer performs the mathematical operation of division, it may make very slight rounding errors which appear far to the right of the decimal point. The computer itself corrects these before printing a quotient on the screen. The problem is that in the computer's memory (where the comparisons are made), the computer may have an answer that is slightly different from what you think it should be. For example, the computer might conclude that 2/4 is .49999999999 rather than .50. Therefore, a student who answers that 2 divided by 4 is .50 might be told that he or she is wrong. This problem is solved by building into your equations a tolerance for rounding errors.

Program Lines

Replace lines like the following:

```
300 PRINT ''WHAT IS '';X;'' DIVIDED BY '';Y;
310 INPUT A
320 IF A = X/Y THEN PRINT ''RIGHT!''
```

with lines like these:

```
300 PRINT ''WHAT IS '';X;'' DIVIDED BY '';Y;
310 INPUT A
330 IF A > X/Y + .00001 THEN 400
340 IF A < X/Y - .00001 THEN 400
350 PRINT ''RIGHT!''
```

Remember that this problem occurs only on some computers and only when comparing a student response with an answer that the computer has obtained by using the process of division.

Module 19

Timing Learner Responses

Objective

To keep track of how long it takes a learner to respond. This information can be used to measure performance or to allow a learner only a certain length of time before the computer will give the answer.

Strategy

Have the computer perform two activities simultaneously: (1) look for a learner response and (2) measure the passage of time. The computer can measure the passage of time by performing an activity of a known duration; for example, the computer can run through a FOR/NEXT loop. If a designated amount of time passes, the computer will stop looking for the learner's response, accept a default response of "no answer," and continue to its next instruction.

Module 20

The Moving and Flashing Cursor

Objective

To enable a learner to enter a response without typing a precise answer at the keyboard. For example, physically handicapped learners can respond by hitting the keyboard at a random location or by using another means to break the electric circuit.

Strategy

Arrange the letters to spell out a word in an appropriate matrix on the screen. An arrangement of six columns with five or six letters in each column is possible (see Figure C.7). Program the cursor to move across the top of the columns of letters. When the cursor is above the letter that the learner wants to type, the learner breaks the circuit by touching the keyboard or by some other means. Then the cursor starts moving down the column. When the cursor reaches the letter the learner wishes to select, the learner breaks the circuit again. This process continues until the learner has spelled out the entire entry. Once the entire entry has been provided as input, the computer treats it exactly as if it had come through a normal INPUT statement.

This strategy is admittedly technical, and not many readers will understand the program lines, as the subroutine requires strategies not discussed in this book. In addition, each model of microcomputer may require a different variation of this strategy. The point is that such a module is possible to develop and that once you develop it (or have someone else develop it), you can "plug it in" wherever you need it.

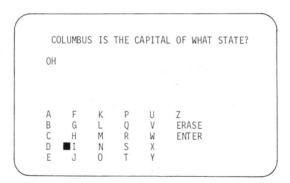

Figure C.7. The moving and flashing cursor. The learner has selected the letters O and H and is about to select I. The cursor first moved horizontally across the top row of letters. When it was above the F, the learner interrupted the circuit by pressing any key or by some other means. The cursor then moved vertically down the F row. Now the learner will interrupt the circuit again while the cursor is next to I. Then the I will appear on the screen next to the OH on the second line, and the computer will again start horizontally scanning the top row. After spelling the entire word, the learner will push ENTER by breaking the circuit when the cursor is next to the ENTER on the screen.

Module 21

Enabling a Computer to Recognize the Names of Students

Objective
To enable the computer to assign a program or a part of a program to a learner, based on the computer's correct identification of that learner.

Strategy
Have the learner enter his or her name or some sort of code word or number. Send the computer to a subroutine in which it will attempt to match the name entered by the learner with a list of names stored in its memory. If there is a match, have the computer assign a corresponding level of instruction. If there is no match, have the computer either restate the request for student identification or assign a default level of instruction.

Program Lines
Insert lines such as the following near the beginning of the program:

```
30 PRINT ''WHAT IS YOUR NAME'';
40 INPUT N$
50 GOSUB 2000
60 ON V GOTO 1100, 1200, 1300, 1400, 1500, 1600
```

Then insert this subroutine:

```
2000 FOR I = 1 TO S
2010 IF N$ = N$(I) THEN V = V(I) GOTO 2050
2020 NEXT I
2030 PRINT ''UNRECOGNIZED NAME.''
2040 GOTO 10
2050 RETURN
```

This subroutine assumes the existence of DATA lines such as the following, which previously may have been stored in an array:

```
5000 DATA JAMES SMITH,5
```

In this example, if James Smith entered his correct name, the computer would assign the value of 5 to V, and then line 60 would route James to the fifth of the six possible levels of the program (the 1500 sequence).

Appendix D
Data Files

DATA files permit the programmer to store data on disks in storage units separate from the program itself. The computer reads the data from the file when the program instructs it to do so. This separate storage has several advantages, one of which is that a computer program can be considerably shortened, because the DATA lines can be omitted from that program and placed instead in a data file. This is especially useful with a very long program, which would exceed the computer's capacity if all the data were included at once.

When data files are used in this way, it is possible to make radical changes in the contents of a program simply by instructing the computer to access a different data file, rather than by changing all the DATA lines. For example, a single disk can contain a program called VOCAB, which is a vocabulary drill for third graders, plus fifteen data files arranged in some hierarchy based on level of difficulty. Simple instructions in the VOCAB program make it possible for different children running the same program to receive completely different vocabulary words, based on their own level of achievement. Many manufacturers of electronic educational games advertise that you can purchase additional modules to increase their capacity. These modules are really data files, and by using data files with your programs, you can increase your program's flexibility and comprehensiveness in the same way that these modules can enhance the games.

Another use of data files is to store a student's responses for later examination by the student, teachers, or parents. This makes it possible to record progress, to score and evaluate tests, and to plan subsequent units of instruction. Likewise, it is possible to enter into the computer data concerning the learner's performance on tasks that do not involve the use of the computer and to use the computer as a monitoring or coordinating system to plan and integrate learner activities.

Finally, data files enable the computer to "learn" from persons who enter information into it. Cybernetic games like ANIMAL (Figures D.1 and D.2) "grow" and "learn" by storing student responses. ANIMAL starts by classifying all animals into four classes: birds, mammals, reptiles, and amphibians. If the learner enters the name of an animal that the computer already "knows," it will identify that animal as specifically as possible. If the learner enters the name of an animal not currently in the computer's memory, then the computer will ask for the name of that animal and for information that distinguishes that animal from others already known by the computer. The computer then stores this new information in a data file so that on future occasions it will "know" another animal.

How to Use Sequential Data Files

Computers use two types of data files: sequential files and random access files. Sequential data files store text, symbols, or numbers in the order in which they are written, and they must be read by the computer in this same order. Random data files differ in that information stored in them can be accessed in any order that the programmer wishes. The third piece of data may be read first, the fifteenth piece may be read second, and so on. Random access files use the computer's time more efficiently in retrieving information, though this advantage of greater efficiency may be offset by several other factors. First, random access files are more complex to use than are sequential files. In addition, the quantity of data stored in files in instructional programs is usually far smaller than the vast amount often stored for business or industrial applications. But an occasional pause for a second or so does not interrupt the instructional process. For these reasons and because computers work at extremely high speeds, most instructional programmers are willing to use sequential files. Therefore, only sequential files will be discussed in this text, but if you are interested in random access files, you should consult your computer's manual.

The following steps describe a common way to use sequential data files:

```
ARE YOU THINKING OF AN ANIMAL? !YES
DOES IT SWIM? !NO
IS IT A REPTILE?!NO
DOES IT FLY?!NO
DOES IT GO BOW WOW? !NO
WHAT LAND ANIMAL DID YOU CHOOSE?!LION
THE ANIMAL YOU WERE THINKING OF WAS A LION.
PLEASE TYPE IN A SHORT QUESTION THAT WOULD
DISTINGUISH A LION FROM A DOG.
MAKE IT A QUESTION WHICH HAS YES FOR ITS ANSWER.
!DOES IT ROAR?
FOR A LION WOULD YES BE THE ANSWER TO THIS QUESTION?
!YES
```

Figure D.1. A screen from ANIMAL. The computer did not guess "lion" correctly and must "learn" this word.

```
ARE YOU THINKING OF AN ANIMAL? !YES
DOES IT SWIM? !NO
IS IT A REPTILE? !NO
DOES IT FLY? !NO
DOES IT GO BOW WOW? !NO
DOES IT ROAR? !YES
IS IT A LION? !YES

** I AM VERY PROUD OF MYSELF **
```

Figure D.2. A screen from ANIMAL. The computer now knows what a lion is.

1. Open the file.
2. Use INPUT# statements to put data into the computer from the file.
3. Use PRINT# statements to take data out of the computer and put it into a file.
4. Close the file.

In actual practice, Steps 2 and 3 can be reversed or omitted, depending on the program's needs. This appendix will briefly describe each of these steps on the TRS-80. More detailed information (and guidelines for other computers) can be found in the manual that gives directions for using your computer's disk drive.

Step 1. To open a file, it is necessary to write a command such as the following:

10 OPEN ''I'',1,''ANIMALS/TXT''

The "I" stands for "input," which means that this file will put data into the computer. The other possibility is to have an "O" (for "output") file. The number 1 after the "I" is a "buffer number," a temporary storage area set up in the computer's memory. The information passing between a disk drive and the computer's memory must pass through such a buffer. The 1 labels the buffer and makes it available for use with the designated file. The term "ANIMALS-TEXT" is the label attached to the file itself. Even when you turn off the computer, take the disk away, and mount it on the same or a different disk drive, this same label will remain attached to this file.

Step 2. To put data into the computer from a sequential data file, use the INPUT# command:

10 INPUT#1,X,Y,Z

This command includes the word INPUT#, a file number, and a list of variable names. In this example, the data will go from the file on the disk into buffer number 1, and the first piece of data will be assigned to the variable X, the second to Y, and the third to Z. You can see that the outcome is the same as a READ X,Y,Z or an INPUT X,Y,Z command, except that the values assigned to X, Y, and Z come from the data file rather than from DATA lines or the person seated at the keyboard. In this example, the variables X, Y, and Z are numeric variables (they have no dollar sign), and therefore the data accessed through buffer number 1 must consist of numeric (as opposed to string) data. Otherwise, an error message will result.

Data files can be used for any type of variable and with arrays as well as single variables. For example, if a data file contains a list of animal names, the following lines will assign values to an array of these names:

```
200 FOR X = 1 TO 5
210 INPUT#1,B$(X)
220 NEXT X
```

In summary, when a computer obtains values for data from a data file, the rules will be exactly the same as when the values come from LET, INPUT, or READ statements. The examples assume that a data file already exists. The strategies for developing such a data file will be described later.

Step 3. To take data from a program and put it into a sequential data file, use the PRINT# command. Remember that in order to do this, you must first follow Step 1 by using a statement such as

```
20 OPEN ''O'',2,''ANIMALS/TXT''
```

The PRINT# command will look like this:

```
10 PRINT#1,A;G
```

This command includes the word PRINT#, a buffer number, and a list of variables. In the example, the data will go from the computer into buffer number 1 and then into the data file currently associated with that buffer. The semicolon is used between the variables to save space on the disk; a comma would work equally well but would waste space on the disk because a series of blank spaces would be inserted between each pair of variables.

In the preceding example, the values of A and G are stored in the next two available spaces in the file currently associated with buffer number 1. In a sense, writing to a data file is the same as printing output onto DATA lines: the values are inserted in the file in the order in which you print them, and delimiters (spaces, semicolons, and commas) have a comparable effect. For example, examine the following line:

```
100 PRINT#2,A$;B$
```

If A$ = "FAT" and B$ = "CAT," then this line will write the single word "FAT-CAT" into the file. If you want "FAT" and "CAT" stored as two separate words, you can store them with this line:

```
100 PRINT#2,A$,B$
```

If you want the output stored as one "word" with a space in the middle ("FAT CAT"), then you can use this line:

```
100 PRINT#2,A$;'' '';B$
```

If the output you wish to store in the file contains commas or semicolons in the string of symbols, such punctuation will be interpreted by the computer as indicating that you are entering several separate variables, even though you wish to store only one long variable. This problem can be resolved by using quotation marks around the output to be sent to the file. We recommend that you consult your computer's manual for details on how to do this.

Step 4. When you are finished using a file, you should close it. Once you have done so, the buffer area reserved for that file can be reassigned to another file with a new OPEN statement. Use the following format:

```
100 CLOSE 1
```

If you have used several files in separate buffer areas, you can close them all at once:

```
100 CLOSE 2,5,8
```

The following is an example of a short program using a data file:

```
10 DIM B$(10)
20 OPEN ''I'',1,''MYFILE''
30 FOR K = 1 TO 10
40 INPUT# B$(K)
50 NEXT K
60 CLOSE 1
70 PRINT ''NOW I CAN PRINT THE FIRST TEN''
80 PRINT ''PIECES OF DATA IN MYFILE.''
```

The sample program assumes that a data file named "MYFILE" already exists and is accessible to the computer. The program opens "MYFILE," reads the first ten pieces of data it finds there into the B$ array, closes access to "MYFILE," and prints a message indicating that it is prepared to print the list of data.

Important caution! Do *not* take a disk out of a drive before you have closed all the files. This is because the last portion of the output to be sent to a file may not yet have been written into that file. When you close the file, you complete that task. Also note that any of the following commands or actions automatically close any files that are currently open:

1. The NEW command.
2. The RUN command.
3. The EDIT command.
4. Adding or deleting any program lines.
5. The CLEAR command.
6. A disk error.

How to Create a File Outside Your Program

This discussion of data files assumes that you want to create a file as a natural part of your program. What if you do not want to do this? What if you want to create a file that can later be appended to an existing program? For example, you might write a program called VOCAB, a vocabulary drill. Then you might wish to have VOCAB access data files called WORDS1, WORDS2, WORDS3, and the like, which would give considerable flexibility to VOCAB. In such a case, you would not put the strategy for developing the data files in VOCAB but, rather, use a short, independent program to develop the data files.

How to Update an Existing File

Suppose that you want to update an existing file by adding more data to it. For example, you may wish to add new scores to a list of students' test scores. How can you do this? If you simply reopen the file for output and load in the new scores, they will be loaded at the beginning of the data file, and the previous scores will be lost. Instead, you should follow these procedures:

1. Open the relevent file.
2. INPUT# the entire file and store it in an appropriate string or array.
3. Close the file.
4. Add the new scores to the array.
5. Open the file for output.
6. PRINT# the updated array to the file.
7. Close the file.

The same procedure can be used to modify a specific piece of information in a file.

Your computer's manual probably has a full chapter on using sequential files. This appendix has attempted to explain to you the basic strategies for using data files, but you should consult that manual if you encounter problems.

Appendix E
Moving Programs To and From the Disk

Loading a Program

If you have a program on a disk and wish to run it, it is necessary to transfer it from auxiliary storage (from the disk) into the computer's active memory. To do this, use the LOAD command.

On the TRS-80, use this format:

```
LOAD ''CAPS''
```

On the Apple, use this format:

```
LOAD CAPS
```

The only difference between the Apple and the TRS-80 is that the Apple requires quotation marks, whereas the TRS-80 does not. Other systems have comparable commands.

The LOAD command simply transfers the program from the disk to the main memory but does not cause the computer to start executing the program's commands.

Loading a program also has the effect of erasing from the computer's active memory any other lines that were there before the LOAD command.

Running a Program

Once a program has been loaded, by typing the word RUN, you can make the computer start executing the program's commands:

```
RUN
```

256

This command is exactly the same on the TRS-80, on the Apple, and on most other computers.

It is also possible to load and run a program in a single step. This is done by typing RUN followed by the name of the program whose commands you wish to execute. On the TRS-80, use this format:

```
RUN ''CAPS''
```

On Apple, use this format:

```
RUN CAPS
```

Again, the only difference between the TRS-80 and the Apple is the presence or absence of the quotation marks. For other systems, check your manual.

It is important to note the difference between the simple RUN command and the RUN name-of-program command. RUN will instruct the computer to go to the lowest numbered line that happens to be in the computer's memory at the time and to start executing the commands there. RUN CAPS, on the other hand, instructs the computer to go to disk drive, look for a program labeled CAPS, transfer that program to the main memory, and then start executing the lines in the program.

Question: A programmer loads his or her program (named CAPS) and modifies a few lines in it, then types RUN CAPS (on an Apple), and is dismayed to see that none of the new lines are in the program. What has the computer done wrong?

Answer: The computer has done nothing wrong: the programmer made a mistake. When the programmer typed RUN CAPS, the computer promptly erased what was currently in its memory (the program with the new lines), loaded the original version of the program, and proceeded to run that old version.

Question: What should the programmer have done in order to run the newly revised program?

Answer: The programmer should have either typed RUN instead of RUN CAPS or saved the program before running it.

Confusing RUN with RUN name-of-program is a *very common error* among beginning programmers.

How to Save a Program

If you wish to transfer a program to a disk from the computer's main memory, use the SAVE command. On the TRS-80, it takes the following format:

```
SAVE ''CAPS''
```

On the Apple, it looks like this:

```
SAVE CAPS
```

Again, the only difference between the TRS-80 and the Apple is the presence or absence of the quotation marks. For other systems, check your manual.

The SAVE CAPS command tells the computer to check the disk to see if there is a program there labeled CAPS. If there is such a program, the computer will erase the version of that program currently on the disk and replace it with the version from the main memory. But if there is no such program, the computer will create a file with that label and store the program in the main memory in that new location.

After the SAVE command has been executed, the program will exist both in the computer's main memory and on the disk.

How to Erase a Program from a Disk

To erase a program on the TRS-80, use the KILL command. The format of this command varies, depending on when you use it. Most frequently, it is used before entering BASIC, and at such times it has the following format:

```
KILL CAPS
```

On the TRS-80, the KILL command can also be used after entering BASIC, and in such cases the format is as follows:

```
KILL ''CAPS''
```

The Apple uses the DELETE command to erase programs. The DELETE command has the following format:

```
DELETE CAPS
```

When it encounters a KILL or DELETE command, the computer goes to the disk, looks to see if there is a program with the designated label, and then erases that program and discards the label. Be careful when you use KILL or DELETE commands, because the program you erase will be gone forever. For other systems, check your manual to find the comparable strategy for deleting programs.

Critical Errors That Can Lead to Physical Harm to Oneself or to the Computer

1. *Never* save a program under the name of a different program. You will erase the old program!

Example: You have a program named CAPS on your disk. You write a new program called PIZZA. After finishing PIZZA, you mistakenly type SAVE CAPS instead of SAVE PIZZA. The computer promptly goes to the disk, finds a file labeled CAPS, erases the contents of that file, and stores the lines of the current program (PIZZA) in the newly vacated file. CAPS now contains nothing but PIZZA!

2. Never save a program without first Loading it. (You will erase the old program!)

Example: You've been working on CAPS, and it almost works. You have saved the program on a disk. While you are away from the computer, you think of the two lines which you think will fix the program. You sit down at the computer and type in the two new lines (without first Loading CAPS). After typing the two new lines, you type SAVE CAPS. The computer immediately goes to the disk, finds CAPS, erases the contents of that file, and stores there the current contents of the main memory. CAPS now contains a grand total of two lines!

How to prevent this error: List or run the program before you save it. If it runs correctly, then the lines are all there. But if you do this, beware of forgetting to save the program afterwards.

3. Never Kill (or delete) a program which you really want to keep.

Example: You write a program called CAPS. You subsequently write a program called PIZZA. You want to erase CAPS and keep PIZZA, but you inadvertently type KILL PIZZA. The outcome is a permanent loss of PIZZA.

How to prevent this error. There are only two ways to overcome this error: (1) Don't make the error, and (2) have a backup copy of the program. To keep you from making the error, some systems (such as the Apple) permit you to "lock" your files. To erase a locked file, you must first unlock it; and it's less likely that you will make two consecutive errors than a single error.

4. Never Save a program to a full disk.

Example: You have a small amount of space left on your disk. You write a program too long to fit in this restricted space. You try to save the program. The computer will then tell you that this is impossible, and you are stuck with a program with no place to put it.

What to do when this happens: (1) Save the program on a different disk. Immediately remove the full disk and insert a properly formatted disk with sufficient room. Then save the program again; or (2) kill (or delete) enough programs to make room for the new program. (On the TRS-80, do this *without* going to the DOS level. On the Apple, this is not a problem.) Then save the new program.

Unlike the previously discussed errors, this mistake is not always fatal. It becomes a serious problem only if you have no extra disks or if you are unable to make room on the present disk.

How to prevent this error: (1) Always allow enough room on your disk to save the program you are writing. (2) Always have at least one formatted disk available for emergencies.

5. Never inflict electromagnetic (or other) damage upon your disk.
Examples:

a. You accidentally demagnetize a disk. This may erase it completely.
b. On the TRS-80, you turn off the power while the disk is in the drive. This puts an unpredictable error in the operating system, and this error may show up later when you least expect it.
c. You walk through a door with a magnetic screening device. This may damage or erase your disk.
d. You expose the disk to static electricity.
e. You put a greasy fingerprint on the plastic surface of the disk. This may make the whole disk inoperable, or it may damage only part of it.
f. You inflict damage on the disk in any other way, such as by letting the dog chew it or leaving it on an automobile dashboard where the temperature becomes excessively hot.

Result: Either the whole disk or part of it may be lost. With ingenuity and help from your manual, you *may* be able to recover what you have lost; but don't count on it. Persons who inflict such damage are usually certain that they have done nothing wrong, but close examination usually reveals that they were careless. Even experts make such mistakes.

How to prevent such problems: (1) Be careful not to make the errors. (2) Have a backup copy of all important programs.

6. Never turn the power off while you are writing the program. This results in the loss of whatever was in the active memory. (On the TRS-80, the damage may be even more severe.)

Example: You have written a large number of lines into a program without saving these lines. A power failure causes the electricity to go off. The result is that any program lines in the computer's active memory at the time the power went off are lost.

How to prevent this problem: Save your program often. The loss of power can affect only what is in the computer's main memory. Programs stored on an auxiliary storage device will not be affected.

7. Never return to DOS before you have saved your program (TRS-80 only).

Example: You write a program. Then you type CMD"S" and DIR to get a directory of all your programs. The result is that when you return to BASIC, the slate will be wiped clean and you will have no program to save.

How to prevent this problem: (1) Always save before you go to the DOS level. (2) If you do make this mistake, type BASIC *. In most cases (unless you have inadvertently made another error in the interim), this will return you to the exact point where you were when you typed CMD"S" or rebooted your system.

The following three guidelines will enable you to minimize the impact of many of these errors:

1. Always have a backup copy of important programs.
2. Save your programs frequently while you are writing them.
3. Keep the disk in a safe place (such as its envelope) when you are not using it. When using it, handle it only by the paper cover.

Appendix F
List of Sources

THE following pages contain a listing of vendors and other sources from which it is possible to obtain good instructional computing programs.

Since the field is rapidly expanding, many significant sources have undoubtedly been omitted. Nevertheless, our intention has been to make the list as comprehensive as possible. Whenever possible, information is given regarding the types of programs and services offered by an individual or organization. Every attempt has been made to include only legitimate vendors who are likely to offer high-quality programs.

Abbott Educational Software
334 Westwood Avenue
E. Longmeadow, MA 01028
Phone: 413-525-3462
Topics: Reading. Levels: Elementary,
   Secondary, College.

Acorn Computer Corporation
400 Unicorn Park Drive
Woburn, MA 01801
Phone: 800-225-8001
Topics: Wide variety of programs. Levels:
   Elementary, Secondary, College.

Active Systems, Inc.
Box A-187
Hanover, NH 03755
Phone: 603-643-2381

Addison-Wesley Publishing Company
Reading, MA 01867
Phone: 617-944-3700
Topics: Math, Science (Biology, Physics),
   Computer Science, Administrative
   Simulation Modeling. Levels:
   Secondary, College.

Addison-Wesley Publishing Company, Inc.
School Division
2725 Sand Hill Road
Menlo Park, CA 94025
Phone: 415-854-0300
Topics: Math. Levels: Elementary,
   Secondary.

Anthro-Digital, Inc.
103 Bartlett-POB 1385
Pittsfield, MA 01201
Phone: 413-448-8278
Topics: Language Arts, Computer Literacy,
    Business, English, Administration.

Apple Computer Co.
20525 Mariani Avenue
Cupertino, CA 95014
Phone: 408-996-1010
Topics: Lanugage Arts, Early Childhood,
    Music, Reading, Teaching Aids.

Applecart Programs for Education
515 N. Franklin
Juneau, AK 99801
Phone: 907-586-3689
Topics: Computer Literacy, Social Studies.
    Levels: Preschool, Elementary,
    Secondary.

Applied Educational Systems
RFD #2 Box 213
Dunbarton, NH 03301
Phone: 603-774-6151
Topics: Administrative Software.

Aquarius
P. O. Box 128
Indian Rocks Beach, FL 33535
Phone: 813-595-7890
Topics: Special Education, Home
    Economics, Language Arts, Reading,
    Math, Science, Social Studies, English,
    Vocational Ed. Levels: Preschool,
    Elementary, Secondary, Adult.

ASK Enterprises
825 West Rosewood St.
Rialto, CA 92376
Topics: Reading, Spelling, Language Arts.

Atari Program Exchange
P. O. Box 3705
Santa Clara, CA 95055
Phone: 408-727-5602
Topics: Language Arts, Reading, Math,
    Science, Social Studies, Music, Business,
    English. Levels: Preschool, Elementary,
    Secondary.

Athena Software
727 Swarthmore Dr.
Newark, DE 19711
Phone: 302-738-6953
Topics: Language Arts, Math, Science,
    English. Levels: Preschool, Elementary,
    Secondary.

Avant Garde Creations
1907 Garden Ave.
Eugene, OR 97403
Phone: 503-345-3043
Topics: Language Arts, Reading, Math, Life
    and Physical Sciences, Computer
    Literacy, English. Levels: Preschool,
    Elementary, Secondary.

Bob Baker Software
3703 Miradera St.
Sacramento, CA 95821
Phone: 916-972-1931
Topics: Math, Business, Administration.

Basics & Beyond
Pinesbridge Road, Box 10
Amawalk, NY 10501
Phone: 914-962-2355
Topics: Language Arts, Math, Computer
    Literacy, Home Economics, Health,
    Social Studies. Levels: Elementary,
    Secondary.

BCD Associates, Inc.
5809 S.W. 5th, Suite 101
Oklahoma City, OK 73128
Phone: 405-948-1293
Topics: Interactive video-prompted
    courseware authoring.

Bell & Howell
Interactive Communications Division
7100 N McCormick Road
Chicago, IL 60645
Phone: 800-323-4338
Topics: Learning Games, Computer
    Literacy, Teacher Aids, Courseware
    Authoring System.

BIPACS
33 West Walnut Street
Long Beach, NY 11561
Phone: 212-685-3459
Topics: Language Arts, English. Levels:
Preschool, Elementary, Secondary,
College, Adult.

James P. Birk
Department of Chemistry
AZ State University
Tempe, AZ 85287
Phone: 602-965-3129
Topics: Chemistry.

Borg-Warner Educational Systems
600 W. University Drive
Arlington Heights, IL 60004
Phone: 800-323-7577
Topics: Language Arts, Reading, Math,
College Entrance Exams.

Brantex, Inc.
Color Software Services
P.O. Box 1708
Greenville, TX 75401
Phone: 214-454-3674
Topics: Math, Business. Levels: Preschool,
Elementary.

Britannica Computer Based Learning
% Encyclopedia Britannica Educational
Corp.
425 North Michigan Avenue
Chicago, IL 60611
Phone: 800-554-9862
Topics: Math, Science, Computer Literacy,
Language Arts, Special Education,
Reading, Computer Science, Social
Studies, English, Vocational Ed, Survival
Skills. Levels: Preschool, Elementary,
Secondary.

The Cactusplot Company
1442 N. McAllister
Tempe, AZ 85281
Phone: 602-945-1667
Topics: Math, Gradekeeping, Math
Utilities.

CALICO, Inc.
Computer Assisted Library Instruction,
Company
P.O. Box 15916
St. Louis, MO 63114
Topics: Library and Reference Skills

University of California
Lawrence Hall of Science
Math-Computer Ed Project
Berkeley, CA 94720
Phone: 415-642-3167
Topics: Math, Computer Science.

Cambridge Development Laboratory
36 Pleasant Street
Watertown, MA 02172
Phone: 617-926-0869
Topics: Math, Science, Equipment-
Computer Interfaces.

Carolina Biological Supply Company
2700 York Road
Burlington, NC 27215
Phone: 800-334-5551
Topics: Science (Biology, Physics,
Chemistry, Space), Math. Level:
Secondary.

Cavri Systems
26 Trumbull Street
New Haven, CT 06511
Phone: 203-562-4979

Children's Computer Workshop
1 Lincoln Plaza
New York, NY 10023
Phone: 212-595-3456
Topics: Language Arts, Readiness Skills.
Levels: Preschool, Elementary.

Classic Software Productions
7566 John Avenue
St. Louis, MO 63129
Topics: Physics, Vocational Ed. Levels:
Secondary, College, Adult.

Class 1 Systems
17909 Mapel Street
Lansing, IL 60438
Phone: 312-474-4664
Topics: Class Management, Test
Generation.

Classroom Computing Consultants
7128 Ontario
Hammond, IN 46323
Phone: 219-845-9840
Topics: Instructional Applications.

CMA Micro Computer
55722 Sante Fe Trail
Yucca Valley, CA 92284
Phone: 619-365-9718
Topics: Math, Statistics, Computer
    Literacy, Business, Educational
    Administration.

Comaldor
P.O. Box 356 Postal Station 0
Toronto, Ontario
Canada, M4A 2N9
Phone: 416-751-7481

Comm-Data Computer House
P.O. Box 325
Milford, MI 48042
Phone: 313-685-0113
Topics: Math, Social Studies, English,
    Teacher Aids.

Commodore
Computer Systems Division
1200 Wilson Drive
West Chester, PA 19380
Phone: 215-431-9100
Topics: Computer Literacy, Business,
    Typing. Levels: Elementary, Secondary,
    College.

COMPress
P.O. Box 102
Wentworth, NH 03282
Phone: 603-764-5831
Topics: Language Arts, Math, Science
    (Chemistry), Computer Literacy,
    English. Levels: Secondary, College.

Compu-Tations, Inc.
P.O. Box 502
Troy, MI 48099
Phone: 313-689-5059
Topics: Language Arts, Math, Social
    Studies, Typing, Special Ed, Foreign
    Languages. Levels: Preschool,
    Elementary, Secondary, College.

Computer Curriculum Corporation
1070 Arastradero Road
Palo Alto, CA 94304
Phone: 800-227-8324
Topics: Language Arts, Reading, Math,
    Computer Literacy, Computer Science
    English, Career Guidance. Levels:
    Elementary, Secondary.

Computer Information Exchange
P.O. Box 159
San Luis Rey, CA 92068
Phone: 714-757-4849

Computer Resources, Inc.
Route 4
Barrington, NH 03825
Phone: 603-868-5337

Computer Systems Design Group
3632 Governor Drive
San Diego, CA 92122
Phone: 415-856-1954

Computerware
P.O. Box 668
Encinitas, CA 92024
Phone: 619-436-3512
Topics: Computer Literacy, Computer
    Science, Health, Music, Business.

Computrex Computer Services
P.O. Box 536
Inman, SC 29349
Topics: Astronomy, Earth Science, Physics.

ComQuest
221 E. Camelback, St. 1
Phoenix, AZ 85012
Phone: 602-264-0324

CONDUIT
University of Iowa
P.O. Box 388
Iowa City, IA 52244
Phone: 319-353-5789
Topics: Language Arts, Math, Science
    (Biology, Chemistry, Physics), Social
    Studies, Music, Business, English,
    Foreign Languages. Levels: Secondary,
    College.

Control Data Publishing
P.O. Box 261127
San Diego, CA 92126
Phone: 800-233-3784
Topics: Language Arts, Reading, Math,
Science, Computer Literacy, Computer
Science, Health, English. Levels:
Elementary, Secondary, College.

Counterpoint Software, Inc.
Early Games Division
4005 W 65th Street-Suite 218
Minneapolis, MN 55435
Phone: 800-328-1223
Topics: Reading, Math, Music. Levels:
Preschool, Kindergarten.

Cove View Press
Box 810
Arcata, CA 95521
Phone: 707-822-7079
Topics: Language Arts, Math, Music,
Typing.

Cow Bay Computing
Box 515
Manhasset, NY 11030
Phone: 516-365-4423
Topics: Language Arts, Math, Science,
Computer Literacy, Administrative
Aids.

Creative Publications
P.O. Box 10328
Palo Alto, CA 94303
Phone: 415-968-3977
Topics: Language Arts, Reading, Math,
Computer Literacy, Computer Science,
Art, Business, English, Classroom
Management. Levels: Preschool,
Elementary, Secondary, College.

Cross Educational Software
1802 N Trenton Street
P.O. Box 1536
Ruston, LA 71270
Phone: 318-255-8921
Topics: Physics, Astronomy, Biology,
Chemistry, Physical Science, Teacher
Aids. Levels: Elementary, Secondary.

Curriculum Applications
P.O. Box 264
Arlington, MA 02174
Topics: Language Arts, Math, English.
Levels: Elementary, Secondary.

Cybertronics International
999 Mount Kemble Avenue
Morristown, NJ 07960

Data Command
P.O. Box 548
Kankakee, IL 60901
Phone: 815-933-7735
Topics: Language Arts.

E. David & Associates
22 Russett Lane
Storrs, CT 06268
Phone: 203-429-1785
Topics: Language Arts, Reading, Math,
Social Studies, Business. Levels:
Elementary, Secondary.

Davidson and Associates
6069 Groveoak Pl. Number 12
Rancho Palos Verdes, CA 90274
Phone: 213-378-3995
Topics: Reading, Language Arts, Math.

Demi-Software
6 Lee Road
Medfield, MA 02052
Phone: 617-359-4502

Developmental Learning Materials
One DLM Park
Allen, TX 75002
Phone: 800-527-4747
Topics: Language Arts, Math.

Dickens Data Systems
478 Engle Drive
Tucker, GA 30084
Phone: 404-923-3028

Diversified Educational Enterprises, Inc.
725 Main Street
Lafayette, IN 47901
Phone: 317-742-2690
Topics: Biology Simulations, Math
Packages, Classroom Management.

Dorsett Educational Systems
P.O. Box 1226
Norman, OK 73070
Phone: 405-288-2300
Topics: Math, Health, English, Spanish,
Social Studies, Vocational Ed, Reading,
Science, Language Arts.

Earthware Computer Services
2386 Spring Blvd.
P.O. Box 30039
Eugene, OR 97403
Phone: 503-344-3383
Topics: Earth Science, Physics, General
Science.

Educational Activities, Inc.
Attn: Charlotte Gray Reiter
1937 Grand Ave.
Baldwin, NY 11510
Phone: 800-645-3739
Topics: Computer Literacy, Reading,
Language Arts, Math, Science, Social
Studies, Health, English, Preschool.

Educational Computing
3144 Valentino Court
Oakton, Va 22124
Phone: 703-255-2356
Topics: Biology (Entomology). Levels:
Secondary, College.

Educational Computer Systems
136 Fairbanks Road
Oak Ridge, TN 37830
Phone: 615-483-4915
Topics: Earth Science, School
Administration.

Educational Courseware
67A Willard Street
Hartford, CT 06105
Phone: 203-247-6609
Topics: Computer Literacy, Math, Teacher
Utilities, Astronomy, Physics. Levels:
Elementary, Secondary, College.

Educational Development Corp.
P.O. Box 470663
8141 East 44th Street
Tulsa, OK 74147
Phone: 918-622-4522
Topics: Reading, Math, Classroom
Management.

Educational Materials & Equipment Co.
P.O. Box 17
Pelham, NY 10803
Phone: 914-576-1121
Topics: Biology, Physics, Chemistry,
Environmental Science, Metrics,
Computer Literacy, Home Economics
(Nutrition). Levels: Secondary, College.

Educational Micro Systems, Inc.
P.O. Box 471
Chester, NJ 07930
Phone: 201-879-5982
Topics: Math. Level: Elementary.

Educational Services Management
P.O. Box 12599
Research Triangle Park
North Carolina 27709
Phone: 919-781-1500

Educational Software, Inc.
4565 Cherryvale Avenue
Soquel, CA 95073
Phone: 408-476-4901
Topics: Computer Literacy, Music. Levels:
Preschool, Elementary.

Educational Software & Design
P.O. Box 2801
Flagstaff, AZ 86003
Topics: Chemistry, Mathematics.

Educational Software Midwest
414 Rosemere
Maquoketa, IA 52060
Phone: 319-652-2334

Educational Testing Service
SIGI Office
Rosedale Road
Princeton, NJ 08541
Phone: 609-734-5165
Topics: Career Education. Levels:
Secondary, College.

EDUCOMP LPS (Library Processes
System)
919 W. Canadian Street
Vinita, OK 74301
Phone: 918-256-7183
Topics: Library Management.

Educulture, Inc.
1 Dubuque Plaza
Dubuque, IA 52001
Phone: 800-553-4858
Topics: English. Levels: Secondary,
   College.

Edupro
P.O. Box 51346
Palo Alto, CA 94303
Phone: 415-494-2790
Topics: Math, Language Arts, Social
   Studies, Science, Computer Literacy,
   Art, Administrative Applications. Levels:
   Elementary, Secondary.

EduSoft
P.O. Box 2560
Berkeley, CA 94702
Phone: 800-227-2778
Topics: Preschool, Elementary Math,
   Language Arts, Secondary Science.

Edu-Soft
4639 Spruce Street
Philadelphia, PA 19139
Phone: 215-747-1284
Topics: Language Arts, Math, Teacher Aids,
   Pascal, Computer Literacy.

EduTech, Inc.
634 Commonwealth Avenue
Newton Centre, MA 02159
Phone: 617-965-4813
Topics: Physics, Astronomy, Biology,
   Chemistry, Math. Levels: Secondary,
   College.

Edutek Corporation
415 Cambridge, #14
Palo Alto, CA 94306
Phone: 415-325-9965
Topics: Language Arts, Reading, Math,
   Computer Literacy, Music, Art. Levels:
   Preschool, Elementary, Secondary.

Edu-Ware Services, Inc.
28035 Dorothy Drive
Agoura Hills, CA 91301
Phone: 213-706-0661
Topics: Language Arts, Reading, Science,
   Math, Computer Literacy. Levels:
   Preschool, Elementary, Secondary,
   College.

Edu-Ware East
P.O. BOx 336
Maynard, MA 01754
Topics: Science, Math.

Eiconics, Inc.
211 Cruz Alta
Box 1207
Taos, NM 87571
Phone: 505-758-1696
Topics: Courseware Authoring System.

Electronic Courseware Systems, Inc.
309 Windsor Rd.
Champaign, IL 61820
Phone: 217-359-7099
Topics: Language Arts, Math, Music,
   English. Levels: Preschool, Elementary,
   Secondary, College.

Ellis Computing
3917 Noriega Street
San Francisco, CA 94122
Phone: 415-753-0186
Topics: Computer Science, Business Ed,
   Utilities.

EMC Publishing
300 York Avenue
St. Paul, MN 55101
Phone: 800-328-1452
Topics: Language Arts, Reading, Math,
   Science, Home Economics, Health,
   Social Studies, English, Foreign
   Languages. Levels: Preschool,
   Elementary, Secondary.

Entelek
Ward-Whidden House - The Hill
P.O. Box 1303
Portsmouth, NH 03801
Phone: 603-436-0439
Topics: Math, Biology, Chemistry, Physics.
   Levels: Secondary, College.

Epyx, Inc.
1043 Kiel Court
Sunnyvale, CA 94086
Phone: 408-745-0700
Topics: Music, Art.

Essertier Software Corporation
919 14th Street
Hermosa Beach, CA 90254
Phone: 213-379-1570
Topics: Math, Administrative Applications.

Evans Newton, Inc.
7650 E. Redfield - Suite D5
Scottsdale, AZ 85260
Phone: 602-998-2777
Topics: Administrative and Teacher Aids.

Eye Gate Media, Inc.
3333 Elston Ave.
Chicago, IL 60618
Phone: 800-621-8086
Topics: Language Arts, Library, Social
    Studies, Math, Science, Computer
    Literacy, Career Education, Reading,
    Home Economics, Health, Music, Art,
    Business. Levels: Preschool,
    Elementary, Secondary, College.

Fireside Computing, Inc.
MicroGnome Division
5843 Montgomery Road
Elkridge, MD 21227
Phone: 301-796-4165

Fisher Scientific Company
Educational Materials Division
4901 W. LeMoyne Street
Chicago, IL 60651
Phone: 800-621-4769
Topics: Math, Science, Administration,
    Testing.

Fullmer Associates
1132 Via Jose
San Jose, CA 95120
Phone: 408-997-1154
Topics: Language Arts, Reading, Math,
    Business, General Purpose Drill
    Generator. Levels: Elementary,
    Secondary.

J. L. Hammett
Hammett Place - Box 545
Braintree, MA 02184
Phone: 800-225-5467
Topics: Language Arts, Reading, Math,
    Science, Computer Literacy, Social
    Studies, Business, Logic Games. Levels:
    Preschool, Elementary, Secondary,
    College.

Harper and Row
10 E. 53rd Suite 4D
New York, NY 10022
Topics: Business and Accounting.

Hartley Courseware, Inc.
P.O. Box 431
Dimondale, MI 48821
Phone: 517-646-6458
Topics: Reading, Language Arts, Math,
    Social Studies, Teacher Utilities.

Hayden Book Company
50 Essex Street
Rochelle Park, NJ 07662
Phone: 201-368-2202
Topics: Computer Literacy, Computer
    Science, Home Economics, Music, Art,
    Business. Levels: Preschool,
    Elementary, Secondary, College.

High Tech Software Products, Inc.
P.O. Box 60406
1611 N.W. 23rd Street
Oklahoma City, OK 73146
Phone: 405-524-4359
Topics: Chemistry, Physics, Teacher Aids,
    Statistics. Levels: Secondary, College.

Holt, Rinehart and Winston
School Department
383 Madison Avenue
New York, NY 10017
Topics: Computer Managed Instruction.

Houghton Mifflin
Department J
One Beacon Street
Boston, MA 02108
Topics: Reading, Language Arts.

Ideal School Supply Company
11000 S. Lavergne Ave.
Oak Lawn, IL 60453
Phone: 312-425-0800
Topics: Language Arts, Reading, Math,
    Science, Computer Literacy.

Ideatech Company
P.O. Box 62451
Sunnyvale, CA 94088
Phone: 408-985-7591
Topics: Language Arts, Reading, Math,
    Science (Basic Electricity). Levels:
    Preschool, Elementary, Secondary,
    Adult.

Indian Head Software
1002 Indian Head Drive
Snow Hill, NC 28580
Phone: 919-747-2839
Topics: Chemistry, Math, Computer
    Literacy. Levels: Elementary, Secondary,
    College.

Information Unlimited Software, Inc.
2401 Marinship Way
Sausalito, CA 94965
Phone: 415-331-6700
Topics: Business, Utilities.

Insoft
P.O. Box 19208
Portland, OR 97219
Phone: 503-244-4181
Topics: Language Arts, Reading, Music,
    Art, Business, English. Levels:
    Secondary, College.

Instant Software
Rte. 101 and Elm Street
Peterborough, NH 03458
Phone: 800-258-5473
Topics: Language Arts, Reading, Math,
    Science, Social Studies, Music, Business,
    English. Levels: Elementary, Secondary.

Instructional-Communications
    Technology, Inc.
10 Stepar Place
Huntington Station, NY 11746
Phone: 516-549-3000
Topics: Language Arts, Reading, Math,
    Basic Skills. Levels: Elementary,
    Secondary, College.

Integral Computer Systems, Inc.
136 Main Street
Putnam, CT 06260
Phone: 203-928-5310
Topics: Business, Administrative
    Applications.

International Institute of Applied
    Technology, Inc.
2121 Wisconsin Ave., N.W., Suite 400
Washington, DC 20007
Phone: 202-965-7410
Topics: Interactive Videodisk Systems,
    PILOT Language, Courseware
    Authoring Language.

International Micro Systems
6445 Metcalf
Shawnee Mission, KS 66202
Phone: 913-677-1137

Interpretive Education Guidance
    Associates
Communications Park,
Box 3000
Mount Kisco, NY 10549
Phone: 800-431-1242
Topics: Home Economics, Math, Business
    (Finance), Special Ed, Job Readiness.
    Level: Secondary.

Island Software
P.O. Box 300
Department F
Lake Grove, NY 11755
Phone: 516-585-3755
Topics: Social Studies, Gifted and
    Talented. Levels: Preschool,
    Elementary, Secondary.

J & S Software
140 Reid Avenue
Port Washington, NY 11050
Phone: 516-944-9304
Topics: Physics, Chemistry, Biology,
    Reading, English, Physical Sciences.

Jadee Enterprises
1799 Meadowlake Drive
Charleston, IL 61920

Jagdstaffel Software
645 Brenda Lee Drive
San Jose, CA 95123
Phone: 408-578-1643
Topics: Language Arts, Reading, Home
    Economics, Health, Social Studies,
    Business, English, Industrial Ed,
    Administration. Levels: Elementary,
    Secondary, College.

Jensen Software
810 Sandalwood
Elyria, OH 44035
Phone: 216-366-9525
Topics: Language Arts, Reading, Math,
    Social Studies. Levels: Preschool,
    Elementary, Secondary.

JMH Software of Minn, Inc.
P.O. Box 41308
Minneapolis, NM 55441
Phone: 612-424-5464
Topics: Language Arts, Math, Social
    Studies, Driver Ed. Levels: Preschool,
    Elementary, Secondary.

Johnson Software
1200 Dale Avenue
Mountain View, CA 94040

K-12 MicroMedia, Inc.
172 Broadway
Woodcliff Lake, NJ 07675
Phone: 201-391-7555
Topics: Math, Language Arts, Reading,
    Science, Art, English, Computer
    Literacy, Business, Social Studies,
    Computer Science. Levels: Preschool,
    Elementary, Secondary, College.

Krell Software
1320 Stony Brook Road
Stony Brook, NY 11790
Phone: 516-751-5139
Topics: Reading, Math. Levels: Elementary,
    Secondary, College.

Kvitle Kourseware
15510 Heimer Road
San Antonio, TX 78232
Phone: 512-434-3681
Topics: Language Arts, Math, English,
    Bilingual, Foreign Languages (French,
    German, Russian, Latin). Levels:
    Elementary, Secondary, College.

The Learning Company
545 Middlefield, Suite 170
Menlo Park, CA 94025
Phone: 415-328-5410
Topics: Language Arts, Math, Science,
    Computer Literacy, Art, Logic, Problem
    Solving. Levels: Preschool, Elementary,
    Secondary.

Learning Tools, Inc.
686 Massachusetts Ave.
Cambridge, MA 02139
Phone: 617-864-8086
Topics: Administrative Planning and
    Reporting, Curriculum Management.

Library Software
P.O. Box 23897
Pleasant Hill, CA 94523
Phone: 415-945-2025

L.I.F.E. Software, Ltd.
Richvale Telecommunications
10610 Bayview Plaza, Un 18
Richmond Hill, Ont L4C 3N8
Phone: 416-491-2230

Life Science Associates
1 Fenimore Road
Bayport, NY 11705
Phone: 516-472-2111
Topics: Math, Biology, Psychology, Special
    Ed. Levels: Secondary, College.

Lightning Software
P.O. Box 11725
Palo Alto, CA 94306
Phone: 415-327-3280

Little Bee Educational Programs
P.O. Box 262
Massillon, OH 44648
Phone: 216-832-4097
Topics: Language Arts, Reading, Math.
    Levels: Preschool, Elementary.

Little Genius Ltd.
3871 Lawrence Place
N Vancouver, BC V7K 2X1
Phone: 604-986-6786
Topics: Computer Literacy, Computer
    Science. Levels: Elementary, Secondary,
    College, Adult.

Longman Micro Software
Longman Group Resources
33-35 Tanner Row
York, England YO1 1JP
Topics: Science, Biology, Chemistry,
    Physics

L & S Computerware
1589 Fraser Drive
Sunnyvale, CA 94086
Phone: 408-738-3416

Math Software
1233 Blackthorn Place
Deerfield, IL 60015
Topics: Math.

MCE, Inc.
Suite 250
157 S. Kalamazoo Mall
Kalamazoo, MI 49007
Phone: 800-421-4157
Topics: Math, Home Economics, Health, Social Studies, Special Ed. Levels: Elementary, Secondary.

McGraw-Hill
1221 Avenue of Americas
New York, NY 10020
Phone: 800-223-4180
Topics: Science and Social Studies.

MED Systems Software
P.O. Box 3558
Chapel Hill, NC 27514
Phone: 919-933-1990
Topics: Health and Science.

Mega-Byte Systems
66 Church Street
Ellenville, NY 12428
Phone: 914-647-5977

Melcher Software
P.O. Box 213
Midland, MI 48640
Phone: 517-631-7607
Topics: Math, Teacher Utilities.

Mentor Software, Inc.
P.O. Box 791
Anoka, MN 55303
Topics: Chemistry.

Mercer Systems, Inc.
87 Scooter Lane
Hicksville, NY 11801

Merlan Scientific Ltd.
247 Armstrong Ave.
Georgetown, ONT L7G 4X6
Phone: 416-877-0171
Topics: Chemistry, Physics, Biology, Math, Administration.

Merry Bee Communications
815 Crest Drive—Papillion
Omaha, NE 68046
Phone: 402-592-3479
Topics: Language Arts, Reading, Music. Levels: Preschool, Elementary.

Metacomet
P.O. Box 31337
Hartford, CT 06108
Phone: 203-549-4464

Meta-Designed Software
P.O. Box 136
Haddonfield, NJ 08033

The Micro Center
P.O. Box 6
Pleasantville, NY 10570
Phone: 800-431-2434
Topics: Math, Language Arts, Computer Literacy, Problem Solving, Science, Social Studies, Art, Teacher Aids, Administrative Aids. Levels: Preschool, Elementary, Secondary, College.

Microcomputer Education Applications Network
256 N. Washington Street
Falls Church, VA 22046
Phone: 703-536-2310
Topics: Special Education Administration.

Microcomputer Software Systems
4716 Lakewood Drive
Metairie, LA 70002
Phone: 504-887-8527
Topics: Math, Social Studies.

Microcomputer Workshops Corporation
225 Westchester Ave.
Port Chester, NY 10573
Phone: 914-937-5440
Topics: Math, Language Arts, Reading, Science (Genetics, Chemistry, Biology), Computer Science, Social Studies, Foreign Languages (French, Spanish).

Microcomputers in Eucation
Independent School District 281
4148 Winnetka Ave North
Minneapolis, MN 55427
Topics: Math, Reading, Language Arts, Spelling, Science, Social Studies, Foreign Language, Media, Music.

MICRO-ED Inc.
P.O. Box 444005
Eden Prairie, NM 55344
Phone: 800-MICROED
Topics: Language Arts, Reading, Math, Science, Social Studies, Music, English. Levels: Preschool, Elementary, Secondary, Adult.

Micro Learn
Division of Micro Lab, Inc.
2699 Skokie Valley Road
Highland Park, IL 60035
Phone: 312-433-7550
Topics: Language Arts, Reading, Math,
   Social Studies, Art, Business, English,
   Couseware Authoring System. Levels:
   Secondary, College.

Micro Learningware
Highway 66 South, Box 307
Mankato, MN 56002
Phone: 507-625-2205
Topics: Math, Language Arts, Foreign
   Language, Social Studies, Science,
   Business Education, Teacher Aids,
   Career Ed.

Micromatics, Inc.
81 North 200 West - Suite 5
Bountiful, UT 84010
Phone: 801-292-2458

Micro Photo Division
Bell and Howell
Old Mansfield Rd.
Wooster, OH 44691
Phone: 800-321-9881
Topics: Career Guidance System.

Microphys Programs
1737 West 2nd Street
Brooklyn, NY 11223
Phone: 212-375-5151
Topics: Physics, Chemistry, Physical
   Sciences, Math (Calculus), Language
   Arts, English. Levels: Elementary,
   Secondary, College.

Micropi
P.O. Box 5524
Bellingham, WA 98227
Phone: 206-733-9265
Topics: Language Arts, Chemistry,
   Computer Science, English. Levels:
   Secondary, College.

Micro Power & Light
12820 Hillcrest Road
Number 219
Dallas, TX 75230
Phone: 214-234-8233
Topics: Science, Math, Library, Statistics,
   Language Arts, Computer Literacy.
   Levels: Elementary, Secondary, College.

Micropute Software
P.O. Box 1943
Rocky Mount, NC 27801

Micro-School Programs - Bertamax, Inc.
101 Nickerson St., Suite 202
Seatle, WA 98109
Phone: 206-282-6249
Topics: Math, Language Arts,
   Administrative and Teacher Aids.

Microsoft Consumer Products
10700 Northup Way
Bellevue, WA 98004
Phone: 206-828-8080
Topics: Typing, Math, Teacher Aids.

Microsoftware Services
P.O. Box 776
Harrisonburg, VA 22801
Phone: 703-433-9485
Topics: Teacher Aids. Levels: Elementary,
   Secondary, College.

Milliken Publishing Company
1100 Research Blvd.
St. Louis, MO 63132
Phone: 314-991-4220
Topics: Language Arts, Math, Reading.

Milton Bradley Company
Education Division
443 Shaker Rd.
E. Longmeadow, MA 01028
Phone: 413-525-6411
Topics: Language Arts, Math, Computer
   Literacy. Levels: Elementary, Secondary.

Minnesota Educational Computing
Consortium Publications
2520 Broadway Drive
St. Paul, MN 55113
Phone: 612-638-0627
Topics: Language Arts, Reading, Math,
   Science, Computer Literacy, Home Ec,
   Health, Social Studies, Music, Art,
   Business, English, Teacher Utilities,
   Special Ed. Levels: Preschool,
   Elementary, Secondary, College.

Modtec
4144 N. Via Villas
Tucson, AZ 85719
Phone: 602-293-5186

Monument Computer Service
Village Data Center
P.O. Box 603
Joshua Tree, CA 92252
Phone: 619-365-6668
Topics: Language Arts, Reading, Math,
  Science, Computer Literacy. Levels:
  Elementary, Secondary, College.

Mount Castor Industries
368 Shays Street
Amherst, MA 01002
Phone: 413-253-9413
Topics: Administrative Applications.

Mu-Microcomputers, Inc.
300 Broad Street
Stamford, CT 06901
Phone: 203-359-4236
Topics: Computer Science, Utilities.

MUSE Software
347 N. Charles Street
Baltimore, MD 21201
Phone: 301-659-7212
Topics: Social Studies, Science Simulations.

Musitronic, Inc.
555 Park Drive-POB 441
Owatonna, MN 55060
Phone: 800-533-0485
Topics: Music.

National Software Marketing
4701 McKinley Street
Hollywood, FL 33021
Phone: 305-625-6062

Opportunities for Learning
8950 Lurline Ave.
Chatsworth, CA 91311
Phone: 818-341-2535
Topics: Computer Science, Business,
  Foreign Language, Social Studies, Math,
  Computer Literacy, Science, Language
  Arts, Teacher Aids, Music, Art, Reading,
  Health, English. Levels: Preschool,
  Elementary, Secondary, College.

Optimized Systems Software, Inc.
10379 Lansdale Avenue
Cupertino, CA 95014
Phone: 408-446-3099
Topics: Utilities.

Orange Cherry Media
7 Delano Drive
Bedford Hills, NY 10507
Phone: 914-666-8434
Topics: Language Arts, Reading, Math,
  Earth Science, Social Studies, English.
  Levels: Preschool, Elementary.

ORDINAFRANCAIS
3591 Dudley Road
N Vancouver, BC V7R 3B9
Topics: French. Levels: Secondary,
  College.

Pearlsoft
Division of Relational Systems
  International Corporation
Box 13850
Salem, OR 97309
Phone: 503-390-6880
Topics: Administration, Courseware
  Authoring.

PIE, Corporation for Public Information in
  Education
1714 Illinois
Lawrence, KS 66044
Phone: 913-841-3095
Topics: Reading, Math, Social Studies,
  Curriculum Management. Levels:
  Preschool, Elementary, Secondary.

Powell Associates, Inc.
3724 Jefferson - Suite 205
Austin, TX 78731
Phone: 512-453-7288
Topics: School Information Management
  System.

Precision People, Inc.
3452 North Ride Cir. S
Jacksonville, FL 32217
Phone: 904-262-1096
Topics: Math, Diagnostics, Special
  Education, Psychological Software.
  Levels: Elementary, Secondary.

Professional Computerware
P.O. Box 409
Morgantown, GA 30560
Phone: 404-374-6045
Topics: Science (Anatomy), Library
  Reference, Program Security Packages.
  Levels: Secondary, College.

The Professor
P.O. Box 301
Swanton, VT 05488
Topics: Computer Literacy, Computer
    Science. Levels: Secondary, College.

Program Design, Inc.
95 East Putnam Ave.
Greenwich, CT 06830
Phone: 203-661-8799
Topics: Language Arts, Math, Reading,
    Computer Literacy. Levels: Preschool,
    Elementary, Secondary.

Programs for Learning, Inc.
P.O. Box 954
New Milford, CT 06776
Phone: 203-355-3452
Topics: Chemistry, Physics.

Quality Educational Designs, Inc.
P.O. Box 12486
Portland, OR 97212
Phone: 503-287-8137
Topics: Math.

Radio Shack
Contact Local Retailers
Topics: Computer Science, Math, Social
    Studies, Administration, Reading.

Rainbow Computing, Inc.
Software Department
9719 Reseda Blvd.
Northridge, CA 91324
Phone: 800-423-5441
Topics: Art, Business. Levels: Secondary,
    College.

Rand McNally and Compay
P.O. Box 7600
Chicago, IL 60680
Phone: 312-673-9100
Topics: Geography.

Random House, Inc.
201 East 50th Street
New York, NY 10022
Phone: 800-638-6460
Topics: Language Arts, Math, Reading,
    Classroom Management and Support
    Tools, Computer Literacy, Career Ed.
    Levels: Elementary, Secondary.

Reader's Digest Services, Inc.
Microcomputer Software Division
Pleasantville, NY 10570
Phone: 800-431-8800
Topics: Language Arts, Math, Strategy
    Games. Level: Elementary.

Redcomp Services
HC 78 Box 624
West Chenango Road
Castle Creek, NY 13744
Phone: 607-648-3275
Topics: Math, Science (Chemistry,
    Physics), Social Studies, English. Levels:
    Elementary, Secondary, College.

Right on Programs
P.O. Box 977
Huntington, NY 11743
Phone: 516-271-3177
Topics: Language Arts, Math, Science,
    Social Studies, English. Levels:
    Elementary, Secondary.

Reston Software
11480 Sunset Hills Rd.
Reston, VA 22090
Phone: 703-437-8900
Topics: Books and a wide variety of
    programs.

Roklan Corp.
3335 N Arlington Heights Rd.
Arlington Heights, IL 60004
Phone: 312-392-2525
Topics: Language Arts, Reading, Math,
    Computer Literacy, English. Levels:
    Elementary, Secondary.

Salsbury Associates, Inc.
608 Madam Moore
New Bern, NC 28560
Phone: 919-638-4456

Sandpiper Software
P.O. Box 336
Maynard, MA 01754
Phone: 617-568-8641

Scholastic, Inc.
P.O. Box 7501
2931 E. McCarty St.
Jefferson City, MO 65102
Phone: 800-325-6149
Topics: Language Arts, Reading, Math,
   Chemistry, Biology, Computer Literacy,
   Computer Science, Social Studies,
   Music, Art, Business, English. Levels:
   Preschool, Elementary, Secondary,
   College.

School & Home Courseware
Suite C
1341 Bulldog Lane
Fresno, CA 93710
Phone: 209-227-4341
Topics: Language Arts, Reading, Math,
   Science, Home Economics, Health,
   Business, English.

School Management Systems
2226 Main Street
Sweet Home, OR 97386
Phone: 503-367-4747
Topics: Administrative Management
   Systems.

Science Research Associates
155 North Wacker Driver
Chicago, IL 60606
Phone: 312-984-7000
Topics: Math, Computer Literacy, Reading,
   Language Arts, Computer Science,
   Business, English, Administrative Aids.
   Levels: Elementary, Secondary, College.

Scientific Software Associates
P.O. Box 208
Wausau, WI 54401
Phone: 715-845-2066
Topics: Administrative Applications, Test
   Scoring and Analysis. Levels: Secondary,
   College.

Science Software Systems, Inc.
11899 West Pico Boulevard
West Los Angeles, CA 90064
Phone: 800-421-6636
Topics: Biology, Chemistry, Physics, Earth
   Science, Computer Science,
   Environmental Science.

Scott Foresman and Company
Electronic Publishing Division
1900 E. Lake Avenue
Glenview, IL 60025
Phone: 312-729-3000
Topics: Elementary Math and Reading,
   Language Arts, Reading, Math, Science
   (Chemistry, Physics), Computer
   Literacy, School Management. Levels:
   Preschool, Elementary, Secondary.

Serendipity Systems
225 Elmira Road
Ithaca, NY 14850
Phone: 607-277-4889
Topics: Teacher Aids

Sheridan College
1430 Trafalgar Road
Oakville, Ontario
Canada L6H 2L1
Phone: 416-845-9430 Ext 142
Topics: Geometry, Descriptive Statistics,
   Typing, Photography. Levels:
   Secondary, College.

Skillcorp Software, Inc.
1711 McGaw Avenue
Irvine, CA 92714
Phone: 800-854-8688
Topics: Language Arts, Reading, Math,
   Courseware Authoring Systems,
   Management System for Reading and
   Math. Levels: Preschool, Elementary.

SLED Software
P.O. Box 16322
Minneapolis, MN 55416
Phone: 612-926-5820
Topics: Language Arts, Special Ed.

Sliwa Enterprises
2360-J George Washington Memorial
   Parkway
Yorktown, VA 23692
Phone: 804-898-8386
Topics: Language Arts, Math, English,
   Foreign Languages. Levels: Secondary,
   College.

B. James Smith
378 Main Street
Shrewsbury, MA 01545
Phone: 617-845-1878
Topics: School Administration Aids.

Society for Visual Education
1345 Diversey Parkway
Chicago, IL 60614

Softech, Ltd.
37 Harcourt Street
Dublin 2 Ireland
Phone: 720822
Topics: Math, Science (Physics), Business,
    School Administration.

Software Connections
1800 Wyatt Drive Suite 17
Santa Clara, CA 95054
Phone: 408-988-3704
Topics: Classroom Management (Local
    Networks)

Software Industries
902 Pinecrest
Richardson, TX 75080

Software Research Corp.
Discovery Pk - PO Box 1700
University of Victoria
Victoria, BC Canada V8W 2Y2
Phone: 604-477-7246
Topics: Special Education, Teacher Aids,
    Math, Social Studies, Art, Business,
    English as a Second Language. Levels:
    Elementary, Secondary.

Solartek
RD 1, Box 255A
West Hurley, NY 12491
Phone: 914-679-5366
Topics: Solar Energy.

So. Micro Systems for Educators
P.O. Box 1981
Burlington, NC 27215
Phone: 919-226-7610
Topics: Special Ed, Administrative Report
    Writing.

SouthWest EdPsych Services, Inc.
P.O. Box 1870
Phoenix, AZ 85001
Phone: 602-253-6528
Topics: Language Arts, Reading, Math,
    Social Studies, Special Ed. Levels:
    Preschool, Elementary, Secondary,
    College.

Special Delivery Software
20525 Mariani Avenue
Cupertino, CA 95014
Phone: 408-996-1010

Spinnaker Software
215 First Street
Cambridge, MA 02142
Phone: 617-686-4700
Topics: Language Arts, Logic, Problem
    Solving. Levels: Preschool, Elementary.

Sterling Swift Publishing Co.
7901 S. IH-35
Austin, TX 78744
Phone: 512-282-6840
Topics: Math, Computer Literacy, Music,
    Courseware Authoring System. Levels:
    Elementary, Secondary.

Storybooks of the Future
P.O. Box 4447
Santa Clara, CA 95054
Phone: 415-386-5184
Topics: Language Arts, Reading

Strategic Simulations, Inc.
883 Stierlin Rd. A-200
Mountainview, CA 94043
Phone: 415-964-1353
Topics: Social Studies, Business,
    Economics.

Sunburst Communications
39 Washington Ave.
Pleasantville, NY 10570
Phone: 800-431-1934
Topics: Math, Language Arts, Computer
    Literacy, Reading, English. Level:
    Elementary.

Synergistic Software
830 N. Riverside Drive
Suite 201
Renton, WA 98055
Phone: 206-226-3216
Topics: Earth Science, Health, Foreign
    Languages.

Syntauri Corporation
4962 El Camino Real Suite 112
Los Altos, CA 94022
Phone: 415-966-1273
Topics: Music. Levels: Secondary, College.

Tamarack Software, Inc.
P.O. Box 247
Darby, MT 59829
Phone: 406-821-4596
Topics: Computer Literacy, Computer
Science, Administrative Aids. Levels:
Elementary, Secondary, College.

TARA Ltd.
P.O. Box 118
Selden, NY 11784
Phone: 516-331-2537
Topics: Language Arts, Reading, Math,
Science, Social Studies, English.

Teacher's Pet Software
P.O. Box 791
Livermore, CA 94550
Phone: 415-449-1084
Topics: Language Arts, Math. Level:
Elementary.

The Teaching Assistant
22 Seward Drive
Huntington Station, NY 11746
Phone: 516-499-8397
Topics: Physics, Language Arts, Aviation
(Flight Planning).

Teach Yourself by Computer Software
2128 W. Jefferson Rd.
Pittsford, NY 14534
Phone: 716-424-5453
Topics: Language Arts, Math, Earth
Science, Biology, Social Studies,
English, Foreign Languages, Classroom
Management. Levels: Elementary,
Secondary.

Teck Associates
P.O. Box 8732
White Bear Lake, MN 55110
Phone: 612-429-5570
Topics: Math, Science, Computer Literacy,
Computer Science, Authoring
Language. Levels: Preschool,
Elementary.

Terrapin, Inc.
678 Massachusetts Ave.
Cambridge, MA 02139
Phone: 617-492-8816
Topics: LOGO Language.

Texas Instruments
P.O. Box 53
Lubbock, TX 79408
Phone: 800-858-4565
Topics: LOGO and software packages.

T.H.E.S.I.S.
P.O. Box 147
Garden City, MI 48135
Phone: 800-354-0550
Topics: Reading, Math, Language Arts.

3R Software
P.O. Box 3115
Jamaica, NY 11431
Phone: 212-658-5196

T.I.E.S. - Minnesota School District
Data Processing Joint Board
1925 West County Road B2
St. Paul, MN 55113
Phone: 612-633-9110
Topics: Language Arts, Reading, Math,
Science, Computer Literacy, Computer
Science, Business, English.

Tycom Associates
68 Velma Avenue
Pittsfield, MA 01201
Phone: 413-442-9771
Topics: French, Spanish, German, Math.

UNICOM
297 Elmwood Avenue
Providence, RI 02907
Phone: 800-556-2828
Topics: Educational Management Tools,
Language Arts, Reading, Math,
Computer Literacy, Networking. Levels:
Preschool, Elementary, Secondary.

Universal System for Education
2120 E. Academy Circle
Colorado Springs, CO 80909
Phone: 303-574-4575

Vernier Software
2920 S.W. 89th
Portland, OR 97225
Phone: 503-297-5317
Topics: Physics. Levels: Secondary,
College.

Vockell Software
6927 Knickerbocker Pkwy
Hammond, IN 46323
Phone: 219-845-8250
Topics: Inexpensive instructional software.

Wadsworth Electronic Publishing
    Company
Statler Office Building
20 Park Plaza
Boston, MA 02116
Phone: 800-322-2208
Topics: Secondary Math.

H. C. Ward
P.O. Box 3412
DeLand, FL 32720
Phone: 904-789-4654
Topics: Math (English and Spanish
    Version). Levels: Elementary,
    Secondary.

Watsoft Products, Inc.
158 University Avenue West
Waterloo, Ont Can N2L 3E9
Phone: 519-886-3700
Topics: Math, Science, Computer Literacy,
    Computer Science, Business. Levels:
    Secondary, College.

Westinghouse Learning Corporation
5005 W 110th Street
Oak Lawn, Il 60453
Topics: Physics.

Wida Software
2 Nicholas Gardens
London, England W5 5HY
Phone: 01-567-6941
Topics: Language Arts, Reading, English,
    Foreign Languages, Authoring Systems,
    Special Ed. Levels: Elementary,
    Secondary.

WIMS Computer Consulting
6723 East 66th Place
Tulsa, OK 74133
Phone: 981-492-9036

Zeitgeist
5150 N 6th, Suite 179
Fresno, CA 93710
Phone: 209-222-8244
Topics: Math. Levels: Elementary,
    Secondary.

Index of Subjects

Index of Examples